ALL·IN·ONE

CRISC®

Certified in Risk and Information Systems Control

EXAM GUIDE

ALL·IN·ONE

CRISC®

Certified in Risk and Information Systems Control

EXAM GUIDE

Second Edition

Peter H. Gregory
Dawn Dunkerley
Bobby E. Rogers

New York   Chicago   San Francisco
Athens   London   Madrid   Mexico City
Milan   New Delhi   Singapore   Sydney   Toronto

CRISC® Certified in Risk and Information Systems Control All-in-One Exam Guide, Second Edition

3 LHN 24

Library of Congress Control Number: 2022930860

ISBN   978-1-260-47333-9
MHID   1-260-47333-3

Sponsoring Editor Wendy Rinaldi	**Technical Editor** Matthew Webster	**Production Supervisor** Thomas Somers
Editorial Supervisor Janet Walden	**Copy Editor** Bart Reed	**Composition** KnowledgeWorks Global Ltd.
Project Manager Nitesh Sharma, KnowledgeWorks Global Ltd.	**Proofreader** Rachel Fogelberg	**Illustration** KnowledgeWorks Global Ltd.
Acquisitions Coordinator Caitlin Cromley-Linn	**Indexer** Ted Laux	**Art Director, Cover** Jeff Weeks

To Rebekah, Nathan, and Shay.

—Peter H. Gregory

For Thomas, Lauren, and Max. I am very, very lucky.

—Dawn Dunkerley

I'd like to dedicate this book to my family, who was very understanding and patient with me while I wrote this book. To my wife Barbara; my children Greg, Sarah, and AJ; and my grandchildren, Sam, Ben, Evey, Emmy, big Caleb, and now, little Caleb: you guys are the world to me.

—Bobby E. Rogers

ABOUT THE AUTHORS

Peter H. Gregory, CRISC, CISM®, CISA®, CDPSE™, CIPM®, CISSP®, DRCE, CCSK™, is a 30-year career technologist and a security leader in a regional telecommunications company. He has been developing and managing information security management programs since 2002 and has been leading the development and testing of secure IT environments since 1990. Peter has also spent many years as a software engineer and architect, systems engineer, network engineer, and security engineer.

Peter is the author of more than 40 books about information security and technology, including *Solaris Security, CISM Certified Information Security Manager All-in-One Exam Guide,* and *CISA Certified Information Systems Auditor All-in-One Exam Guide.* He has spoken at numerous industry conferences, including RSA, Interop, (ISC)² Congress, ISACA CACS, SecureWorld Expo, West Coast Security Forum, IP3, Source, Society for Information Management, the Washington Technology Industry Association, and InfraGard.

Peter serves on advisory boards for cybersecurity education programs at the University of Washington and the University of South Florida. He was the lead instructor for nine years in the University of Washington certificate program in applied cybersecurity, a former board member of the Washington State chapter of InfraGard, and a founding member of the Pacific CISO Forum. Peter is a 2008 graduate of the FBI Citizens Academy and a member of the FBI National Citizens Academy Alumni Association. Peter is an executive member of the CyberEdBoard and the Forbes Technology Council.

Peter resides with his family in Washington state and can be found online at www .peterhgregory.com.

Dawn Dunkerley received a PhD in information systems from Nova Southeastern University in 2011 with a doctoral focus on information security success within organizations. Her research interests include cyberwarfare, cybersecurity, and the success and measurement of organizational cybersecurity initiatives. Dr. Dunkerley holds a number of professional certifications, including CRISC, CISSP, CISSP-ISSAP®, CISSP-ISSEP®, CISSP-ISSMP®, CSSLP®, and CompTIA Security+™ certifications.

Bobby E. Rogers is an information security engineer working as a contractor for Department of Defense agencies, helping to secure, certify, and accredit their information systems. His duties include information system security engineering, risk management, and certification and accreditation efforts. He retired after 21 years in the U.S. Air Force, serving as a network security engineer and instructor, and has secured networks all over the world. Bobby has a master's degree in information assurance (IA). His many certifications include CRISC, CISSP-ISSEP, CEH™, and MCSE: Security, as well as the CompTIA A+™, Network+™, Security+, and Mobility+™ certifications.

About the Technical Editor

Matthew Webster has more than 25 years of experience in both IT and cybersecurity and is the author of *Do No Harm: Protecting Connected Medical Devices, Healthcare, and Data from Hackers and Adversarial Nation States*. Within his realm of experience has been multiple security officer positions, including chief information security officer. Matthew clearly has a passion for cybersecurity, which is evidenced by the fact that he has earned more than 20 IT and cybersecurity certifications, including Certified in Risk and Information Systems Control (CRISC), Certified Information Systems Auditor (CISA), GIAC Law of Data Security & Investigations (GLEG), and Certified Information Systems Security Professional (CISSP).

Matthew has worked in and around many companies throughout the northeast U.S. in a variety of capacities, and he has built many cybersecurity programs from the ground up. As a skilled professional, Matthew has spoken in a range of contexts, including in person and at online events.

CONTENTS AT A GLANCE

CONTENTS

ACKNOWLEDGMENTS

From Peter:

I am immensely grateful to Wendy Rinaldi for affirming the need to have this book published on a tight timeline. My readers, including current and future risk managers, deserve nothing less.

Heartfelt thanks to Wendy Rinaldi and Janet Walden for proficiently managing this project, facilitating rapid turnaround, and equipping us with the information and guidance we needed to produce the manuscript.

Many thanks to Janet Walden and Nitesh Sharma for managing the editorial and production ends of the project and to Bart Reed for copyediting the book and further improving readability. I appreciate KnowledgeWorks Global Ltd. for expertly rendering my sketches into beautifully clear line art and laying out the pages. Like stage performers, they make hard work look easy, and I appreciate their skills.

Heartfelt thanks to Matt Webster (the author of *Do No Harm* and former CISO at Galway Holdings) for his invaluable tech review of the entire manuscript. Matt's experience in security leadership and risk management resulted in many improvements in the manuscript. A thanks also to others, including Mark Adams.

Many thanks to my literary agent, Carole Jelen, for her diligent assistance during this and other projects. Sincere thanks to Rebecca Steele, my business manager and publicist, for her long-term vision and for keeping me on track.

Bobby and Dawn, thank you for including me and welcoming me to this project. The first edition of this book was entirely yours, and I'm honored to have been included in this edition. I have enjoyed working with you and on this project. But most important to me: it has been a pleasure getting to know both of you better. You both have my deepest respect.

Despite having written more than 40 books, I have difficulty putting into words my gratitude for my wife, Rebekah, for tolerating my frequent absences (in the home office) while I developed the manuscript. This project could not have been completed without her loyal and unfailing support and encouragement.

From Dawn:

I continue to be proud to call Bobby Rogers my coauthor and friend. I couldn't ask for a better partner in crime.

Many thanks to Peter Gregory for jumping in and improving our work. Thank you, Peter, for the guidance and support!

McGraw Hill continues to provide both excellent editors and excellent people to guide our projects along the way; we could not have pulled off this project without them and their consistent support.

A big thank you to our technical editor, Matthew Webster. You did a great job keeping us on our toes.

Finally, I heartily acknowledge the contribution of my family and friends who have supported me throughout my various crazy endeavors. I could not ask for more than the love and encouragement I receive every day toward pursuing my goals. Thank you all.

From Bobby:

First, I'd like to thank all the good folks at McGraw Hill and their associates for guiding us throughout this book, helping us to ensure a quality product. Wendy Rinaldi, Caitlin Cromley-Linn, and Janet Walden were awesome to work with, making sure we stayed on track and doing everything they could to make this a wonderful experience. We're very grateful to them for giving us the chance to write this book and believing in us every step of the way. Nitesh Sharma of KnowledgeWorks Global Ltd. was great to work with as project manager, and I'm happy to work again with Bart Reed, our copy editor on this project, who always manages to make me sound far more intelligent with his improvements to my writing.

Dawn Dunkerley has been one of my best friends for several years now, and I also consider her one of the smartest folks in our profession, so I was doubly happy to have her coauthor this book once again. She has added some fantastic insight and knowledge to this book; we couldn't have done it without her. Thanks much, Dawn!

I would also like to offer a profound thanks to Peter for agreeing to be our coauthor on this project. Three minds are definitely better than two, and Peter brought a new insight into ISACA's certifications and processes that we did not have for the first edition. His work in rewriting, revamping, redesigning, and rearranging the book material to make it more closely align to ISACA's exam requirements was a critically needed improvement for this book to continue to be a great reference and study guide for the exam.

Matthew Webster deserves some special thanks because, as the technical editor, he had a difficult job, which was to make sure we stayed reasonable and technically accurate throughout the book. Matthew definitely contributed to the clarity, understanding, and technical accuracy of the text. Thanks for all your help, Matthew!

Most importantly, I would like to thank my family for allowing me to take time away from them to write, especially during the difficult times we live in right now. To my wife, Barb, my children and their families, Greg, Sarah and Sara, AJ and Audra, and my grandchildren, Sam, Ben, Evey, Emmy, and big Caleb, and now, my first great-grandson, little Caleb: I love all of you.

From Peter, Dawn, and Bobby:

We are so grateful for Matthew Webster's contributions to the completeness and quality of this book. Through his experience in risk management and control, Matthew provided expert commentary and many suggested changes that made the book that much better. Thank you, Matthew!

INTRODUCTION

Welcome to the *All-in-One Exam Guide* for ISACA's Certified in Risk and Information Systems Control (CRISC) exam! This book will help you study for, and successfully pass, one of ISACA's premier certification exams, the CRISC exam. This exam is designed to test your knowledge of a wide variety of topics related to risk management and information systems controls. The exam focuses on business and IT risk management in enterprise infrastructure and designing and implementing IT security controls to mitigate risk.

Every day, it seems, data is breached at some of the largest organizations in the world. Recently we've seen breaches in the U.S. government, in the healthcare industry, and even at tech giants such as Microsoft, LinkedIn, and Facebook. Ransomware attacks alone are a plague on thousands of companies in nearly every country in the world. No organization, no matter what size, is immune to the threat of data breaches or, for that matter, data theft or loss. However, effective risk management can reduce the possibility of data breaches and strengthen business processes and IT infrastructures and even contribute to their efficient use. Information system controls reduce the likelihood of adverse events having a significant impact on the organization and should be carefully planned for and considered.

This book covers basic risk concepts, risk assessments, standards and frameworks, and information security control design and implementation. We also cover the essential concepts, terminology, and definitions that risk management practitioners and security professionals need to be effective in these areas. In the book's four main chapters, we cover all four of the top-level domains as well as the task and knowledge statements listed in the official ISACA exam objectives. Appendix A discusses the pragmatic ways in which a security leader can successfully implement a risk management program.

While you don't have to be an expert already in all the areas we discuss, having experience in some of these areas, such as risk concepts, helps. A good, broad background of experience and knowledge in information security will give you an advantage in your studies for this exam. Of course, you'll get a good background in all these subjects throughout the book.

Passing the CRISC exam not only places you in a class of professionals recognized for their experience and expertise in this field, but it also serves to quantify and validate your knowledge of advanced risk management and security topics. After passing this exam, you'll be able to show that not only are you qualified, but you are certified in these areas. This book is designed to help get you there.

Purpose of This Book

Let's get the obvious out of the way: this is a comprehensive study guide for the information security and risk management professional who needs a reliable reference for individual or group-led study for the CRISC certification. This book contains the information that CRISC candidates are required to know. While this book is one source of information to help you prepare for the CRISC exam, it should not be thought of as the ultimate collection of *all* the knowledge and experience that ISACA expects qualified CRISC candidates to possess—no one publication covers all this information. The other thing you'll need, just as important as suitable study material in our minds, is experience. There's no substitute for practical, hands-on experience. You should make every effort to learn all aspects of the ISACA CRISC exam material we discuss in this book.

This book also serves as a reference for aspiring and practicing security and risk professionals and leaders. The content required to pass the CRISC exam is the same content that practicing security and risk professionals need to be familiar with in their day-to-day work. This book is a definitive CRISC exam study guide as well as a desk reference for those who have already earned their CRISC certification.

The pace of change in the information security and risk management industry and profession is high. Rather than contain every detail and nuance of every law, practice, standard, and technique in information security and risk management, this book shows the reader how to stay current in the profession. Indeed, the pace of change is one of many reasons that ISACA and other associations require continuous learning to retain one's certifications. It is crucial to understand key facts and practices in security and risk management and learn how to stay current as they continue to change. However, despite the high rate of change in information security, there's good news: the techniques for risk management itself change very slowly. The principles of risk assessments, risk management, and risk treatment are solid and time-proven. Much of this book is devoted to these practices.

This book is also invaluable for security and risk management professionals who are not in a leadership position. You will gain considerable insight into today's security and risk management challenges. This book is also helpful for IT, privacy, and business management professionals who work with risk management professionals and need a better understanding of what they are doing and why.

Finally, this book is an excellent guide for anyone exploring a career in information security and risk management. The study chapters explain all the relevant technologies, techniques, and processes used to manage a modern risk management program. This is useful if you are wondering what the risk management profession is all about.

How to Use This Book

This book covers everything you'll need to know for ISACA's CRISC certification examination. Each chapter covers specific objectives and details for the exam, as defined by ISACA in its job practice areas. The chapters and their sections correspond precisely to the CRISC job practice that ISACA updates from time to time.

Each chapter has several components designed to effectively communicate the information you'll need for the exam.

- The topics covered in each chapter are listed in the first section to help you to map out your study.

- **Tips** are included in each chapter that offer great information on how concepts you'll study apply in a place that we like to call "the real world." Often, they give you a bit more information on a topic covered in the text.

- **Exam Tips** are included to point out areas you need to focus on for the exam. Note that they won't give you any exam answers, but they will help you know about important topics you may see on the test.

- **Notes** may be included in a chapter as well. These are bits of information that are relevant to the discussion and that point out extra information.

- **Fifteen practice questions** appear at the end of each chapter and are designed to allow you to attempt some exam questions on the topics covered in the domain.

Appendix A is designed to help you understand the practical side of risk management, particularly for security leaders who need to develop or improve the risk management function in an organization. All three of us have many years of experience; this is our gift to you so that you have the greatest chance to succeed.

Appendix B contains information on how to access the online practice exam questions that accompany this book. The TotalTester engine allows you to test yourself in either Practice or Exam mode, or by narrowing down to a specific domain.

About This Second Edition

ISACA, like other certification organizations, periodically updates the job practice for CRISC and its other certifications. In 2020, we expected that ISACA would update the CRISC job practice in 2021, which prompted us to prepare to write this second edition reflecting these updates.

The first edition of this book was organized by subject matter and included a mapping from the book to the CRISC job practice. This arrangement allowed the book to tell the risk and control story logically, and the mapping table in the book helped readers understand what parts of the book corresponded to what parts of the CRISC job practice.

This second edition has been rearranged: the chapters and sections in the book now precisely correspond to the areas of the CRISC job practice, so it is no longer necessary to include a practice-to-book mapping. This new structure simplifies readers' desire to read more about a particular topic in the job practice.

ISACA is somewhat academic in its approach to the arrangement of the CRISC job practice areas. For this reason, we added an appendix that describes the development and operation of a risk management program from a practical point of view. This appendix helps to fill the gap between the CRISC job practice and what it really takes to succeed.

Bobby and Dawn, the coauthors of the first edition, asked the publisher if Peter Gregory could be added to the writing team for the second edition. Peter's familiarity with ISACA, its certifications, and his experience writing *All-In-One Exam Guides* for ISACA and IAPP certifications have helped improve this second edition. This book is the finished product of our collective service to you, our readers.

Becoming a CRISC Professional

To become a CRISC professional, you are required to pay the exam fee, pass the exam, prove that you have the necessary education and experience, and agree to uphold ethics and standards. To keep your CRISC certification, you are required to take at least 20 continuing education hours each year (120 hours in three years) and pay annual maintenance fees. This life cycle is depicted in Figure 1.

The following list outlines the primary requirements for becoming certified:

- **Experience** A CRISC candidate must submit verifiable evidence of at least three years of professional work experience in IT risk management and IS control. Experience must be verified and gained within the ten-year period preceding the application date for certification or within five years from passing the exam. No waiver options are available.

- **Ethics** Candidates must commit to adhering to ISACA's Code of Professional Ethics, which guides the personal and professional conduct of those certified.

- **Exam** Candidates must receive a passing score on the CRISC exam. A passing score is valid for up to five years, after which the passing score is void. A CRISC candidate who passes the exam has a maximum of five years to apply for CRISC certification; candidates who pass the exam but fail to act after five years will have to retake the exam if they want to become CRISC certified.

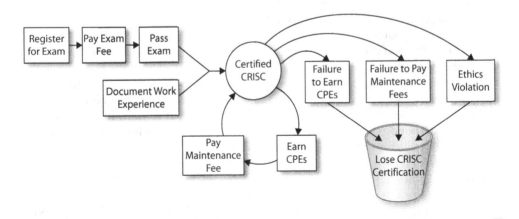

Figure 1 The CRISC certification life cycle

- **Education** Those certified must adhere to the CRISC Continuing Professional Education Policy, which requires a minimum of 20 continuing professional education (CPE) hours each year, with a total requirement of 120 CPEs over the course of the certification period (three years).

- **Application** After successfully passing the exam, meeting the experience requirements, and having read through the Code of Professional Ethics and Standards, a candidate is ready to apply for certification. An application must be received within five years of passing the exam.

Experience Requirements

To qualify for CRISC certification, you must have completed the equivalent of three years of total work experience in at least two of the CRISC domains. Additional details on the minimum certification requirements, substitution options, and various examples are discussed next.

 NOTE Although it is not recommended, a CRISC candidate can take the exam before completing any work experience directly related to information security management. As long as the candidate passes the exam and the work experience requirements are filled within five years of the exam date, and within ten years from the application for certification, the candidate is eligible for certification.

Direct Work Experience

You are required to have a minimum of three years of work experience in IT risk management and IS control. This is equivalent to 6000 actual work hours, which must be related to at least two of the CRISC job practice areas, listed next. One of these two job practice areas must be in Governance or IT Risk Assessment.

- **Governance** Establish and maintain organizational governance and risk governance programs and frameworks. Determine roles and responsibilities as well as develop policies, standards, business processes, risk appetite, and risk tolerance, aligned with business culture and compliance with legal, regulatory, and contractual requirements.

- **IT Risk Assessment** Establish and maintain processes to identify and analyze risk, including vulnerability management, threat modeling, risk assessments, and business impact analysis. Develop and maintain a risk register.

- **Risk Response and Reporting** Establish and maintain risk treatment and risk response, controls and control ownership, third-party risk management processes, and control testing and remediation. Establish and publish metrics, key performance indicators, key risk indicators, and key control indicators.

- **Information Technology and Security**   Understand the principles of information technology and security, including enterprise architecture, IT operations, project management, business continuity and disaster recovery planning, data life cycle, systems development life cycle, security awareness training, and privacy.

All work experience must be completed within the ten years before completing the certification application or within five years from initially passing the CRISC exam. You will need to complete a separate Verification of Work Experience form for each segment of experience.

Substitution of Experience

Unlike most other ISACA certifications, there are no available experience waivers or substitutions. Instead, you are required to have three or more years of experience in IT risk management and IS control, as described in the preceding section.

 NOTE   We recommend you also read the CRISC certification qualifications on the ISACA website. From time to time, ISACA does change the qualification rules, and we want you to have the most up-to-date information available.

ISACA Code of Professional Ethics

Becoming a CRISC professional means you agree to adhere to the ISACA Code of Professional Ethics, which is a formal document outlining those things you will do to ensure the utmost integrity and that best support and represent the organization and certification.

Specifically, the ISACA Code of Professional Ethics requires ISACA members and certification holders to do the following:

- Support the implementation of, and encourage compliance with, appropriate standards and procedures for the effective governance and management of enterprise information systems and technology, including audit, control, security, and risk management.

- Perform their duties with objectivity, due diligence, and professional care, in accordance with professional standards.

- Serve in the interest of stakeholders in a lawful manner, while maintaining high standards of conduct and character and not discrediting their profession or the association.

- Maintain the privacy and confidentiality of information obtained in the course of their activities unless disclosure is required by legal authority. Such information shall not be used for personal benefit or released to inappropriate parties.

- Maintain competency in their respective fields and agree to undertake only those activities they can reasonably expect to complete with the necessary skills, knowledge, and competence.

- Inform appropriate parties of the results of work performed, including the disclosure of all significant facts known to them that, if not disclosed, may distort the reporting of the results.

- Support the professional education of stakeholders in enhancing their understanding of the governance and management of enterprise information systems and technology, including audit, control, security, and risk management.

Failure to comply with the ISACA Code of Professional Ethics can result in an investigation into a member's or certification holder's conduct and, ultimately, disciplinary measures, including the forfeiture of their hard-won certification(s).

You can find the full text and terms of enforcement of the ISACA Code of Professional Ethics at www.isaca.org/credentialing/code-of-professional-ethics.

The Certification Exam

The certification is offered throughout the year in several examination windows. You have several ways to register; however, we highly recommend you plan and register early regardless of your chosen method.

In early 2022, the schedule of exam fees in U.S. dollars was

- CRISC application fee: $50
- Regular registration: $575 member/$760 nonmember

As we write this, we're emerging from the global COVID-19 pandemic. During the pandemic, ISACA and other certification bodies adapted and developed remotely proctored exams that permitted test-takers to sit for a certification exam from their residence. We have observed that ISACA has returned to tests administered at testing centers while continuing to offer remotely proctored exams for those who prefer remote testing. We'll discuss both options in this section.

 NOTE   We recommend you pay close attention to information on ISACA's website regarding testing logistics and locations.

Once registration is complete, you will immediately receive an e-mail acknowledging your registration. Next, you will need to schedule your certification exam. The ISACA website will direct you to the certification registration page, where you will select a date, time, and (optionally) location to take your exam. When you confirm the date, time, and location for your exam, you will receive a confirmation via e-mail. You will need the confirmation letter to enter the test location—make sure to keep it unmarked and in a safe place until test time.

Onsite Testing Center

When you arrive at the test site, you will be required to sign in, and you may be required to sign an agreement. Also, you will be required to turn in your smartphone, wallet or purse, and other personal items for safekeeping. The exam proctor will read aloud the rules you are required to follow while you take your exam. These rules will address matters such as breaks, drinking water, and snacks.

While you take your exam, you will be supervised by the proctor, and possibly you will be monitored by video surveillance in the test center to make sure no one can cheat on the exam.

Remote Proctored Testing

If you have registered for a remote proctored exam, you need to make sure you meet all the technical requirements. ISACA has published the "Remote Proctoring Guide," which includes all the necessary technical requirements and describes the step-by-step procedures for taking the exam.

A remote proctored exam means you'll be taking the exam on your own computer in your residence or other location. You'll be in live contact with an exam proctor, and your webcam will be turned on throughout the exam so that the proctor can observe you while taking the exam to ensure you are not cheating through the use of reference materials (books or online). The proctor may ask you to show them the room where you are taking the exam to ensure you do not have reference materials or information anywhere in view.

To be eligible for a remote proctored exam, you must have a supported version of Windows or macOS, a current Google Chrome or other Chromium browser (such as Brave or SRware Iron), a webcam with at least 640×480 resolution, a microphone, and a stable broadband Internet connection. You must have the ability to install the PSI Secure Browser and modify firewalls and other administrative tasks on the day of the exam (this requires you have administrative privileges on the computer you are using—which might be a problem if you are using a company-issued computer).

You'll be required to log in to your My ISACA account when your exam is scheduled. Next, you'll navigate to your certifications, find the exam you have scheduled, and launch the exam. You'll be directed to perform several tasks, including installing the secure browser and closing several other programs on your computer, including other web browsers and programs like Adobe Reader, Word, Excel, and any others that could include reference material.

You are not permitted to speak or perform gestures at any time during the exam. In short, you cannot be seen to perform any action that might be an indication of aid by an accomplice or the presence of reference material.

You'll be required to verify your ID by holding it near your webcam so that the proctor can see it to confirm that you are not having someone else take the exam for you. You will also be required to use your webcam to show the entire room to your proctor.

After all steps have been completed, the proctor will release the exam to you, and you may begin.

Exam Questions

Each registrant has four hours to take the multiple-choice question exam. There are 150 questions on the exam, representing the four job practice areas. Each question has four answer choices, of which you can select only one best answer. You can skip questions and return to them later, and you can also flag questions that you want to review later if time permits. While you are taking your exam, the time remaining will appear on the screen.

When you have completed the exam, you are directed to close it. At that time, the exam will display your pass or fail status, with a reminder that your score and passing status are subject to review.

You will be scored for each job practice area and then provided one final score. All scores are scaled. Scores range from 200 to 800; however, a final score of 450 is required to pass.

Exam questions are derived from a job practice analysis study conducted by ISACA. The areas selected represent those tasks performed in a CRISC's day-to-day activities and represent the background knowledge required to develop and manage an information security program. You can find more detailed descriptions of the task and knowledge statements at https://www.isaca.org/credentialing/crisc/crisc-exam-content-outline.

Exam Coverage

The CRISC exam is quite broad in its scope. The exam covers four job practice areas, as shown in Table 1.

Independent committees have been developed to determine the best questions, review exam results, and statistically analyze the results for continuous improvement. Should you come across a horrifically difficult or strange question, do not panic. This question may have been written for another purpose. A few questions on the exam are included for research and analysis purposes and will not be counted against your score. The exam contains no indications in this regard.

Domain	CRISC Job Practice Area	Percentage of Exam
1	Governance	26%
2	IT Risk Assessment	20%
3	Risk Response and Reporting	32%
4	Information Technology and Security	22%

Table 1 CRISC Exam Practice Areas

Preparing for the Exam

The CRISC certification requires a great deal of knowledge and experience from the CRISC candidate. You need to map out a long-term study strategy to pass the exam. The following sections offer some tips and are intended to help guide you to, through, and beyond exam day.

Before the Exam

Consider the following list of tips on tasks and resources for exam preparation. They are listed in sequential order.

- **Read the candidate's guide** For information on the certification exam and requirements for the current year, see the ISACA Exam Candidates Information Guide: go to www.isaca.org/credentialing/crisc and look for the Exam Candidate Information Guide download links.

- **Register** If you are able, register early for any cost savings and solidify your commitment to moving forward with this professional achievement.

- **Schedule your exam** Find a location, date, and time, and commit.

- **Become familiar with the CRISC job practice areas** The job practice areas serve as the basis for the exam and requirements. Beginning with the 2021 exam, the job practice areas have changed. Ensure your study materials align with the current list, shown at https://www.isaca.org/credentialing/crisc.

- **Know your best learning methods** Everyone has preferred learning styles, whether self-study, a study group, an instructor-led course, or a boot camp. Try to set up a study program that leverages your strengths.

- **Self-assess** Run through practice exam questions available online (see Appendix B for more information). ISACA may offer a free CRISC self-assessment.

- **Study iteratively** Depending on how much work experience in information security management you have already, we suggest you plan your study program to take at least two months but as long as six months. During this time, periodically take practice exams and note your areas of strength and weakness. Once you have identified your weak areas, focus on those areas weekly by rereading the related sections in this book, retaking practice exams, and noting your progress.

- **Avoid cramming** We've all seen the books on the shelves with titles that involve last-minute cramming. Just one look on the Internet reveals various websites that teach individuals how to cram for exams most effectively. Research sites claim that exam cramming can lead to susceptibility to colds and flu, sleep disruptions, overeating, and digestive problems. One thing is certain: many people find that good, steady study habits result in less stress and greater clarity and focus during the exam. Because of the complexity of this exam, we highly recommend the long-term, steady-study option. Study the job practice areas thoroughly. There are many study options. If time permits, investigate the many resources available to you.

- **Find a study group**   Many ISACA chapters and other organizations have formed specific study groups or offer less-expensive exam review courses. Contact your local chapter to see whether these options are available to you. In addition, be sure to keep your eye on the ISACA website. Also, use your local network to find out whether there are other local study groups and other helpful resources.

- **Recheck your confirmation letter**   Do not write on or lose your confirmation letter. Put it in a safe place and note what time you will need to arrive at the site. Note this on your calendar. Confirm that the location is the one you selected and is located near you.

- **Check logistics**   Check the candidate's guide and your confirmation letter for the exact time you are required to report to the test site (or log in from home if you registered for a remote proctored exam). A few days before the exam, check the site—become familiar with the location and tricks to getting there. If you are taking public transportation, be sure you are looking at the schedule for the day of the exam: if your CRISC exam is scheduled on a Saturday, public transportation schedules may differ from weekday schedules. If you are driving, know the route and where to park your vehicle.

- **Pack**   Place your confirmation letter and a photo ID in a safe place, ready to go. Your ID must be a current, government-issued photo ID that matches the name on the confirmation letter and must not be handwritten. Examples of acceptable forms of ID are passports, driver's licenses, state IDs, green cards, and national IDs. Ensure you leave food, drinks, laptops, cell phones, and other electronic devices behind, as they are not permitted at the test site. For information on what can and cannot be brought to the exam site, see the CRISC exam candidate guide at https://www.isaca.org/credentialing/crisc.

- **Make a notification decision**   Decide whether you want your test results e-mailed to you. You will have the opportunity to consent to e-mail notification of the exam results. If you are fully paid (zero balance on exam fee) and have agreed to the e-mail notification, you should receive a one-time e-mail approximately eight weeks from the date of the exam with your results.

- **Sleep**   Make sure you get a good night's sleep before the exam. Research suggests that you should avoid caffeine at least four hours before bedtime, keep a notepad and pen next to the bed to capture late-night thoughts that might keep you awake, eliminate as much noise and light as possible, and keep your room a suitable temperature for sleeping. In the morning, rise early so as not to rush and subject yourself to additional stress.

Day of the Exam

On the day of the exam, follow these tips:

- **Arrive early** Check the Bulletin of Information and your confirmation letter for the exact time you are required to report to the test site. The confirmation letter or the candidate's guide explains that you must be at the test site *no later* than approximately 30 minutes *before* testing time. The examiner will begin reading the exam instructions at this time, and any latecomers will be disqualified from taking the test and will *not* receive a refund of fees.

- **Observe test center rules** There may be rules about taking breaks. This will be discussed by the examiner, along with exam instructions. If you need something at any time during the exam and are unsure as to the rules, be sure to ask first. For information on conduct during the exam, see the ISACA CRISC candidate guide at https://www.isaca.org/credentialing/crisc.

- **Answer all exam questions** Read the questions carefully, but do not overanalyze them. Remember to select the *best* solution. There may be several reasonable answers, but one is *better* than the others. If you aren't sure about an answer, you can mark the question and return to it later. After going through all the questions, you can return to the marked questions (and others) to read them and consider them more carefully. Above all, don't try to overanalyze questions, and do trust your instincts. Do not try to rush through the exam, as there is plenty of time to take as much as a few minutes for each question. However, at the same time, do watch the clock so that you don't find yourself going too slowly that you won't be able to answer every question thoughtfully.

- **Note your exam result** When you have completed the exam, you should see your pass/fail result. Your results may not be in large, blinking text; you may need to read the fine print to get your preliminary results. If you passed, congratulations! If you did not pass, do observe any remarks about your status; you will be able to retake the exam—there is information about this on the ISACA website.

If You Did Not Pass

Don't lose heart if you did not pass your exam on the first attempt. Instead, remember that failure is a stepping stone to success. Thoughtfully take stock and determine your improvement areas. Go back to this book's practice exams and be honest with yourself regarding those areas where you need to learn more. Reread the chapters or sections where you need to know more. If you participated in a study group or training, contact your study group coach or class instructor if you feel you can get any advice from them on how to study up on the topics you need to master. Take at least several weeks to study those topics, refresh yourself on other topics, then give it another go. Success is granted to those who are persistent and determined.

After the Exam

A few weeks from the exam date, you will receive your exam results by e-mail or postal mail. Each job practice area score will be noted in addition to the overall final score. All scores are scaled. Should you receive a passing score, you will also receive the application for certification.

Those unsuccessful in passing will also be notified. These individuals will want to closely look at the job practice area scores to determine areas for further study. They may retake the exam as many times as needed on future exam dates, as long as they have registered and paid the applicable fees. Regardless of pass or fail, exam results will not be disclosed via telephone, fax, or e-mail (except for the consented e-mail notification).

NOTE You are not permitted to display the CRISC moniker until you have completed certification. Passing the exam is *not* sufficient to use the CRISC anywhere, including e-mail, résumés, CVs, correspondence, or social media.

Applying for CRISC Certification

To apply for certification, you must submit evidence of a passing score and related work experience. Keep in mind that you have five years to use this score on a CRISC certification application once you receive a passing score. After this time, you will need to retake the exam. In addition, all work experience submitted must have been within ten years of your new certification application.

To complete the application process, you need to submit the following information:

- **CRISC application**   Note the exam ID number as found in your exam results letter, list the information security management experience and any experience substitutions, and identify which CRISC job practice area (or areas) your experience pertains to.

- **Verification of Work Experience forms**   These must be filled out and signed by your immediate supervisor or a person of higher rank in the organization to verify your work experience noted on the application. You must fill out a complete set of Verification of Work Experience forms for each separate employer.

As with the exam, after you've successfully mailed the application, you must wait approximately eight weeks for processing. If your application is approved, you will receive an e-mail notification, followed by a package in the mail containing your letter of certification, certificate, and a copy of the Continuing Professional Education Policy. You can then proudly display your certificate and use the "CRISC" designation on your résumé, e-mail and social media profiles, and business cards.

NOTE You are permitted to use the CRISC moniker *only* after receiving your certification letter from ISACA.

Retaining Your CRISC Certification

There is more to becoming a CRISC professional than merely passing an exam, submitting an application, and receiving a paper certificate. Becoming a CRISC professional is an ongoing and continuous lifestyle. Those with CRISC certification agree to abide by a code of ethics, meet ongoing education requirements, and pay annual certification maintenance fees. Let's take a closer look at the education requirements and explain the costs involved in retaining certification.

Continuing Education

The goal of continuing professional education requirements is to ensure that individuals maintain CRISC-related knowledge to better develop and manage security management programs. To maintain CRISC certification, individuals must obtain 120 continuing education hours within three years, with a minimum requirement of 20 hours per year. Each CPE hour is to account for 50 minutes of active participation in educational activities.

What Counts as a Valid CPE Credit?

For training and activities to be utilized for CPEs, they must involve technical or managerial training that is directly applicable to information security and information security management. The following list of activities has been approved by the CRISC certification committee and can count toward your CPE requirements:

- ISACA professional education activities and meetings.
- If you are an ISACA member, you can take Information Systems Control Journal CPE Quizzes online or participate in monthly webcasts. For each webcast, CPEs are rewarded after you pass a quiz.
- Non-ISACA professional education activities and meetings.
- Self-study courses.
- Vendor sales or marketing presentations (ten-hour annual limit).
- Teaching, lecturing, or presenting on subjects related to job practice areas.
- Publication of articles and books related to the profession.
- Exam question development and review for any ISACA certification.
- Passing related professional examinations.
- Participation in ISACA boards or committees (20-hour annual limit per ISACA certification).
- Contributions to the information security management profession (ten-hour annual limit).
- Mentoring (ten-hour annual limit).

For more information on what is accepted as a valid CPE credit, see the Continuing Professional Education Policy (https://www.isaca.org/credentialing/how-to-earn-cpe/#cpe-policy).

Tracking and Submitting CPEs

Not only are you required to submit a CPE tracking form for the annual renewal process, but you also should keep detailed records for each activity. Records associated with each activity should have the following:

- Name of attendee
- Name of sponsoring organization
- Activity title
- Activity description
- Activity date
- Number of CPE hours awarded

It is in your best interest to track all CPE information in a single file or worksheet. ISACA has developed a tracking form for your use, which can be found in the Continuing Professional Education Policy. To make it easy on yourself, consider keeping all related records such as receipts, brochures, and certificates in the same place. Documentation should be retained throughout the three-year certification period and for at least one additional year afterward. Evidence retention is essential, as you may someday be audited. If this happens, you would be required to submit all paperwork. So why not be prepared?

For new CRISCs, the annual and three-year certification period begins January 1 of the year following certification. You are not required to report CPE hours for the first partial year after your certification; however, the hours earned from the time of certification to December 31 can be utilized in the first certification reporting period the following year. Therefore, should you get certified in January, you will have until the following January to accumulate CPEs. You will not have to report them until you report the totals for the following year, in October or November. This is known as the *renewal period*. During this time, you will receive an e-mail directing you to the website to enter CPEs earned over the course of the year. Alternatively, the renewal will be mailed to you, and then CPEs can be recorded on the hard-copy invoice and sent with your maintenance fee payment. CPEs and maintenance fees must be received by January 15 to retain certification.

Notification of compliance from the certification department is sent after all the information has been received and processed. Should ISACA have any questions about the information you have submitted, it will contact you directly.

Sample CPE Submission

Table 2 contains an example of a CPE submission.

Name_____Chris Jacobs_____

Certification Number___67895787_____

Certification Period____1/1/2022_____to____12/31/2022_____

Activity Title/Sponsor	Activity Description	Date	CPE Hours	Support Docs Included?
ISACA presentation/lunch	PCI compliance	2/11/2022	1 CPE	Yes (receipt)
ISACA presentation/lunch	Security in SDLC	3/11/2022	1 CPE	Yes (receipt)
Regional Conference, RIMS	Compliance, risk	1/12–14/2022	6 CPEs	Yes (CPE receipt)
BrightFly webinar	Governance, risk, & compliance	2/16/2022	3 CPEs	Yes (confirmation e-mail)
ISACA board meeting	Chapter board meeting	4/8/2022	2 CPEs	Yes (meeting minutes)
Presented at ISSA meeting	Risk management presentation	6/21/2022	1 CPE	Yes (meeting notice)
Published an article in XYZ	Journal article on SOX ITGCs	4/12/2022	4 CPEs	Yes (article)
Vendor presentation	Learned about GRC tool capability	5/12/2022	2 CPEs	Yes
Employer-offered training	Change management course	3/25/2022	7 CPEs	Yes (certificate of course completion)

Table 2 Sample CPE Submission

CPE Maintenance Fees

To remain CRISC certified, you must pay CPE maintenance fees each year. These fees are (as of early 2022) $45 for members and $85 for nonmembers each year. These fees are in addition to ISACA membership and local chapter dues (neither of which is required to maintain your CRISC certification).

Revocation of Certification

A CRISC-certified individual may have their certification revoked for the following reasons:

- Failure to complete the minimum number of CPEs during the period.
- Failure to document and provide evidence of CPEs in an audit.

- Failure to submit payment for maintenance fees.
- Failure to comply with the Code of Professional Ethics can result in investigation and ultimately can lead to revocation of certification.

If you have received a revocation notice, you will need to contact the ISACA Certification Department at certification@isaca.org for more information.

Living the CRISC Lifestyle

Being a CRISC involves a lot more than passing the exam, participating in continuous learning, and paying the annual maintenance fees. There are numerous opportunities to get involved in local, national, and global activities and events that will help you grow professionally and meet other risk management professionals.

Find a Local Chapter

ISACA has over 200 local chapters in nearly 100 countries around the world. Chances are there is a chapter near you. Peter attended many ISACA chapter meetings and other events in Seattle when he lived there, where engaging speakers spoke on new topics, and where he met many like-minded security and audit professionals over the years.

Local chapters rely entirely on volunteers, and there is room for you to help in some way. Better chapters have various programs, events, study groups, and other activities that enrich participants professionally. For us, most of our ISACA experience happens in our local chapter.

Attend ISACA Events

ISACA puts on fantastic in-person conferences with world-class keynote speakers, expert presentations, vendor demonstrations and exhibits, a bookstore, and opportunities to meet other security, risk, and audit professionals. We find ISACA conferences enriching to the point of being overwhelming. There are so many learning and networking opportunities that we find ourselves nearly exhausted at the end of an ISACA conference.

Join the Online Community

ISACA has an online community known as Engage, in which participants can discuss any topic related to security, risk, audit, privacy, and IT management. You can read and participate in online discussions, ask questions, help others with their questions, and make new professional connections. You can join Engage at https://engage.isaca.org/.

Pay It Forward Through Mentorship

If you are at the point in your career where you qualify for and have a reasonable prospect of passing the CRISC exam, chances are you have had a mentor or two earlier in your career, and maybe you have one now. As you grow in your professional stature, others will look to you as a potential mentor. Perhaps someone will come out and ask you if you would consider mentoring them.

The world needs more, and better, information security professionals and leaders. Mentoring is a great way to "pay it forward" by helping others get into the profession and grow professionally. You will also find that mentoring will enrich you as well.

Volunteer

As a nonprofit organization, ISACA relies on volunteers to enrich its programs and events. There are many ways to help, and one or more of these volunteer opportunities might be suitable for you:

- **Speaking at an ISACA event** Whether you do a keynote address or a session on a specific topic, speaking at an ISACA event is a mountaintop experience. You can share your knowledge and expertise on a particular topic with attendees, but you'll learn some things, too.

- **Serving as a chapter board member** Local chapters don't run by themselves—they rely on volunteers who are working professionals who want to improve the lot of other professionals in the local community. Board members can serve in various ways, from financial management to membership to events.

- **Starting or helping a CRISC study group** Whether as a part of a local chapter or at large, consider starting or helping a group of professionals who want to learn the details of the CRISC job practice. We are proponents of study groups because study group participants make the best students: they take the initiative to take on a big challenge to advance their careers.

- **Writing an article** ISACA has online and paper-based publications with articles on a wide variety of subjects, including current developments in security, privacy, risk, and IT management from many perspectives. If you have specialized knowledge on some topic, other ISACA members can benefit from this knowledge if you write an article.

- **Participating in a credential working group** ISACA works hard to ensure that its many certifications remain relevant and up to date. Experts around the world in many industries give their time to ensure that ISACA certifications remain the best in the world. ISACA conducts online and in-person working groups to update certification job practices, write certification exam questions, and publish updated study guides and practice exams. Peter contributed to the first working group in 2013 when ISACA initially developed the CRISC certification exam; he met many like-minded professionals, some of whom he is still in regular and meaningful contact with.

- **Participating in ISACA CommunITy Day** ISACA organizes a global effort of local volunteering to make the world a better, safer place for everyone. Learn about the next CommunITy Day at https://engage.isaca.org/communityday/.

- **Writing certification exam questions**   ISACA needs experienced subject matter experts who are willing to take the time to write new certification exam questions. ISACA has a rigorous, high-quality process for exam questions that includes training. Who knows—you could even be invited to an in-person workshop on writing exam items. You can find out more about how this works at https://www.isaca.org/credentialing/write-an-exam-question.

You can learn about these and many other volunteer opportunities at https://www.isaca.org/why-isaca/participate-and-volunteer.

Please take a minute to reflect on the quality and richness of the ISACA organization and its many world-class certifications, publications, and events. These are all fueled by volunteers who made ISACA into what it is today. Only through your contribution of time and expertise will ISACA continue in its excellence for future security, risk, privacy, and IT professionals. And one last thing you can only experience on your own: volunteering not only helps others but enriches you as well. Will you consider leaving your mark and making ISACA better than you found it?

Continue to Grow Professionally

Continuous improvement is a mindset and a lifestyle that is built in to IT service management and information security—it's even a formal requirement in ISO/IEC 27001! We suggest that you periodically take stock in your career status and aspirations, be honest with yourself, and determine what mountain you will climb next. If needed, find a mentor who can guide you and give you solid advice.

While this may not immediately make sense to you, know this: helping others, whether through any of the volunteer opportunities listed previously or in other ways, will enrich you personally and professionally. We're not talking about feathers in your cap or juicy items on your résumé, but rather the growth in character and wisdom that results from helping and serving others, particularly when you initiated the helping and serving.

Professional growth means different things to different people. Whether it's a better job title, more money, a better (or bigger or smaller) employer, a different team, more responsibility, or more certifications, embarking on long-term career planning will pay dividends. Take control of your career and your career path—this is yours to own and shape as you will.

Summary

Becoming and being a CRISC professional is a lifestyle, not just a one-time event. It takes motivation, skill, good judgment, persistence, and proficiency to be a strong and effective leader in the world of information security management. The CRISC was designed to help you navigate the security management world with greater ease and confidence.

Each CRISC job practice area will be discussed in detail in the following chapters, and additional reference material will be presented. Not only is this information helpful in studying prior to the exam, but it is also meant to serve as a resource throughout your career as an information security management professional.

Governance

In this chapter, you will:

- Understand the concepts of organizational governance and how goals and objectives support it
- Learn about structure, roles, and responsibilities
- Analyze how organizational risk culture is facilitated through the definition of risk appetite and risk tolerance
- Understand the concepts of enterprise risk management, associated frameworks, and the ethics of risk management

This chapter covers Certified in Risk and Information Systems Control Domain 1, "Governance." The domain represents 26 percent of the CRISC examination.

The CRISC Task Statements relevant to this domain focus on governance and how it applies in this context to the organization, particularly executive management. The governance aspects of risk for an organization, as well as the relationships between enterprise risk and IT risk, are also explored. The chapter also examines risk management governance and how it is implemented in the organizational structure and culture. Governance also applies to overall laws, regulations, and even risk frameworks, so we will discuss those at length. In those governance discussions we will explain both external governance and internal governance, including policies and standards. Internal governance also includes management oversight, such as business process reviews, risk appetite and tolerance, as well as contractual obligations regarding risk management. Other topics related to the Task Statements we will touch on here and look at in depth in other chapters include elements of risk such as assets and their value, threats, vulnerabilities, likelihood, and impact.

Although many organizations will "do the right thing" in terms of due diligence and care, upholding their legal and ethical responsibilities and such, many other organizations either do not or don't do it to the same standards. This is why governance is so vitally important to an organization. Governance ties all these elements together. Governance sets standards, whether they are legal, ethical, or otherwise, and attempts to "standardize" what organizations do in terms of their obligations to stakeholders and society in general. As you'll see in this chapter, governance comes from different sources, both outside the organization and within it. It is a synthesis of enforced requirements and organizational leadership culture. Also, governance is necessary to ensure that organizations treat systems and data with care and, again, perform their due diligence and due care duties when dealing with data protection and risk.

In this chapter, we will focus on organizational governance and how it applies to all the different elements of an information security management system: mission, strategy, goals and objectives, roles and responsibilities, culture, risk, and even ethics.

Organizational Governance

Governance is the glue that holds all the different framing elements of an organization together: its mission, strategy, goals, and objectives. Governance establishes the requirements an organization must meet and consists of both internal and external governance. External governance comes in the form of laws, regulations, professional and industry standards, and other sources of requirements imposed on the organization from the outside. Internal governance typically supports external governance through policies, procedures, and processes. For example, if a law imposes requirements to protect certain sensitive data using specific controls or to a certain standard, then policies and procedures further support those requirements by formalizing and codifying them within the organization. Policies and procedures can also be independent of external governance and simply reflect the organization's culture, needs, and values, usually established by its executive management. In any event, governance is the controlling factor for the organization; governance keeps the organization on the right focus and ensures that it is meeting its compulsory requirements, such as obedience to laws, as well as performing its due diligence and due care responsibilities.

In addition to imposing requirements on the organization, governance also refers to the structure by which the organization is led and regulated. Again, this could come from external or internal sources. External sources for governance could consist of an external board of directors or regulatory agencies. These entities ensure that the organization is led from the perspective of responsibility and accountability. Internal governance comes from internal business leaders and reflect business drivers not related to externalities. In reality, good governance typically reflects a balance between both internal and external business drivers.

The infrastructure framework of the organization—in the form of strategy, goals, objectives, mission statements, and so on—supports governance, as we will discuss further in this chapter.

Organizational Strategy, Goals, and Objectives

Businesses exist with clear missions, goals, and objectives. The organization is in business for a particular purpose, not merely because people want to come to work every day and socialize. Missions, goals, and objectives directly relate to why the organization is in business in the first place, whether that is to develop and market a product or provide a service. Organizational senior management defines the business's mission, goals, and objectives, typically on a strategic or long-term level. Senior management also defines the levels of risk tolerance and appetite based on factors that include the market space, the operational environment, the economy, governmental regulation, and so on. These risk levels directly articulate with and support the business mission, balancing business opportunities that can generate revenue and move the business forward with potential negative events that may cause the business to fail or at least have a detrimental impact on the organization.

 EXAM TIP Remember that risk appetite and tolerance are directly related to the business mission, although different business pursuits may have varying levels of each. Senior management sets those levels based on the potential rewards from risky opportunities and the amount of loss the organization could endure if those rewards don't materialize.

Organizational Structure, Roles, and Responsibilities

How the business is organized can help drive how it deals with risk in several ways. Most businesses are organized from a functional perspective; in other words, departments and other hierarchical structures are established to take care of specific functions that contribute to the business goals and objectives. For example, in a production-driven business, there may be a manufacturing or production department, an engineering department, a research and development department, and an assembly line. There will likely be additional departments that cover support functions, such as marketing, accounting and finance, public relations, and so on. A hospital, on the other hand, will be organized according to its specific functions, such as the emergency department, surgery, neurology, radiology, and so on. Businesses in other markets or areas will be organized differently as well. In any case, the organization of the business is structured as its mission and business purposes dictate. Certain functions can be found in any business, such as information technology, information security, and even legal compliance. These functional areas may have the primary function of dealing with risk, but an important thing to consider is that all different organizational structures, from lower-level work sections to higher-level departments and divisions, have responsibilities regarding risk.

The organization must look at its structure and decide how each individual unit will manage risk at its own level, understanding that risk management should be uniform throughout the entire organization. Another consideration is that risks tend to "roll up" or be combined at the higher levels of an organization. For example, risks that the accounting department incurs are only a part of the risks at higher organizational levels and are included in their risk management processes. Each lower-level unit in an organizational hierarchy has risks that are part of the next higher level's risk considerations. While individual units may be responsible for only a small piece of the overall organizational risk, their parent units also bear responsibility for managing that risk, as well as the risk of other subordinate units. Another concept relating to organizational structures is that the risk incurred by one part of the organization is borne by all parts of the organization; there is almost no such thing as a risk that only affects one small part of the business. Risk ripples across the entire organization in some way.

Each individual unit, whether it is a unit in the lower levels of the business hierarchy or at the highest levels, should take steps to identify, evaluate, and assess risks at its level. Risks may be thought of as tactical, operational, and strategic. Tactical risks are those that are encountered by smaller-level production sections—those that carry out the day-to-day work of the organization. Operational risks can span several work units and relate to how the business conducts its functions, as well as how the different work units interact with each other. Strategic risk is borne at the higher levels of the organization, including senior management, and involves risks incurred by leading the business toward opportunities and away from decisions that exceed the organization's capacity for risk appetite and tolerance. Respectively, these three types of risks also correspond to short-term, mid-term, and long-term risks as well.

Regardless of the level of risk incurred within the organization, there should be an enterprise risk management strategy and program in place to deal with the lower-tier, middle-tier, and higher-tier risks as well as ensure that the risk management strategy handles risks consistently and uniformly in alignment with the organization's risk tolerance and appetite. Governance from the higher levels of the organization affects risk appetite and tolerance and shapes the organization's risk management strategy throughout all the different hierarchical levels. The organizational structure must support that governance, as well as clearly define lines of authority and responsibility in terms of risk leadership and management.

Organizational Culture

Organizational *culture* is the term that describes how people treat each other and how people get things done. Many organizations establish a set of values that define the norms of behavior. Terms like *respect*, *collaboration*, and *teamwork* are often seen in these values. Some organizations will publish formal value statements and print them for display in lobbies, offices, and conference rooms.

The way that an organization's leaders treat each other and the rest of the organization sets an example for behavioral norms. Often, these norms reflect those formal values, but sometimes they may differ. One could say that an organization's stated culture and its actual culture may vary a little, or a lot. The degree of alignment itself is a reflection of an organization's culture.

An organization also has a risk culture, which is essentially how the organization as an entity feels about and deals with risk. This culture is developed from several sources. First, it can come from the organization's leadership, based on their business and management philosophies, attitudes, education, and experience. It can also come from the organization's governance. Remember that governance is essentially the rules and regulations imposed on the organization by either external entities (in the form of laws, for example) or internally by the organization itself. In any case, the culture of the organization really defines how the organization feels about risk and how it treats risk over time. We will talk later about how two concepts, risk tolerance and risk appetite, support the organizational risk culture.

Policies and Standards

Different types of controls work together to protect an organization, many of which have a technical focus. However, while the more technical approaches are quite often the stars of the cybersecurity show, the importance of the good old policy cannot be understated. In fact, without a policy, quite often, the security program will fall flat due to a lack of governance, management involvement, and accountability. This objective covers different types of policies and how they work together to form the underlying foundation of human and process control, ensuring a balanced and effective security program.

To provide effective security, security policy and procedure creation must begin at the top of an organization with senior management that understands, supports, and holds personnel accountable to the written policies. Remember that organizational policies must articulate with external governance, such as requirements found in laws and regulations, or the management philosophies and tolerances of the organization's leadership. These policies and procedures must then flow throughout the organization to ensure that security is useful and functional at every level of the organization. Understanding organizational security must begin with an understanding of the basic laws, regulations, and legal jurisdiction that policies must be informed by in order to protect not only the organization and its assets but also its employees and customers.

Management creates policies based on its leadership philosophies, culture, industry standards and requirements, and, most importantly, external governance. Policies articulate with all these items and represent management's directives in upholding these requirements. Policies specific to risk governance include a body of documents that may start with the Risk Management Strategy, which details the organization's overall strategy, methodology, and long-term desires for managing risk. Policies support the strategy, as well as governance requirements, such as those that may be found in laws or regulations that dictate that certain risk management activities must take place within the organization. An example of a risk-related policy would be a risk management or risk assessment policy, which dictates the organization's requirements for risk management, assessment and analysis, risk treatment, and risk monitoring. This policy may be brief or detailed but will usually state roles and responsibilities, the risk management methodology adopted by the organization, and the requirement to implement detailed risk management procedures.

Business Processes

The organization's mission is the reason that it exists, whether this is producing goods, offering services, and so on. A shoe manufacturer is in the business of making shoes; therefore, its mission is to make good quality shoes. Most businesses have a mission statement that describes their mission. While the mission is the overall reason for existence, business processes are the activities that carry out that mission. A shoe manufacturer's business processes could be as high level as manufacturing, sales, and marketing, but even those higher-level processes are broken down into activities, such as sewing cloth and leather, developing types and styles of shoes, and selling them to retailers. These are all processes that support the business. Each of these business processes also incurs some level of business risk. There could be risks in the manufacturing process due to the types of materials or specific manner of attaching the shoe soles to the rest of the shoe. A faulty process could mean that the shoes are of lesser quality than other competitors or that the styles don't meet the demands of consumers. This, in turn, will lead to fewer sales or more consumer returns. Regardless of whether they are higher-level processes or more detailed activities and tasks, each of these is supported by one or more systems or sets of data. These systems also incur risk, but of a different nature. The risk incurred by the systems includes the ability to effectively use those systems and data to support the different business processes. Therefore, IT (or even cybersecurity) risk directly informs business process risk since it could affect the ability of the organization to carry out its business processes and, in turn, its overall mission.

Business processes are "owned" by different managers within the organization. This means that the business process owners are responsible for both the day-to-day and long-term operations and success of the process. This also means, ordinarily, that they are the primary owners of the business risk associated with the process. Of course, higher-level management bears ownership and responsibility for both the process and risk also, but these are typically the people in charge of the business process.

Better organizations will take a formal approach with regard to the development and management of business processes. Documents that describe processes, roles and responsibilities, and key assets may be formally managed with business process change management and periodic review and be kept in official repositories to ensure that no unauthorized changes occur.

Organizations with higher maturity will develop metrics and even key performance indicators (KPIs) associated with each business process. This allows management to understand the quantity and quality of business process output, which can be used to determine tactical and strategic improvements that can make processes more effective and efficient. Risk practitioners must work hand-in-hand with business process owners to develop these KPIs, as well as associated key risk indicators (KRIs) and key control indicators (KCIs).

NOTE   KPIs, as well as KRIs and KCIs, are covered in more detail in Chapter 3, where we discuss risk response and reporting as part of Domain 3.

Organizational Assets

Company assets can include physical items, such as computer and networking equipment, office machines (for example, scanners and copiers), work facilities, and information processing centers, as well as nonphysical items, such as valuable data. Asset identification involves identifying both types of assets and determining their value. Asset values must be established beyond the mere capital costs; a true asset valuation should consider several factors. For example, a consideration should be the cost to repair or recover the asset versus simply replacing the asset outright. Often, repairing the asset may be less expensive in the short run, but the cost of the different components required to conduct a repair should be considered. Also, it's important to remember that this might only be a temporary solution—one that could come back to haunt you (and your pockets) in the long run.

Asset management is the collection of activities used to oversee the inventory, classification, use, and disposal of assets. Asset management is a foundational activity, without which several other activities could not be effectively done, including vulnerability management, device hardening, incident management, data security, and some aspects of financial management.

In information security, asset management is critical to the success of vulnerability management. If assets are not known to exist, they may be excluded from processes used to identify and remediate vulnerabilities. Similarly, it will be difficult to harden assets if their existence is not known. What's more, if an unknown asset is attacked, the organization may have no way of directly realizing this in a timely manner. If an attacker compromises an unknown device, the attack may not be known until the attacker pivots and selects additional assets to compromise. This time lag could prove crucial to the impact of the incident.

Asset Identification

A security management program's main objective (whether formally stated or not) is the protection of the organization's assets. These assets may be tangible or intangible, physical, logical, or virtual. Here are some examples of assets:

- **Buildings and property**   These assets include real estate, structures, and other improvements.

- **Equipment**   This can include machinery, vehicles, and office equipment such as copiers, printers, and scanners.

- **IT equipment**   This includes computers, printers, scanners, tape libraries (the devices that create backup tapes, not the tapes themselves), storage systems, network devices, and phone systems.

- **Virtual assets**   In addition to the tangible IT equipment cited, virtual assets include virtual machines and the software running on them.

- **Supplies and materials**   These can include office supplies as well as materials used in manufacturing.

- **Records**   These include business records, such as contracts, video surveillance tapes, visitor logs, and far more.

- **Information**   This includes data in software applications, documents, e-mail messages, and files of every kind on workstations and servers.

- **Intellectual property**   This includes an organization's designs, architectures, patents, software source code, processes, and procedures.

- **Personnel**   In a real sense, an organization's personnel *are* the organization. Without its staff, the organization cannot perform or sustain its processes.

- **Reputation**   One of the intangible characteristics of an organization, reputation is the individual and collective opinion about an organization in the eyes of its customers, competitors, shareholders, and the community.

- **Brand equity**   Similar to reputation, this is the perceived or actual market value of an individual brand of product or service that is produced by the organization.

Sources of Asset Data

An organization that is building or improving its security management program may need to build its asset inventory from scratch. Management will need to determine where this initial asset data will come from. Some sources include the following:

- **Financial system asset inventory**   An organization that keeps all of its assets on the books will have a wealth of asset inventory information. However, it may not be entirely useful: asset lists often do not include the location or purpose of the asset and whether it is still in use. Correlating a financial asset inventory to assets in actual use may consume more effort than the other methods for creating the initial asset list. However, for organizations that have a relatively small number of highly valued assets (for instance, an ore crusher in a gold mine or a mainframe computer), knowing the precise financial value of an asset is highly useful because the actual depreciated value of the asset is used in the risk analysis phase of risk management. Knowing the depreciated value of other assets is also useful, as this will figure into the risk treatment choices that will be identified later.

 TIP   Financial records that indicate the value of an asset do not include the value of information stored on (or processed by) the asset.

- **Interviews**   Discussions with key personnel for the purposes of identifying assets are usually the best approach. However, to be effective, several people usually need to be interviewed to be sure to include all relevant assets.

- **IT systems portfolio**   A well-managed IT organization will have formal documents and records for its major applications. While this information may not encompass every IT asset in the organization, it can provide information on the assets supporting individual applications or geographic locations.

- **Online data**   An organization with a large number of IT assets (systems, network devices, and so on) can sometimes utilize the capability of online data to identify those assets. An organization with cloud-based assets can use the asset management portion of the cloud services dashboard to determine the number and type of assets in use there. Also, a systems or network management system often includes a list of managed assets, which can be a good starting point when creating the initial asset list.

- **Security scans**   An organization that has security scanning tools can use them to identify network assets. This technique will identify authorized as well as unauthorized assets.

- **Asset management system**   Larger organizations may find it more cost effective to use an asset management application dedicated to this purpose, rather than rely on lists of assets from other sources.

None of these sources should be considered accurate or complete. Instead, as a formal asset inventory is being assembled, the security manager should continue to explore other sources of assets.

Collecting and Organizing Asset Data

It is rarely possible to take (or create) a list of assets from a single source. Rather, more than one source of information is often needed to be sure that the risk management program has identified at least the important, in-scope assets it needs to worry about.

 NOTE   As part of IT governance, management needs to determine which person or group is responsible for maintaining asset inventories.

It is usually useful to organize or classify assets. This will help to get identified assets into smaller chunks that can be analyzed more effectively. There is no single way to organize assets, but here are a few ideas:

- **Geography**   A widely dispersed organization may want to classify its assets according to their location. This will aid risk managers during the risk analysis phase since many risks are geographic-centric, particularly natural hazards.

- **Service provider**   An organization utilizing one or more Infrastructure as a Service (IaaS) providers can group its assets by service provider.

- **Business process**   Because some organizations rank the criticality of their individual business processes, it can be useful to group assets according to the business processes they support. This helps the risk analysis and risk treatment phases because assets supporting individual processes can be associated with business criticality and treated appropriately.

- **Organizational unit**   In larger organizations, it may be easier to classify assets according to the organizational unit they support.

- **Sensitivity**   Usually ascribed to information, sensitivity relates to the nature and content of that information. Sensitivity usually applies in two ways: to an individual, where the information is considered personal or private, and to an organization, where the information may be considered a trade secret. Sometimes sensitivity is somewhat subjective and arbitrary, but often it is defined in laws and regulations.

- **Regulation**   For organizations that are required to follow government and other legal obligations regarding the processing and protection of information, it will be useful to include data points that indicate whether specific assets are considered in scope for specific regulations. This is important because some regulations specify how assets should be protected, so it's useful to be aware of this during risk analysis and risk treatment.

There is no need to choose which of these methods will be used to classify assets. Instead, an analyst should collect several points of metadata about each asset (including location, process supported, and organizational unit supported). This will enable the security manager to sort and filter the list of assets in various ways to better understand which assets are in a given location or which ones support a particular process or part of the business.

TIP   Organizations should consider managing information about assets in a fixed-assets application.

Risk Governance

Risk governance has several different aspects. As mentioned earlier, governance provides the overall requirements of what the organization must adhere to and could include legal, ethical, safety, and professional requirements. Risk governance, then, describes the requirements that the organization must adhere to in terms of managing both business and IT risk. Laws, regulations, and other external governance can dictate portions of risk governance, as can internal governance, which comes in the form of policy. Risk governance is also set forth by executive management in the form of risk appetite and tolerance, risk strategy, and throughout the various policies that support risk management. Risk governance includes adopting a risk assessment and analysis methodology, risk treatment and response options, risk monitoring processes, and so on. A multitude of risk governance and management frameworks have been published to assist in this process, which we will discuss next.

Enterprise Risk Management and Risk Management Frameworks

Enterprise risk management (ERM) is the practice of identifying and managing strategic risk in an organization. This includes topics such as macroeconomics, market risk, regulations, workforce, information technology, and cybersecurity. The individual risks in ERM will cite various uncertainties and scenarios that, if realized, may have a negative impact on the organization's long-term viability.

Standards and frameworks help provide a standardized, industry-accepted approach toward managing risk. While they're certainly not perfect, they provide a baseline for an organization to recognize the key steps toward understanding and categorizing the risks to its business, implementing the appropriate security controls to lower risk to an acceptable level, and continually monitoring the residual risk and report the status to management. Each standard and framework has its own pluses and minuses, and we will discuss two of the more commonly used: the ISACA Risk IT Framework and the National Institute of Standards and Technology (NIST) Risk Management Framework. Keep in mind that this discussion serves only to introduce you to the frameworks.

ISACA Risk IT Framework

Originally published in 2009, the ISACA Risk IT Framework is a common risk management framework you should be aware of. ISACA wanted to create a framework that merges the traditional IT models with a more risk-focused mindset. Within the ISACA model, the activities considered key are grouped into processes, which in turn are grouped into three domains: Risk Governance, Risk Evaluation, and Risk Response. You will see many of the same concepts that you'll find within this book (and even this chapter), so it's definitely a worthwhile model to review. The Risk Governance domain discusses risk appetite, risk tolerance, and communicating risk to leadership. The Risk Evaluation domain includes an understanding of the impacts to the business and the risk scenarios, developed through the inclusion of internal and external environmental factors, risk management capability, IT capability, and IT-related business capability. The Risk Response domain covers the risk response definition, risk response prioritization, and key risk indicators (KRIs). The framework also describes risk response options such as risk avoidance, risk mitigation, risk sharing and transfer, and risk acceptance.

NIST Risk Management Framework

NIST Special Publication 800-37, Revision 2, "Guide for Applying the Risk Management Framework to Federal Information Systems," along with other supporting publications from NIST (part of the U.S. Department of Commerce), makes up the defining volumes of the Risk Management Framework (RMF). The RMF is composed of seven steps:

1. Prepare.
2. Categorize information systems.
3. Select security controls.
4. Implement security controls.
5. Assess security controls.
6. Authorize information systems.
7. Monitor security controls.

Security categorization requires the information systems and associated information to be categorized based on an impact analysis. When selecting a set of security controls, you must take into account the security categorization as well as any previous assessments of risk. Following this step, you implement the security controls that were previously selected and then assess their effectiveness and the overall success of the controls in lowering the risk to the accepted level. Finally, the security controls need to be continually monitored so that you're sure they continue to operate as intended. You also need to consider any changes that come into effect across the organization (think location, mission, security classification, or other underlying factors).

You will notice many additional concepts within NIST Special Publication 800-37 that are germane to the CRISC exam; for example, the early steps of the RMF discuss categorizing and selecting appropriate security controls (which we will discuss later in the book), while other steps correspond to the implementation, assessment, and continuous monitoring of controls (covered throughout this book). For these reasons alone, it's a great idea to read this document to understand how the steps work together and how they are similar (and sometimes different) from other frameworks.

Three Lines of Defense

ISACA makes a distinction of three lines of defense in managing enterprise risk. These are operational management, risk management and compliance functions, and auditing and accountability. These lines are different events which are implemented at different levels of the organization, across business processes, as part of the wider enterprise risk management program. The personnel responsible for these three lines of defense are the risk owner, who is ultimately accountable and responsible for how risk is treated, and the risk practitioner, who is responsible for the day-to-day risk management functions.

Operational Management

Operational management refers to the tactical management activities that take place at the business unit or business process level. At this level, risk is managed on a day-to-day basis by monitoring control effectiveness as well as any risk associated with the business process itself or its supporting systems. This line of defense may be implemented by the risk practitioner, the business process owner, or even IT and cybersecurity personnel. This is the layer in which controls are operated as a part of business processes and often implemented as a part of information systems.

Risk and Compliance Management

This line of defense involves proactively monitoring and managing risk associated with IT support systems, security controls that are implemented to protect the systems, and risk associated with overall business processes. This is where the organization's risk management program shines; implementing the activities associated with the risk governance framework is part of this critical line of defense. This includes overall risk assessment and analysis, risk response, and continuous risk monitoring.

Compliance management involves ensuring that the organization, its business processes, and the supporting IT systems comply with any governance requirements, whether they come from inside the organization or from external entities. Compliance directly leads to auditing processes and systems, discussed next.

While risk and compliance management are connected, they are separate and distinct entities. Risk can be variable in nature and changes over time, whereas compliance is typically a binary (yes/no, compliant/noncompliant) mentality. However, there is usually some overlap between these two areas, particularly in control assessments and risk analysis, as both risk management and compliance management often require control and risk assessments. Business process owners and senior managers, as well as senior risk practitioners, typically are involved with this line of defense.

Auditing and Accountability

In the world of risk management, auditing involves continuously monitoring risk levels to ensure they fall within acceptable levels of risk appetite and tolerance, as well as monitoring the controls, management processes, and responses that maintain acceptable risk levels. This could mean auditing at the process level (account management, for instance) or even at the overall organizational risk level, and every area of interest in between. Auditing ensures that processes and activities are being conducted in accordance with governance and serves to further ensure accountability.

While auditing and accountability are not exactly the same thing, they are complementary. Accountability, in terms of risk management, ensures that risk owners are both responsible and accountable for managing risk at an acceptable level within their area of responsibility. In short, accountability ensures they are doing their job. Accountability is connected to auditing in the respect that only through auditing processes and activities do we determine if those processes and activities are fulfilling the governance and risk management requirements that risk owners are responsible for meeting.

Risk Profile

A *risk profile* encompasses an overall asset, organization, or business process under review and includes detailed information on all aspects of those items and how they contribute to, mitigate, or influence risk. The risk profile for a system, for instance, would present detailed information on all the different characteristics of the system, its security controls, the risk assessment and analysis for the system, the risk responses for the system, and ongoing management for that risk. Risk profiles periodically change based on a variety of factors, including the criticality or sensitivity of the system, the vulnerabilities inherent to the system, the threats that may exploit those vulnerabilities, and the mitigating security controls that protect the system. Regulations and societal norms also influence risk profile, particularly in areas such as data privacy. The risk profile is used to actively manage ongoing risk and ensure that it remains within acceptable levels.

Risk Appetite and Risk Tolerance

As discussed previously, the culture of the organization really defines how the organization feels about risk and how it treats risk over time. *Risk capacity* is the amount of loss an organization can incur without seriously affecting its ability to continue as an organization. More resilient organizations can endure greater loss than those that aren't as resilient. How resilient an organization is can sometimes be informed by its risk culture. As part of the organization's risk culture, there are its *risk appetite* and *risk tolerance*. These are different terms you also need to know to understand risk. Risk appetite is, in effect, how much risk an organization is willing to deal with in any given endeavor. This is the general level of risk that an organization is willing to accept in the course of its business.

An organization's risk appetite is driven by the corporate risk culture and by the environment in which the organization exists (market, regulation, and other external factors).

Risk tolerance, on the other hand, is the acceptable level of deviation in risk for a particular endeavor or business pursuit. Risk tolerance is how much variation from the expected level of risk the organization is willing to put up with. There's a certain amount of risk in every business enterprise or pursuit; however, the organization may not be able or willing to tolerate large deviations from what it considers its acceptable level of risk on an endeavor.

 EXAM TIP Know the differences between risk appetite and risk tolerance; *risk appetite* involves how much risk the organization is willing to endure, whereas *risk tolerance* is how much variation from that amount is acceptable to the business for a particular venture. Risk culture drives both of these factors.

Legal, Regulatory, and Contractual Requirements

Governance imposed by entities external to the organization usually takes the form of laws, regulations, professional standards and requirements, and so on. Often, it is simply enough for laws and regulations to be in place, or for a company to formally accept professional standards for these requirements to be imposed on an organization. Sometimes, however, governance is also imposed as part of contractual requirements between organizations. Including governance requirements in contracts, even if an organization would otherwise not be required to meet those requirements, makes them legally enforceable. In any event, organizations are required to fulfill their obligations imposed by these external governance sources.

Additionally, laws, regulations, and other governance sources often conflict with or even supplement each other. For example, one regulation may require a specific level of protection for sensitive data, and another law or regulation may require additional layers of protection based on the characteristics of the data, the organization, or the industry. For example, privacy data and healthcare data are often regulated by multiple sources of governance. In this event, the organization must implement internal policies and procedures to fulfill the requirements of all governance imposed on it. Even in the case of professional standards, such as those imposed by the Payment Card Industry Data Security Standard (PCI DSS), organizations must fulfill the requirements imposed on them if they have agreed to do so through contract or by virtue of their industry. In this example, organizations aren't legally required to comply with this standard, but by virtue of the fact that they process credit card transactions, they are required by the credit card industry and can be censured or banned from processing transactions by the credit card companies if they do not comply with the requirements.

Compliance with legal and regulatory requirements is a critical factor in most organizations, and many of these requirements also impose risk management requirements as well, so risk management is often dictated, to a degree, by governance. In fact, many laws and regulations, such as the Health Insurance Portability and Accountability Act (HIPAA), require a formalized risk management program. Risk governance frameworks, such as the NIST Risk Management Framework, also require formalized risk management. These frameworks can also be included in any other laws, regulations, contracts, or other governance requirements imposed on an organization.

Professional Ethics of Risk Management

Most organizations, particularly professional ones, have requirements for a code of conduct or professional ethics. This is especially true in the cybersecurity and risk management professions. These codes of ethics regulate the behavior of professionals and ensure that they maintain high standards of behavior. Most of the industry-recognized professional certifications also require adherence to a code of ethics, and ISACA is no exception.

ISACA's Code of Professional Ethics can be found at https://www.isaca.org/credentialing/code-of-professional-ethics and is imposed on all organizational members and certification holders. ISACA also implements procedures for filing complaints against professionals bound to uphold those ethical standards in the event they fail to do so. The ISACA Code of Professional Ethics (paraphrased here) includes provisions for the following:

1. Supporting and complying with standards and procedures for governance and management of information systems and technology

2. Performing duties professionally, with due diligence and care, as required by professional standards

3. Conducting activities in a lawful manner and maintaining the high standards of conduct and character required by the profession and ISACA

4. Ensuring privacy and confidentiality of sensitive information obtained in the course of professional duties

5. Maintaining competency in the professional field

6. Full disclosure and impartiality regarding results of work performed to ensure that the results of that work are not distorted

7. Supporting professional education in the areas of governance and management of enterprise information systems and technology, including auditing, controls, security, and risk management

Chapter Review

Organizational governance drives how an organization conducts itself within legal, regulatory, and even self-imposed constraints. Governance focuses on legal compliance, due diligence and care, and ethical behavior. This governance can come from both external and internal sources in the form of laws, regulations, professional standards, and internal policies and procedures. Risk management is often a requirement included in governance standards.

Quick Review

- Governance guides the conduct of an organization in terms of legal and ethical behavior.
- Governance can come from external and internal sources.
- External governance is imposed through laws, regulations, professional standards, risk frameworks, and contract requirements.
- Internal governance comes from internal policies and procedures.
- The organization's mission, goals, and objectives must include and support governance requirements.
- Senior management defines risk appetite and tolerance for the organization.
- Risk capacity is the amount of loss an organization can incur without its very existence being threatened.
- Risk appetite is the amount of risk an organization is willing to take on in pursuit of its mission.
- Risk tolerance is the level of variance from the appetite an organization is willing to permit for any particular business venture.
- An organization's mission, goals, and objectives are typically defined at the strategic or long-term level.
- Organizational structure can affect an organization's ability to deal with risk in terms of its risk culture, appetite, tolerance, and resilience.
- Organizational business units, which consist of various business processes, must deal with both business and IT risk at the process level.
- Business process risk contributes to the overall organizational risk and is managed at various levels, starting with the risk owner, who is responsible and accountable for risk management for a particular set of business processes or business units.
- An enterprise risk management strategy and program must be in place to deal with lower-, middle-, and higher-tier risks. Risk governance drives the enterprise risk management program.
- Organizational risk culture defines how an organization feels about and deals with risk and comes from the organization's leadership and governance.
- Organizational policies are internal governance that reflects the management philosophy, culture, and directives of senior leaders.
- Policies are intended to articulate with external governance.
- Organizational assets include anything of value to the organization, including physical equipment, facilities, human assets, and information.
- Asset management is a collection of activities used to manage the inventory, classification, use, and disposal of assets.
- The three lines of defense in managing enterprise risk are operational management, risk and compliance management, and auditing accountability.

- The risk profile consists of detailed information on all aspects of an asset and how those aspects contribute to, mitigate, or influence risk.
- The risk profile is used to manage risk for an asset.
- Governance can be imposed by laws, regulations, and contracts, which are legally enforceable.
- Codes of conduct and ethics dictate the behavior of risk management professionals.

Questions

1. An organization is subject to healthcare regulations that govern the protection requirements of individual health data. Which of the following describes this type of governance?

   A. External

   B. Internal

   C. Regulatory

   D. Professional

2. Your company handles credit card transaction processing as part of its business processes. Which of the following best describes the source and type of governance it may incur because of these business processes?

   A. Internal, policies and procedures

   B. External, industry standards

   C. External, laws and regulations

   D. Internal, industry standards

3. Your organization is structured into various departments, and each of these has its own activities that support the mission, goals, and objectives of the organization. These activities are decomposed from a high level and include various tasks to support the various business units. Which the following best describes these activities?

   A. Operational management

   B. Organizational strategy

   C. Business processes

   D. Risk management functions

4. An organizational culture that is averse to risk and change is more likely to have the following in terms of risk appetite and tolerance?

   A. High risk appetite, low risk tolerance

   B. Low risk appetite, high risk tolerance

   C. Low risk appetite, low risk tolerance

   D. High risk appetite, high risk tolerance

5. Which of the following roles is the lowest level of responsibility in terms of risk ownership for a business process or unit?

   A. Organizational CEO or president

   B. VP for risk management

   C. Risk practitioner

   D. Business process owner

6. Which of the following is the level of variation or deviance an organization is willing to accept for a particular business venture?

   A. Risk appetite

   B. Risk tolerance

   C. Risk acceptance

   D. Risk capacity

7. A small business unit in the production department is incurring risk for one of its lower-level business processes. Although this risk is focused on the business process and not at the organizational level, it must be accounted for in the overall organizational risk assessment. At what level should this risk be considered?

   A. Organizational risk

   B. Operational risk

   C. Strategic risk

   D. Tactical risk

8. An organization needs to create its internal risk management program and begins with risk governance. Which of the following should the organization create first?

   A. Risk strategy

   B. Risk management policy

   C. Risk assessment procedure

   D. Risk management methodology

9. Which of the following describes why the organization exists?

   A. Organizational mission statement

   B. Organizational strategy

   C. External governance

   D. Organizational policy

10. Which of the following activities is considered foundational, without which other management activities, such as vulnerability management, incident management, and data security, could not be accomplished?

   A. Configuration management

   B. Risk management

    C. Asset management

    D. Financial management

11. Which of the following is *not* one of the three domains listed in ISACA's Risk IT Framework?

    A. Risk Governance

    B. Risk Evaluation

    C. Risk Assessment

    D. Risk Response

12. Which of the following requires that a risk practitioner perform duties professionally, with due diligence and care, as required by professional standards?

    A. Risk IT Framework

    B. NIST Risk Management Framework

    C. ISACA Code of Professional Ethics

    D. Laws and regulations

13. A risk manager is analyzing a risk item and intends to recommend that risk acceptance be the recommended treatment. Which of the following must the risk manager consider to make this determination?

    A. Risk awareness

    B. Risk capacity

    C. Risk tolerance

    D. Risk appetite

14. The organization's legal counsel is considering the prospect of real estate prices, including office space leasing costs, increasing significantly in the next five years. What level of risk management should be used to manage this risk?

    A. Asset

    B. ERM

    C. Program

    D. Market

15. All of the following are factors that influence an organization's culture *except* which one?

    A. Published values

    B. Policies

    C. Leadership behavior

    D. Behavioral norms

Answers

1. **A.** Laws and regulations are a form of external governance.

2. **B.** This describes an external source of governance in the form of industry standards, specifically the Payment Card Industry Data Security Standard (PCI DSS).

3. **C.** Business processes are the activities that support the organizational mission and can be broad or broken down into detailed activities and tasks.

4. **C.** An organization that is risk averse likely has both a low risk appetite and low risk tolerance.

5. **D.** Although various levels of organizational management may be responsible and accountable for risk, the lowest level of risk ownership for a business process or unit is the business process owner.

6. **B.** Risk tolerance is the amount of variation or deviation an organization is willing to accept from its risk appetite that a particular business venture may incur.

7. **D.** Tactical risks are those encountered by smaller production sections—those that carry out the day-to-day work of the organization. A lower-level business process may be considered to have a tactical risk.

8. **A.** The risk strategy for the organization should be created first because it provides long-term direction for the risk management program. The risk management strategy also supports external governance. Policies and procedures are created afterward to support the strategy as well as implement external governance.

9. **A.** The organizational mission statement is developed by the organization to describe its overall mission, which is its very reason for existence.

10. **C.** Asset management is one of the foundational activities on which other activities depend (vulnerability management, configuration management, and so on) because assets must be inventoried and accounted for first.

11. **C.** Risk Assessment is not one of the domains covered in the Risk IT Framework. The three domains are Risk Governance, Risk Evaluation, and Risk Response.

12. **C.** The ISACA Code of Professional Ethics establishes requirements for ethical conduct and behavior that all certified professionals must adhere to, including the requirement to perform all duties professionally, with due diligence and care, as required by professional standards.

13. **C.** Risk tolerance determines the amount of risk an organization will accept for any individual risk situation.

14. **B.** A risk matter such as macroeconomic risk generally will be managed by an organization's enterprise risk management (ERM) program.

15. **B.** Of the available choices, an organization's policies are the least likely to influence an organization's culture.

IT Risk Assessment

In this chapter, you will:

- Understand the role of risk assessments and risk analysis in the risk management life cycle
- Learn about the techniques used to identify various types of risks
- Become familiar with risk identification and risk analysis techniques such as threat modeling, vulnerability analysis, control deficiency analysis, root cause analysis, and risk scenario development
- Understand the concepts and steps taken in a risk assessment
- Be familiar with the role and structure of a risk register
- Understand the concepts of inherent risk and residual risk

This chapter covers Certified in Risk and Information Systems Control Domain 2, "IT Risk Assessment." The domain represents 20 percent of the CRISC examination.

The CRISC Task Statements relevant to this domain address several key activities present in a risk management program, starting with conducting IT risk assessments and the impact of IT risks on the organization's objectives or operations. These risk assessments should identify and evaluate threats, vulnerabilities, and risks, and they should be recorded in an IT risk register. In many organizations, the IT risk register would be integrated into an enterprise risk management program, if it exists. IT risk assessments should evaluate the existence and effectiveness of IT controls and identify the need for new or changed controls based on risk. This risk and control information should be reported to stakeholders to facilitate risk-driven decision-making, aligning with the organization's established risk appetite and risk tolerance. IT risk personnel should periodically evaluate new and changing technologies for changes to risk. The risk management program should be aligned to industry frameworks and standards.

IT risk assessments are performed to identify risks associated with a specific scope of business operations or information technology in an organization. The purpose of identifying risks is the need for an organization to be aware of specific hazards that, if unchecked, could interrupt business operations and incur additional cost. Business executives and owners don't want bad and unexpected things to happen; rather than stick their heads in the sand, it's wiser to identify those risks and see what can be done about them. The alternative means flying blind and being unaware of risk scenarios, some of which may be highly likely to occur.

Figure 2-1
The components
of risk
management

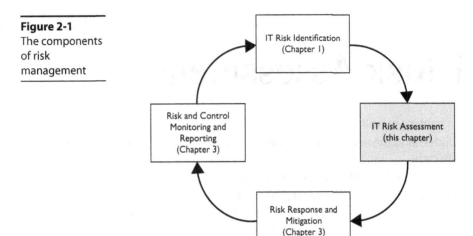

This chapter explores the broad picture of IT risk assessment, which is the search for—and identification of—various risks. We also explore the detailed view of risk analysis, which is the careful examination of individual risks, to better understand them in detail and explore various remedies. Conceptually, risk assessment and risk analysis are simple enough, but because there are so many ways in which risk assessments and risk analyses may occur, and many standards and techniques for each, all of this can become a clutter.

In our opinion, ISACA's layout of this domain, IT Risk Assessment, isn't quite right. Both the macro (risk assessment) and micro (risk analysis) are scattered throughout the two main parts of the domain. We will, however, stay true to the structure of the domain, like it or not, but we'll be sure to clarify the context within risk management in each section.

IT risk assessments and risk analysis, covered in this chapter, are a part of the overall risk management life cycle, depicted in Figure 2-1. Risk governance, including risk profile, risk appetite, and risk tolerance, are covered in Chapter 1, while risk treatment, emerging risks, third-party risk management, controls, and risk reporting are covered in Chapter 3.

IT Risk Identification

IT risk identification comprises the activities performed to identify various types of risks associated with an organization's use of information technology. The types of IT risks that can be identified fall into these categories:

- **Strategic**   This category represents broad themes, including whether IT is aligned to the business and providing services required by the business, and whether IT can support and respond to changes in business strategy.

- **Operational**   This category represents many issues, including IT service management, service quality, production schedule, resilience, and tactical matters such as scheduling and availability.

- **Cybersecurity**   This represents issues related to the ability of internal and external threat actors to compromise information systems or the information stored in them.

- **Privacy**   This represents both cybersecurity-related risks as well as business practices related to the handling of personal information.

- **Supply chain**   This includes the availability of products such as laptops, servers, and components, plus services like tech support, and service providers, including SaaS, PaaS, and IaaS. Supply chain itself has both operational and cybersecurity-related risks.

- **Compliance**   This represents IT-related activities that an organization may be required to perform due to a regulation, policy, or contract terms.

Security professionals need to train themselves to recognize new risks. While at times they may be bold and obvious, sometimes they will be subtle and easily missed for what they are. Often, significant risks are identified when they are least expected. In many organizations, IT risks are not apparent until a threat event occurs. The activities that may lead to the realization of new risks include the following:

- **Audits**   An audit may identify a deficiency in a business process or system that warrants more than remediation-and-forget-it treatment. Often, this requires that a security analyst or risk manager study the audit deficiency to understand its root cause. Rather than think of the deficiency as a one-time (or repeated) mistake, perhaps the design of the control is the cause, or something even broader such as the overall design of a system or set of business processes. Where there's smoke, there's fire—sometimes.

- **Security and privacy incidents**   A security or privacy incident may reveal a latent problem that has been waiting to be discovered. The risk may not be directly related to the incident or its cause. It could be discovered by accident while an incident responder or security analyst investigates an incident more deeply.

- **Penetration tests**   While penetration tests can identify specific vulnerabilities, sometimes it's essential to read between the lines and understand the overall theme or meaning of the penetration test results.

- **News and social media articles**   Information about breaches, cybercriminal organizations, new tools and innovations, and other cybersecurity topics can spur a risk manager to identify a risk inside their organization. We have all experienced this in our careers; an example that comes to mind is this: news of a critical website vulnerability at a competitor's organization was widely reported. Our management contacted us to see whether we had the same or a similar exposure.

- **Security advisories**   Advisories on vulnerabilities and active attacks draw attention to specific actions and technologies. A formal cyberthreat intelligence or attack surface reduction program will subscribe to and consume all such advisories to determine whether the organization is vulnerable and then take action if needed. We consider these advisories to be more tactical than we would include in overall risk identification. However, sometimes an advisory will help us realize that something systemic isn't quite right in our organization and that we want to capture that idea while it's on our minds.

- **Networking**   Discussions about information technology, security, or privacy with professionals in other organizations can trigger the realization of a risk in one's own organization. We do caution you on this point: a risk in one organization, even when similar practices or technologies are in play, does not necessarily mean that another organization has the same risk.

- **Whistleblowers**   A disgruntled or concerned employee may choose to remain anonymous and disclose information about a condition or practice that may represent a genuine risk to the organization.

- **Passive observation**   During the course of work, a risk manager or other cybersecurity staff may realize a heretofore undiscovered risk. Sometimes a risk can lie before us for an extended period of time until some conversation or thought triggers a new realization.

- **Threat modeling**   This is a particular type of risk assessment, typically focused on an individual information system or business process, to identify likely threat scenarios.

- **Secure configuration assessments**   Configurations that are insecure or out of compliance can be a source of critical risks. This can be out of compliance with configuration baselines like the Center for Internet Security. Others can be basic settings such as password strength or length.

- **Governance assessments**   Governance can be a huge impact on how well the process runs. For example, if there are not status checks on systems, the systems may not be configured properly, thus increasing the risk to the organization.

- **Data governance risks**   For some organizations, how data is used or shared can be very risky. For example, if a contract explicitly forbids the sharing of data, but data is being shared anyway, there can be legal repercussions. Reviewing the data governance process is an important part of protecting the data.

- **Privacy assessments**   For some companies, privacy is becoming a greater concern due to enhanced regulation. Not being aware of the laws can have a huge impact on the privacy of data and can lead to fines and lawsuits.

- **Risk-aware culture**   The extent to which leaders, management, and staff in an organization are trained to recognize risk will result in better outcomes, including more effective security and privacy by design, and a willingness to accept that risks are always present and can be managed. Security awareness training should include risk awareness.

- **Risk assessments**   This is the wide gate through which many risks will be identified and analyzed. We're putting this last on the list for a few reasons: risk assessments generally have a specified scope and are aligned to a specific framework of controls, so risk analysts are, by design, looking only for particular types of risks in specific places. These blinders can sometimes prevent someone from seeing certain types of risks, or risks in specific contexts or places.

Our hope here is that you will realize the discovery of risk can occur in many ways. The best tool the risk manager can obtain is an open mind, which is free to explore the possibilities of IT risk in the organization.

 NOTE   The context of IT risks includes on-premises and cloud and service-provider uses of information technology.

Brainstorming and Risk Identification

Brainstorming some concept or idea in front of a whiteboard with other colleagues is one of our favorite activities (and one that we miss—we write this during the COVID-19 pandemic in which most office workers are isolated in their homes). In a brainstorming session, participants each have whiteboard pens and write down ideas that come to mind on some specific topic. Alternatively, one person writes down ideas spoken by others in the room.

The rule of brainstorming is this: silly ideas are not to be rejected, because that silly idea could lead to a great idea. For example, office workers are brainstorming ideas on what color to paint the office. Let's join the discussion.

"White."

"Light brown."

"Light gray."

"Plaid."

Wait a minute. Plaid isn't a color. But they write it down anyway. This prompts another to say, "Let's paint it two colors: white on interior walls to reflect light, and light gray on other walls."

Rejecting "plaid" might not have led the team to the solution they ultimately chose, which was a bit different from what they all expected: a single color.

Thought and discussions about risk are no different. Dare to think outside the box and consider other ideas, which could lead you to new discoveries.

Risk Events

Risk events are the specific scenarios that, if they occurred, would inflict some impact on an organization's ongoing operations. A risk event includes a description of one or more threat scenarios, the identification of the types of threat actors, statements of vulnerabilities that could enable a threat scenario to occur, the value of relevant assets, and the probability of occurrence.

The Vocabulary of Risk

Every profession has its own lexicon—big words that represent complex topics. We aren't experts in every field, so for each of us, sometimes we overhear conversations on some professional topic that are sprinkled with words whose meaning we may not fully comprehend. Our profession, cybersecurity risk management, is no different in this regard. Those of us in the industry occasionally hear "lay" persons misuse these words. For example, we may overhear someone in IT say, "That missing patch is a serious threat." A risk manager might hear that and think to themselves, that person is using the term *threat* incorrectly. However, we should not fault them for trying.

Here are the primary terms in the profession:

- **Asset**   A tangible or intangible possession, such as a server, device, program, database, other data, intellectual property, or equipment.

- **Vulnerability**   A specific weakness in a system, process, or person that could fail to prevent some unwanted event. An example of a vulnerability is an easily picked lock on a door.

- **Threat**   An event, should it occur, that would bring harm to some asset. An example of a threat is a person who wants to break into a building and has lock-picking tools in their possession (and the skills to use them).

- **Impact**   The result on an organization should a threat occur.

- **Attack**   An offensive action that results in potential harm to an asset.

- **Risk**   The possibility and impact of harm that could occur to an asset, based on the asset's value, and any related vulnerabilities and threats.

Here are some additional terms that are often used:

- **Threat actor**   The person or thing that would carry out a threat if they chose to. Examples of threat actors include a lone hacker and a military-based cyberhacking unit.

- **Threat realization**   A threat that is carried out and causes some harm to an asset.

- **Threat modeling**   A specific type of analysis performed to better understand likely attack scenarios.

- **Event**   A more common term that is synonymous with threat realization.

- **Exploit (noun)**   A specific tool or method that can be used to carry out a threat.

- **Exploit (verb)**   The act of attacking an asset, made easier by the presence of a vulnerability.

- **Inherent risk**   The risk associated with a specific type of activity, before controls are considered.

- **Probability (also known as *likelihood*)**   The chance that a specific threat event would occur, generally within a period such as one year.
- **Residual risk**   The risk that remains after any risk reduction has been applied.
- **Risk register**   A listing of risks that have been identified.
- **Risk analysis**   The examination of one or more specific risks.
- **Risk assessment**   An examination of a process or system to identify and describe one or more risks.
- **Risk treatment**   A decision made about potential action to be taken concerning a specific risk.
- **Risk management**   The life-cycle process that includes risk assessments, risk analysis, and risk treatment.

These are just the basic terms used in risk management, defined briefly here. These terms, and several others, are explained in detail throughout this chapter. Figure 2-2 depicts threat agent, threat, vulnerability, impact, and risk concepts.

Here are some statements you might overhear in a conversation with IT risk managers:

- "A threat actor could exploit that vulnerability on Internet-facing assets, resulting in a serious incident."
- "Threat modeling revealed additional vulnerabilities in the new system."
- "The risk assessment identified new risks that have been entered into the risk register."

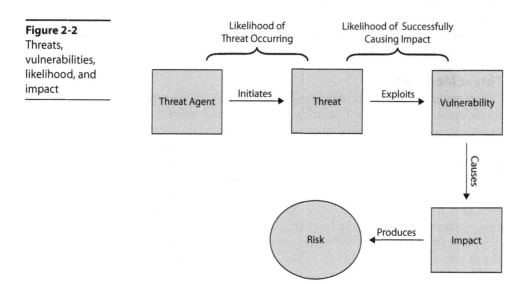

Figure 2-2
Threats, vulnerabilities, likelihood, and impact

Types of Risk Events

Several types of risk events can occur that are related to an organization's uses of information technology. The potential range of risk events includes scenarios such as the following:

- Breaches
- Equipment failure
- Extortion
- Natural disasters
- Fires and floods
- Sabotage
- Intrusion, data theft, and ransomware
- New regulations
- Regulatory fines
- Staff turnover
- Supplier shortages
- Strikes, riots, and demonstrations
- Terrorist attacks and acts of war

Threat Modeling and Threat Landscape

A common approach to assessing risk is the consideration of the universe of relevant threats that are reasonably likely to occur. Such an occurrence may compromise information or information systems, thus impacting business processes. Threat assessments and threat modeling are the primary activities used to identify relevant threats and how they may harm systems or processes.

Threat Modeling

Threat modeling is a risk identification technique that involves examining every possible threat agent, action or event, attack vector, and vulnerability for a given system, asset, or process, and then modeling or simulating how it could progress and the damage that could occur. Threat modeling has its origins in the U.S. and U.K. defense industries. A threat assessment examines how these threats could affect the particular asset, organization, or system you are looking at, in context, and it can be done on one of several levels, either simultaneously or separately. For example, you could perform a threat assessment on a new system being developed or installed. You would examine the different threat agents and threats that could affect that particular system. You could also look at an organizational process, or even the entire organization itself, and perform a comprehensive threat assessment. In addition to *scaling* a threat assessment, as we just described, you could look at threats from a particular perspective, performing a threat assessment specifically for technical threats, physical ones, or even external operating environment threats.

Figure 2-3
Scoping and
scaling a threat
assessment

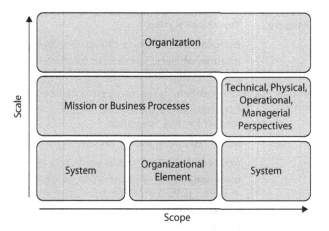

Scale

Organization

Mission or Business Processes

Technical, Physical,
Operational,
Managerial
Perspectives

System

Organizational
Element

System

Scope

This relates to the *scope* of the assessment. For example, you could look at the technical aspects of a given system or examine threats inherent to the processes and procedures associated with a particular business unit. Figure 2-3 shows this scoping and scaling process.

As this figure illustrates, you could scale an assessment to include only specific systems within some functional regions. You could scope it by examining not only all the threats that apply to the technical aspects of systems in those particular functional areas but also threats that affect associated business or management processes. You could have any combination of scope and scale that the organization needs to fulfill its assessment goals.

Threat landscape is a term that connotes a visual metaphor for considering all the threats that have been examined and identified as relevant to a given system or process. A risk manager could be overheard as saying, "The threat landscape for our online commerce system is particularly hostile," meaning there are many significant threats that need to be considered as controls and defenses are designed.

Table 2-1 illustrates how threat agents and threats could be categorized, given factors such as intent, relationships, skills, and so on. Note that these could affect any number or combination of elements (processes, systems, and so on) within an organization. You could categorize threats and threat agents using these characteristics and develop others that frame and define threats and threat agents for your organization.

Note that this information is only a sampling of what you may come up with in a threat assessment. You may also break down some of these elements into far more specific ones, based on your needs and the organization and systems you are focused on. For example, a defense contractor or military organization would likely have a more specific set of threats and agents in its assessment than a nonprofit, charitable organization.

NOTE Appendixes D and E in National Institute of Standards and Technology (NIST) Special Publication 800-30, "Guide for Conducting Risk Assessments," offer a more comprehensive list of threat agents and their related threats.

Threat Category	Threat Description
Intent	**Accidental:** Untrained or careless employee and business partner
	Intentional: Hacktivist, competitor, disgruntled employee, foreign agent, unbalanced individual, organized crime, terrorist, thief, and script kiddie
Relationship to organization	**Internal:** Employees, managers, and executives
	External: Contractor, supplier, vendor, government agency, nation-state, competitor, and civil activist
Skills	None, basic, intermediate, and advanced
Objectives	**Accidental:** Workarounds or cut corners as well as faster/less work
	Intentional: Theft, destruction, sabotage, embarrassment, blackmail, monetary gain, competitive advantage, and intelligence
Methods	**Accidental:** Inattentiveness, ignorance, arrogance, complacency, and poor planning
	Intentional: Social engineering, hacking, theft, physical damage, data alteration, and impersonation
Results	System/data theft, modification, or destruction as well as unauthorized access, compromised information, loss of business, loss of customer confidence, loss of revenue or reputation, and facility damage

Table 2-1   Characteristics of Threat Agents

Threat modeling is sometimes easier when preceded by a vulnerability assessment. You may wish to perform a threat assessment to determine what threats and threat agents exist to exploit those vulnerabilities. These threats can be internal or external, human-made, or natural, and they should match up with a discovered vulnerability. To complete the development of a given risk scenario, you should also consider the time and location characteristics of a potential scenario. Remember that you are developing scenarios down to the most practical level of detail possible; you will have developed many different possible scenarios for an asset, each covering a particular threat–vulnerability pairing by the time you are done. You should then look at the existing controls you have in place to determine how effective they are in protecting an asset.

Organizations considering adopting new technology should include threat modeling in their analysis as a part of an evaluation. Threat modeling will give the organization a glimpse into the scenarios that could occur if proper safeguards and controls were not implemented.

 TIP   Threat and vulnerability assessments are discussed a great deal in this chapter. These two assessment processes are critical to understanding the elements that formulate the risk for an asset.

Vulnerability and Control Deficiency Analysis

Vulnerability and control deficiency analysis are important parts of risk analysis. These focus on the weaknesses in a system or process that could result in a potentially serious incident if exploited by a threat actor. The basic question that a risk analyst would ask about a given asset is, "What weakness in this system or process could be exploited by a threat actor in a successful attack?"

When stated this way, a risk analyst might think only of human-initiated incidents and overlook a broad class of vulnerabilities that are not associated with a human threat actor. Examples of non-human-initiated threats include the following:

- Lack of off-site backup media that makes disaster recovery difficult in the case of a fire or flood that damages on-site systems and backup media.

- Excessive current load on power supply circuits that could result in overtemperature or power failure.

Vulnerability Analysis

Vulnerability analysis is a detailed examination of vulnerabilities that may exist or vulnerabilities that have been determined to exist. A *vulnerability assessment* can give you information about the weaknesses inherent to one or more assets. The vulnerability assessment might include examining all aspects of an asset or capability to determine any vulnerability it has, including the physical, technical, and operational vulnerabilities inherent to the asset. For example, technical vulnerabilities can be related to configuration issues or lack of hardening on a network device. Physical vulnerabilities could relate to the lack of physical protection for the network device. Operational vulnerabilities might include the lack of backup processes or configuration control exercised for the device.

Control Deficiency Analysis

In this section, we will discuss control analysis in detail. It's essential to understand how controls fit into the overall risk analysis process; you perform a control analysis before determining risk since existing controls that are already in place may be effective to varying degrees in mitigating risk. Simply examining threats, vulnerabilities, assets, impact, and likelihood without considering existing controls and protections in place doesn't do justice to the risk analysis process. Not accounting for existing controls would dramatically skew risk assessments and render an unrealistic risk determination. The goal here is to examine existing controls, determine how effective they are, and use that determination in analyzing the impact to assets if threats exploit vulnerabilities and the likelihood of that exploitation. Typically, results of your documentation, observation, interviews, and testing will likely also be part of your control analysis. We'll look at different aspects of control analysis in the following sections. You'll also receive some more in-depth information on controls in Chapter 3, focusing on various aspects of how they are designed, implemented, and used to respond to risk.

Evaluating Existing Control Effectiveness

As we stated earlier, risk analysis often involves evaluating the effectiveness of existing controls. This is because risk doesn't exist in a vacuum filled with only threats, vulnerabilities, and assets. Almost all assets have controls that serve to protect them from harm. These controls may or may not be sufficient to protect against particular threats. In some cases, however, a control may be implemented that significantly lowers the risk to an asset by decreasing the likelihood of a threat exploiting a vulnerability or by protecting the asset sufficiently enough to reduce the impact in the event a threat is realized. This is part of the risk assessment and analysis process, which involves identifying and prioritizing assets, performing threat and vulnerability assessments, and determining what controls exist and how effective they are in protecting against identified risks.

Controls fall into broad categories: administrative, technical, and physical or operational. Controls can also be categorized based on function, classifying them as preventive, detective, and deterrent. When identifying controls that apply to a given resource, process, asset, or system, you should look at all these different categories to determine what controls exist. Administrative controls will be in the form of policies or procedures and can protect an asset by detailing requirements that users must abide by. Technical controls can protect assets by providing logical protections, including strong authentication, restrictive permissions, and other access controls. Physical and operational controls can provide asset protection in the form of operational procedures and physical barriers, which separate unauthorized persons from the asset and prevent them from physically accessing the asset. Consider all these different categories of controls when attempting to identify any controls that may be protecting assets.

Once you have identified all the different controls protecting a given asset, you should determine what functions they are required to serve and how well they're performing those functions. Controls are designed to perform different functions (in some cases, only one function, but often many functions). Economy of use is a critical aspect of applying controls to assets; organizations that can use fewer controls to cover more security functions can reduce costs and more effectively use the resources they have.

Just as threats and vulnerabilities are often paired together, controls are often identified to counter specific threats or vulnerabilities. While we discuss the value of performing threat and vulnerability assessments, seemingly as different activities, often they are conducted simultaneously, along with control analysis, to get a better idea of how these three elements balance with each other. Threats exploit vulnerabilities; however, controls can reduce the likelihood or impact of threat realization and mitigate the weaknesses that vulnerabilities provide. So, there is a relationship among these three elements, making it valuable to sometimes look at all three of them simultaneously in a concerted effort.

In assessing control effectiveness, you should examine how well a particular control protects against a given threat or reduces a specific vulnerability. This can be a subjective process, but can be more objective if performed as part of an in-depth penetration test (discussed later in this chapter in the section, "Risk Assessment Concepts, Standards, and Frameworks"). For example, a threat assessment may give you only the potential threat events that could affect a given asset, and a vulnerability assessment may tell you only what potential vulnerabilities exist on the system. Neither tells you how effective a control may be in reducing the effects of the threat or vulnerability unless you attempt to exploit the vulnerability during penetration testing. However, by also understanding the Common Vulnerability Scoring System (CVSS) score associated with a vulnerability, you can better understand the effort required to perform an attack, and the potential harm that can result from an attack. Only then will you truly know how effective the control is; if a given vulnerability isn't easily exploitable, then, realistically, the control may be more effective than a cursory review would indicate. Likewise, a penetration test may indicate that a control is not as effective as you might have thought initially. Vulnerability assessments describe theoretical weaknesses, whereas penetration tests attempt to exploit vulnerabilities and give more realistic estimates of how effective controls are.

When evaluating controls as part of a risk analysis, you may report them as ineffective, partially effective, or effective in reducing impact or likelihood. You also might use a semiquantitative scale that indicates control effectiveness from a range of numerical values. Each of the various control frameworks often provides guidance on assessing the effectiveness of the controls in that particular framework. For example, the catalog of controls found in NIST Special Publication 800-53, "Security and Privacy Controls for Federal Information Systems and Organizations," is supplemented by an assessment methodology found in its companion volume, Special Publication 800-53A, "Assessing Security and Privacy Controls in Federal Information Systems and Organizations," which describes how to assess and report the effectiveness of each control. Figure 2-4 shows an example of an NIST control from SP 800-53 R5, and Figure 2-5 shows the corresponding assessment guidance for the same control in SP 800-53A R5.

 EXAM TIP Control analysis includes identifying controls, determining their required function, determining whether they are effective in meeting that function, and identifying gaps between the desired and end states of how well controls protect assets.

AC-5   SEPARATION OF DUTIES

Control:

a.   Identify and document [*Assignment: organization-defined duties of individuals requiring separation*]; and

b.   Define system access authorizations to support separation of duties.

Discussion: Separation of duties addresses the potential for abuse of authorized privileges and helps to reduce the risk of malevolent activity without collusion. Separation of duties includes dividing mission or business functions and support functions among different individuals or roles, conducting system support functions with different individuals, and ensuring that security personnel who administer access control functions do not also administer audit functions. Because separation of duty violations can span systems and application domains, organizations consider the entirety of systems and system components when developing policy on separation of duties. Separation of duties is enforced through the account management activities in AC-2, access control mechanisms in AC-3, and identity management activities in IA-2, IA-4, and IA-12.

Related Controls: AC-2, AC-3, AC-6, AU-9, CM-5, CM-11, CP-9, IA-2, IA-4, IA-5, IA-12, MA-3, MA-5, PS-2, SA-8, SA-17.

Control Enhancements: None.

References: None.

Figure 2-4   The AC-5 control from NIST SP 800-53 R5

AC-05	SEPARATION OF DUTIES	
	ASSESSMENT OBJECTIVE: *Determine if:*	
	AC-05_ODP	*duties of individuals requiring separation are defined;*
	AC-05a.	*<AC-05_ODP duties of individuals>* are identified and documented;
	AC-05b.	system access authorizations to support separation of duties are defined.
	POTENTIAL ASSESSMENT METHODS AND OBJECTS:	
	AC-05-Examine	[SELECT FROM: Access control policy; procedures addressing divisions of responsibility and separation of duties; system configuration settings and associated documentation; list of divisions of responsibility and separation of duties; system access authorizations; system audit records; system security plan; other relevant documents or records].
	AC-05-Interview	[SELECT FROM: Organizational personnel with responsibilities for defining appropriate divisions of responsibility and separation of duties; organizational personnel with information security responsibilities; system/network administrators].
	AC-05-Test	[SELECT FROM: Automated mechanisms implementing separation of duties policy].

Figure 2-5   Assessing the AC-5 control, from NIST SP 800-53A R5

Control Gaps

A *control gap* is a situation where controls either do not exist or are not sufficient to provide adequate protection for an asset to reduce either impact or likelihood (and thereby risk) to an acceptable level. In this situation, after the lack of existence or effectiveness of the control is established, the organization must remediate the problem. We won't go into much depth on remediation here; that's the subject of the Risk Response and Reporting domain, which you'll read about in Chapter 3. However, during your analysis, you must identify control gaps and make recommendations for possible response options that would close those gaps. You may identify gaps in physical, technical, or administrative controls, even when other types of controls perform some security and protection functions. For example, suppose an organization implements account management processes, such as creating accounts in a standardized fashion, verifying identities before user accounts are created, and so on. In that case, the organization has operational and technical controls in place that help provide secure account management. However, if the organization has no written policy that requires this process and dictates that it be performed consistently, how can the organization be assured that these procedures will always be followed uniformly and in a secure manner? If there is no policy, the organization leaves it up to individual account operators to perform this function as they want, regardless of how "most people do it." In this case, a control gap would be that, although the organization is applying some level of control over this process, there is no written policy ensuring that it is standardized.

Control Recommendations

Once you've identified existing controls, determined how effective they are, and identified gaps between the current and desired end states of controls, you should be able to make sound, risk-based recommendations to senior managers on how controls should be supplemented, added, or changed. Recommending controls is a risk-based process; remember that there is a risk that you are trying to minimize, but you must balance this between control functionality and economy of resources. You have several considerations to keep in mind when making control recommendations:

- What more could be done to supplement or change existing controls to close the gap between current and desired end states of risk?
- Should new or different controls be applied to replace existing ones?
- What are the costs involved in applying additional controls, and do they exceed the value of the asset or the costs to replace it?
- Would additional controls require retooling or significantly changing the infrastructure, processes, or asset itself?
- Would additional controls require new personnel or training for current personnel?
- Can additional controls be implemented that also reduce risks in other areas (economy of use)?

The answers to these questions, at least some of them, will determine how you make the recommendations to management about closing the "control gap." Both the cost of implementation and the return on investment (ROI) received from implementing new controls or strengthening existing ones will affect management's acceptance of the recommendations. The asset value, or impact if it were significantly damaged or lost, will also affect how well the recommendation is received. Implementing a costly control to protect an asset worth less in terms of impact is not usually an economically sound decision. Organizational levels of risk appetite and tolerance will also affect control recommendations since any new or additional control must reduce risk enough to fall within those levels. In general, when recommending ways to close the control gap, whether it is by introducing new controls, modifying existing ones, or modifying the infrastructure to reduce likelihood or impact, you should do the following:

- Try to leverage existing controls that can be used across the board to include additional assets.
- Look for "quick wins" first—controls that are quickly and inexpensively implemented (such as policies, training, procedure changes, and so on).
- Prioritize control recommendations with risk; the greater the risk, the more attention to those particular control gaps.
- Be realistic in your recommendations: You can't reduce risk to absolute zero, you don't have all the resources you would like at your disposal, and you don't have to offer a 100 percent solution. Sometimes a 70 percent solution is better than a 0 percent solution.
- Provide alternatives to your primary recommendation for each control gap. Give management alternatives based on cost, level of risk reduction, and effectiveness.

Considering Risk and Control Ownership

Risk and control ownership are issues that must be considered during a risk analysis. Depending on how the organization is structured and the risk management strategy, risk ownership may be assigned to one or several different managers, spanning multiple functional areas. This is because the risk that affects one area likely affects other areas, so many different people may have responsibility for affected areas and be required to deal with and respond to risk. Control ownership should also be examined; often, controls that provide protections for a given asset or many systems may not fall under the operational purview of the risk owner. Some controls span the entire organization and protect multiple assets rather than only a specific system. These are referred to as *common controls,* and the responsible entity for these controls is the *common controls provider.* For example, consider physical security controls. There may be a physical security officer for the organization that oversees guards, personnel security, and access to secured areas. They may also be responsible for locks, closed-circuit televisions (CCTVs), and physical intrusion detection systems and alarms. These controls serve to protect information systems and data assets that might be in a secure data center. Risks may be presented to the person who is responsible for information systems in the data center. However, the controls that serve to protect them may belong to the physical security functional area. This will require some coordination between the different functional areas if controls managed by one functional area are insufficient to protect assets managed by another area. This may also affect organizational structures, budgets, and resource allocations.

 CAUTION   Risk, asset, and control owners are not always the same person, functional area, department, or organization. It's essential that you identify these particular owners early in the assessment process and maintain careful coordination and communication between these and other relevant stakeholders within the boundaries of your authority and assessment scope. Different types of owners can result in politically sensitive issues that revolve around resourcing, responsibility, accountability, and, sometimes, blame.

Root Cause Analysis

Root cause analysis, or RCA, is a method of problem-solving that seeks to identify the root cause of an event, situation, or problem. Often, when an event that disrupts business operations occurs, an organization wants to perform an RCA to determine what happened, why it occurred, and what changes can be made to help prevent a recurrence of the incident.

An example of RCA that is often the subject of publicity is the analysis of an airplane crash. Here, investigators carefully attempt to reconstruct the crash to determine the ultimate cause, whether it was the failure of a component, pilot error, or something else. In cybersecurity, an organization besieged by ransomware will perform an RCA to determine how and where the attack originated.

Here are the steps in a typical root cause analysis:

1. **Identification**   The RCA begins with a concise description of the incident or situation being analyzed. This is the starting point in an RCA.

2. **Chronology**   Using available event data, analysis of the incident or situation includes a detailed look at how the incident or situation unfolded.

3. **Differentiation**   Here, an investigator identifies all the details related to the event or situation to determine which details are causal (contributed to the event or situation) and which are non-causal (did not contribute to the event or situation). Investigators realize that many events have more than one causal factor.

4. **Causal analysis**   Each detail or factor is analyzed to determine the degree to which it contributed to the incident or situation. This often leads to the identification of the one causal factor, the root cause, that represents the initiation of the events that led to the incident being investigated.

5. **Identification of corrective actions**   For each causal action that contributed to the incident or situation, the RCA will identify corrective actions that would reduce the probability or impact of a similar incident in the future.

A simplistic approach to RCA is known as the *five whys*. This is an iterative technique in which the analyst looks at the incident or situation (or a causal factor) and asks, why did that occur? In the following example, a ransomware attack encrypted numerous files on a file server:

1. First track: Focus on the end user's PC.
   - Why? Ransomware successfully implanted itself on an end user's PC.
   - Why? The PC's antivirus was not up to date.
   - Why? The PC was on a new network segment not monitored by the antivirus server.
   - Why? Network engineers did not inform IT security of the new network segment (a causal factor).

2. Second track: Focus on the file server.
   - Why? The end user had global write permissions on the file server.
   - Why? It is a standard practice to grant global write access to end users, which reduces the number of access requests (a causal factor).
   - Why? There are not enough service desk technicians to fulfill access requests in a more restrictive environment (a causal factor).

3. Third track: Focus on the end user.

- Why? The end user opened an attachment containing malware in an e-mail message.
- Why? The end user believed that the e-mail was sent from an executive in the company.
- Why? The end user did not recognize the indicators of a phishing message.
- Why? The end user did not attend security awareness training.
- Why? Security awareness training is not required (a causal factor).
- Why? Company executives do not believe that employees should be required to spend time away from their duties in training.

In this situation, three broad root causes were identified: first, the end user's PC was on a network not being monitored by central antivirus software because of a communication breakdown; second, the end user had excessive permissions on the file server because of a practice of loose permissions; third, end users are not required to attend security awareness training. Corrective actions will likely be recommended for all three tracks.

Risk Scenario Development

A *risk scenario* is a business-impacting event that consists of a threat, threat actor, vulnerability, and asset. You could say that a risk scenario is a statement about a hypothetical risk event that could reasonably occur, based on known facts about threats, threat actors, and an asset's vulnerabilities. Such a description of a risk event can help risk managers and business executives better understand what would otherwise be an abstract concept.

Risk scenario development is performed during a risk assessment after assets, threats, and vulnerabilities have been tabulated. Risk scenarios are the potential real-world events identified in risk assessment data that communicate the risks that have a tangible impact on business operations.

Risk managers can approach scenario development from two perspectives: top-down and bottom-up. Both are explained here.

NOTE Threat actors are not only human entities but also events such as natural disasters.

Top-Down Risk Scenario Development

Top-down risk scenario development associates risks with business goals and objectives. The purpose of top-down risk scenario development is to identify scenarios that, if realized, would adversely impact those business goals and objectives. Similarly, top-down risk scenario development can associate risks with key business assets. Again, top-down risk scenarios would be related to those assets. Figure 2-6 depicts the extraction of top-down risk scenarios from risk assessment results.

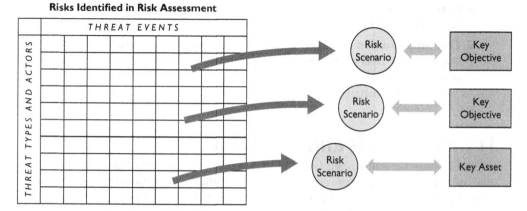

Figure 2-6 Extracting top-down risk scenarios from a risk assessment

Risk assessment and risk analysis are logical, analytical activities. Risk scenario development, on the other hand, particularly top-down risk scenario development, is by far an intuitive, creative activity. In pop culture, one would associate risk assessment and analysis as left-brain activity, with top-down risk scenario development as right-brain activity.

The primary benefit of using top-down risk scenarios is the ability to communicate risks more clearly to executive management. As the developers and promoters of corporate goals and objectives, senior executives should understand the various types of IT risks that could threaten to delay or increase the effort or cost required to achieve them.

Risk managers should look to outside sources to identify realistic risk scenarios. Trade journals and even mainstream media report on cybersecurity and other disruptive IT-related events. Developing a more compelling narrative than "this scenario happened to them, and it could also happen to us" can be difficult.

Bottom-Up Risk Scenario Development

Bottom-up risk scenario development focuses on specific assets (or groups of assets) or threats. Bottom-up risk scenarios are more technical than top-down scenarios and less likely to be conveyed to executive management. However, this technique can help risk managers better understand the scope and nature of various types of risks. Ultimately this may help risk managers refine their top-down risk scenario development by giving them additional information about the universe of risks they are dealing with.

Risk Scenario Development Considerations

Risk scenario development is vital in risk analysis and management, where risks that may initially be abstract are refined and translated into tangible statements of risks to business operations. Absent this transformation, risk scenarios will be little more than an intellectual exercise.

To be successful, risk managers need to ensure that the risk scenarios are:

- **Relevant to the business** Risk scenarios should indicate specific relevance and impact to the organization instead of being generic.

- **Kept current**   An organization's use of technology (at both the macro and micro levels) changes over time, meaning risks will vary in magnitude.

- **Communicated to management with a purpose**   Often, risk scenarios are the way that new risks are shared with management to proceed to risk treatment—that is, to make decisions about what to do about new risks. This is often the only time that management is informed of risks.

IT Risk Analysis and Evaluation

After a risk has been identified (which is covered in the first part of this chapter), it can next be examined. *Risk analysis* is the detailed examination of a risk to better understand basic factors, including the likelihood and impact of risk occurrence and the development of a measure that might be enacted to reduce probability or impact. Risk analysis helps determine the overall level of risk for a particular system, an asset, business process, or even the entire organization. Part of risk analysis involves discussions of findings with risk and control owners, as well as senior managers in the organization. During these discussions, you may discover other factors that influence the likelihood and impact levels or even affect threats, vulnerabilities, and assets. You'll also look at the existing controls and determine how effective they are in meeting risk, as well as look at recommended additional controls. Finally, you will report risk analysis results to senior managers and generate a risk report after this process is complete. We'll discuss these topics in more detail in this section. Figure 2-7 shows a familiar variation of the 5×5 likelihood and impact table, demonstrating how different levels of likelihood and impact are evaluated together to produce a qualitative risk level.

Risk Assessment Concepts, Standards, and Frameworks

Risk assessments are performed to identify, understand, and enable organizations to make intentional decisions about individual risks. There is considerable detail within the workings of risk assessments, as discussed in this section.

Many of the terms you'll encounter on the CRISC exam are generic and may have different definitions based on the different frameworks or standards you are using in practice. The term *assessment* is one such term that may confuse you. For the purposes of taking the exam, and in this book, an assessment refers to the overall combination of steps of identifying, evaluating, and analyzing risk. Remember that *risk identification*

Likelihood	Impact				
	Very Low	Low	Medium	High	Very High
Very High	Very Low	Low	Medium	High	Very High
High	Very Low	Low	Medium	High	Very High
Medium	Very Low	Low	Medium	Medium	High
Low	Very Low	Low	Low	Low	Medium
Very Low	Very Low	Very Low	Very Low	Low	Low

Figure 2-7   Likelihood and impact are evaluated together to produce a risk level.

involves identifying the threats, vulnerabilities, assets, and existing controls. On the other hand, *evaluation* focuses on determining the likelihood and impact if the vulnerabilities are exploited by the threats, resulting in damage to the asset. Risk analysis puts everything together, informs the organization about the risk involved, and helps determine how effective existing controls are and the gaps between current and desired risk states.

Risk assessment processes sometimes include the risk identification piece of the process but are often separate from this part, depending on the framework or standard you are using. In general, this process includes threat source and event identification, vulnerability identification, control analysis, likelihood determination, impact analysis, risk determination, control recommendations, and results documentation; these steps follow the same pattern and path as we're describing here for you in terms of identifying risk and then evaluating it. We'll describe some of these generic processes here in this chapter.

NOTE Different risk analysis methodologies and frameworks use varying terms with the same or different definitions. You should always look at a term given its context and particular framework or methodology.

Types of Assessments

Several types of assessments can be performed to determine the presence of risks, threats, or vulnerabilities in a system or process. Some of the techniques discussed here involve different ways of thinking about risk, while others employ manual or automated tools to examine information of some type.

- **Risk assessment**   An assessment technique used to identify and classify various risks associated with systems or processes.

- **Gap assessment**   An assessment of processes and/or systems to determine their compliance to policies, standards, or requirements.

- **Threat modeling**   Also known as a *threat assessment*, this is a threat-centric technique used to identify specific threat scenarios that may occur. Threat modeling is discussed in more detail earlier in this chapter.

- **Vulnerability assessment**   An assessment used to identify specific vulnerabilities that may be present in processes and/or systems.

- **Maturity assessment**   An assessment of processes or capabilities to determine their maturity, generally according to a maturity standard such as the capability maturity model integration (CMMI) or the NIST cybersecurity framework (CSF).

- **Penetration test**   This is an examination of systems, networks, or applications that identifies exploitable vulnerabilities. Tools used in a penetration test include port scanners, sniffers, protocol analyzers, fuzzers, password crackers, and specialized tools to identify specific vulnerabilities. A penetration test not only identifies but also validates a vulnerability by exploiting it—or demonstrating how it can be exploited if actual exploitation would bring harm to the asset (important when pen testing a production system).

- **Data discovery**   A manual or automated activity in which tools or techniques are used to examine the contents of a target system to determine the presence of specific types of data. Data discovery may also involve an examination of access rights to specific types of data.

- **Architecture and design review**   A manual activity in which the architecture or design of a process or system is examined to identify potential weaknesses.

- **Code review**   A manual activity in which software source code is examined for logic errors and security vulnerabilities.

- **Code scan**   An automated activity in which a code-scanning program or tool examines software source code to identify vulnerabilities and other defects.

- **Audit**   A formal inspection of a control or process to determine whether it is being followed and meets its objectives. Audits are discussed briefly in this book and fully in *CISA Certified Information Systems Auditor All-In-One Exam Guide*.

Scope of an Assessment

Before an assessment can begin, its *scope* needs to be determined. By this, we mean that the systems, processes, locations, teams, and/or time periods that are the focus of the assessment need to be formally established and communicated.

The opposing forces that influence scope are the desire to make it large enough to identify hard-to-find risks, but small enough to be efficient and complete in a reasonable period. A balance must be reached that enables the assessment to succeed.

Collecting Data for an Assessment

One of the challenges for a risk assessor is collecting and managing all the data for an assessment. On one end of the spectrum, the assessor may find it challenging to get the bare minimum of relevant data for a particular asset, including threats and threat actors, and vulnerabilities, as well as protective controls. On the other end of that same spectrum, the assessor may gather so much data that it is overwhelming to analyze and gauge its relevance to the assessment effort.

Another challenge is the source of the data. While the best data comes from authoritative sources with expertise in various areas, such as the asset or system in question, current threats, and so on, the assessor must be able to separate fact from opinion and collect truly objective data versus subjective data. Objective data is evidence that supports an assertion about an asset or risk that can be proven or verified through independent means. Subjective data, on the other hand, is data whose validity is subject to opinion. For example, auditing typically produces objective data in the form of audit logs (assuming they are secured) that detail events that occur on a system and trace those events back to individuals, thus ensuring accountability. Events in question can be verified through the audit logs. However, system administrators who assert that they regularly audit system activities but have no audit logs to prove this can't have their claims verified. Additionally, if no policies or procedures require auditing or show how to perform those tasks, these events can't be independently verified either.

Data can come in various forms, including performance data, statistical analysis, historical data, trends, and narrative form. The assessor should establish the relevance of data as it is collected and determine how it relates to relevant risk questions concerning threats, vulnerabilities, likelihood, impact, assets, and controls. Overwhelming amounts of data can be reduced to relevant summaries and analyzed, sometimes in aggregate, using various automated statistical analysis and database tools.

Data collection typically uses a combination of four methods designed to gather various types of qualitative and quantitative data from different sources. These collection methods complement and support one another, filling in gaps from one method and verifying information collected from another. The four main data collection methods are conducting interviews, reviewing documentation, observing systems and assets in operation, and performing technical testing on assets. They are described in more detail in the following sections.

Conducting Interviews   One of the best methods to start collecting data involves interviewing key personnel, such as asset owners, system administrators, security personnel, and other people with direct knowledge of essential aspects of the asset, relevant threats and vulnerabilities, and controls. These interviews are known as *walkthroughs*. Interviews should be scheduled with key personnel and consist of relevant questions that answer questions relating to security posture, processes and procedures, asset characteristics, and implemented security controls. The assessor should carefully record the results of the walkthrough through concise meeting notes or recording devices for later reference. Keep in mind that while interview data should usually be considered subjective in nature, it can be used as a starting point to gather knowledge and facts about a system that can be later verified using other means, such as documentation, system observation, and testing.

Reviewing Documentation   Documentation is a mainstay of a risk assessment. A well-documented process or system indicates its characteristics, security requirements, and whether the people responsible for the process or system have defined measures in place to fulfill security responsibilities. Documentation gives an assessor a wide variety of information on how the process or system is routinely used, whether a security patch program is in place, who has access to systems and data, what policies exist to define security requirements, and how the system is securely configured. Documentation can be either paper-based or electronic; it can come from spreadsheets, databases, network devices, systems, written procedures, physical access logs, and so on. Examples of documentation include organizational policies, processes and procedures, backup and restore procedures, security officer appointment letters, and so on. While not strictly documentation (unless printed), audit logs and configuration files could also be considered in this category since they provide documentary evidence that supports an assertion of how events were recorded or how a system was configured. Documentation also serves to verify data collected from other sources, such as interviews. Remember, if you don't document something in the security assessor world, you can't prove that you've done it.

Observing and Verifying Systems and Assets   Sometimes it's not enough to interview personnel and review documentation. Unfortunately, people can lie or be mistaken in interviews, and documentation can be falsified. Observing a process or system in operation can verify whether it is secure and whether its security functions and controls are working as intended to protect systems and data. The same is true for physical security controls. An assessor can easily determine whether a control is functioning by observing a system operator perform a security function or visually inspecting a control to ensure it is in place and implemented properly. Examples requiring the observation method include gates, guards, and locks; other examples are watching a system through the boot process, observing a screen lock go into effect, having a system administrator demonstrate various security features, and so on.

Performing System Testing   Not all data can come from talking to people, reading system architecture documents, and watching the system administrator assign permissions to shared folders and files. Some data must come from examinations of the system's configuration, as well as obtaining relevant data related to patching, vulnerabilities, user accounts, configuration files, registry settings, and other technical data. This data is used to determine if a system is configured properly and securely and what potential vulnerabilities might exist on the system. This is where the technical assessment portion of data collection comes into play. Since technical data can be overwhelming in size and volume, automated tools are typically used to perform system security testing. These tools include vulnerability scanners, sniffers, and other hardware and software tools described later in this chapter.

During security testing of a system, various types of host-based and network scans may be performed, along with an in-depth examination of patches and updates applied to the system, configuration settings, user accounts, and other security settings. The system's rights, permissions, and privileges and its resources are examined and compared against security requirements and control functions to ensure they match. Network protocols and connections are studied, and the network architecture may be examined to ensure a sound network design has been implemented. Application software code reviews and testing, including fuzzing, may be performed. Authentication and encryption mechanisms are examined in depth to ensure they are strong and effective and meet governance and best-practice requirements where applicable. Physical access controls may be tested to ensure that physical separation away from systems for unauthorized users is maintained.

The results of system security assessments (usually in the form of vulnerability assessments or penetration testing, discussed in this chapter) are consolidated with the results from interviews, documentation reviews, and system observations to form a comprehensive data picture of the system or asset; these results further inform the controls analysis and impact determination aspects of risk. Table 2-2 summarizes the different data collection methods you can use during an assessment.

Method	Examples
Walkthrough	System administrators, facilities personnel, security personnel, asset managers, common control providers, risk management personnel, and control owners
Documentation review	Architectural diagrams, printed system configuration files, printed audit logs, access control logs, risk and incident reports, and security procedures
Observation	System configuration, resource access controls, physical controls, security processes and procedures as they are being performed, and system functions
Test	Systems, networks, devices, controls, procedures, ports, protocols, services, system security configuration, and vulnerability scanning

Table 2-2   Summary of Data Collection Methods During a Risk Assessment, with Examples

NOTE While you may not be directly tested on data collection methods, it is a good idea to understand these methods, as in actual practice, you will likely use them extensively.

Techniques used to examine systems or processes, evidence collection, sampling, and other considerations are covered in greater detail in ISACA's Certified Information Systems Auditor (CISA) certification and described fully in the book *CISA Certified Information Systems Auditor All-In-One Exam Guide*.

Risk Assessment Standards and Frameworks

Some organizations see risk assessment as one large monolithic process, but many frameworks and standards break it down into different steps. We'll look at several important frameworks, including the National Institute of Standards and Technology (NIST) SP 800-30, OCTAVE, the ISACA Risk IT Framework, ISO/IEC 27005, and others. We will go into detail and examine them from a risk assessment perspective.

Business Alignment

One of the most important considerations for selecting standards and frameworks is business alignment. When selecting a standard, whether for risk assessment, risk management, security controls, or integrated risk management systems, the risk management leader must select a framework or standard that best aligns with the organization's needs. Selection considerations include the following:

- Industry sector
- Customer expectations and requirements
- Applicable regulations
- Risk appetite
- Organizational maturity
- Current and future technology in use

Security and risk professionals who strive for business alignment will achieve better outcomes by building and selecting processes, frameworks, and standards that are more likely to succeed.

NIST Special Publication 800-30

NIST Special Publication 800-30, "Guide for Conducting Risk Assessments," is a step-by-step guide to performing qualitative and quantitative risk assessments. The standard also briefly describes the overall risk management life-cycle process to provide context for individual risk assessments. The steps of a risk assessment are as follows:

1. *Prepare for assessment.* The scope, techniques, records, personnel, schedule, and other resources are identified. We also like to consider the threat landscape, although this is not expressly a part of NIST 800-30.

2. *Conduct assessment.* The following are the actual risk assessment steps performed on each target asset defined in the assessment scope:

   a. *Identify threat sources and events.* All reasonable threat sources, events, and actors are identified.

   b. *Identify vulnerabilities and predisposing conditions.* Vulnerabilities in the in-scope processes or systems are identified. Often, vulnerabilities and threats are paired and listed. For instance, a threat actor with a lock pick set is paired with an exterior door with a substandard key core.

   c. *Determine the likelihood of occurrence.* The probability that each specific threat will occur is determined. Often this is an estimation, as there is generally insufficient data to reliably determine an accurate probability.

   d. *Determine the magnitude of impact.* This is generally expressed in qualitative terms in the form of descriptions of impact on business operations. Also, this can be expressed in quantitative terms that might include response and recovery costs.

   e. *Determine risk.* The risk associated with each threat scenario is calculated, generally as Risk = Impact × Probability × Asset Value.

3. *Communicate results.* The results of the risk assessment are tabulated as determined at the start of the assessment. The results are communicated to various stakeholders in the organization. Often, results are developed for specific audiences; for instance, an executive summary may be produced for executives, while detailed charts will be produced for lower management and those who will participate in remediation activities.

4. *Maintain assessment.* This generally refers to the activity of *risk monitoring,* in which a risk manager will periodically re-examine the assets to determine whether any changes have occurred in threats, threat actors, vulnerabilities, impact, or probability of occurrence.

NIST SP 800-30 contains additional resources, including the following:

- **Appendix D: Threat Sources**   This includes taxonomies of adversarial and non-adversarial threat sources, capabilities, intent, and scale.

- **Appendix E: Threat Events**   This includes numerous adversarial and non-adversarial threat activities that represent reconnaissance or attack.

- **Appendix F: Vulnerabilities and Predisposing Conditions**   This is a taxonomy of vulnerabilities and their characteristics.

- **Appendix G: Likelihood of Occurrence**   This includes taxonomies related to the probability of threats occurring.
- **Appendix H: Impact**   This includes various types of impact on organizations when threats occur.
- **Appendix I: Risk Determination**   This includes taxonomies used to determine the magnitude of individual risks.

OCTAVE Methodology

As part of a U.S. government contract with Carnegie Mellon University, the Operationally Critical Threat, Asset, and Vulnerability Evaluation (OCTAVE) methodology was developed to assist organizations in identifying and assessing information security risk. The methodology was initially developed by the Software Engineering Institute (SEI) at Carnegie Mellon University in 1999 and has been updated over the years to its current version, OCTAVE Allegro, in 2007. OCTAVE uses a concept called *workshops,* made up of members of an organization, sometimes including outside facilitators with risk management and assessment expertise. The methodology has prescribed procedures, including worksheets and information catalogs to assist organizational members, drawn from all functional areas of an organization, to frame and assess risk based on internal organizational context (infrastructure, governance, business environment, and so on). OCTAVE has three iterations: the original OCTAVE, OCTAVE-S, and OCTAVE Allegro.

OCTAVE and OCTAVE-S   The original OCTAVE methodology was released in 1999 and was designed for organizations with at least 300 employees. The assumptions for using OCTAVE included that the organization operates and maintains multitiered information infrastructure and performs vulnerability assessments. While OCTAVE is flexible and allows an organization to tailor its use based on its own assessment needs, the methodology is performed as three sequential phases. The first phase covers identifying assets, threats, protection practices, vulnerabilities, and security requirements. You can see where this maps to the practices we've described throughout this chapter as determining threats, identifying assets and their vulnerabilities, and evaluating existing controls. In the second phase, the members of the workshop perform assessment activities and evaluate the infrastructure. In the third phase, the workshop members develop response strategies for the identified risks.

OCTAVE-S is fundamentally the same as the original OCTAVE, with a few minor differences. First, OCTAVE-S was designed to assess smaller organizations, usually with fewer than 100 people. Second, this iteration relies more on internal personnel with extensive knowledge of the organization and its infrastructure and less on outside risk experts or facilitators. The number of workshop members will also be considerably less; the team may rely on fewer than ten key experts in the organization. OCTAVE-S processes and procedure documents were also written to include more detailed security-related information. This approach does not rely on outside security experts or risk facilitators to assist the team.

OCTAVE Allegro   The OCTAVE Allegro methodology, introduced in 2007, expands the previous two iterations but does not necessarily replace them. It includes a more business-centered and operational risk approach to the assessment. It is also asset-centered in its approach; it focuses on assets and their use or misuse, the environment they are used in, and how threats and vulnerabilities specifically target and affect the assets. Allegro can be used on a scaled basis; either individuals or workshop teams can use this method without requiring a high degree of risk management or assessment knowledge and experience. OCTAVE Allegro is divided into four phases, which include eight steps. These phases and steps are described next.

Phase 1: Establish Drivers   *Step 1: Establish risk measurement criteria.* This step serves to develop and establish the organization's methodology and measurement criteria used to assess risk. OCTAVE uses a qualitative assessment methodology and measurements but can use quantitative methods for certain aspects of the overall process, such as determining likelihood and impact.

Phase 2: Profile Assets   *Step 2: Develop an information asset profile.* In this step, the organization develops an asset profile, which is a collection of information that describes the asset, including its characteristics, priority, impact on the organization, and value. This profile also contains security requirements the asset may have.

Step 3: Identify information asset containers. The information asset container describes how data is stored, where it is processed, and how it is transported. Containers are usually networks and systems, including those that the organization directly operates and those that it outsources.

Phase 3: Identify Threats   *Step 4: Identify areas of concern.* In this step, potential risk factors are identified and are used to develop threat scenarios.

Step 5: Identify threat scenarios. In the context of OCTAVE, threat scenarios describe categories of actors and the relevant threats in each category. The scenarios are typically identified by using a threat tree, which simply maps actors and scenarios.

Phase 4: Identify and Mitigate Risks
Step 6: Identify risks. In this step, consequences such as impact and likelihood are identified and measured, which inform risk.

Step 7: Analyze risks. Once impact and likelihood have been identified and measured, risks are analyzed. During this step, risk scores are developed. These come from developing impact and likelihood values, emphasizing impact in particular, since this is an asset-driven assessment.

Step 8: Select mitigation approach. In this step, risk response strategies are developed, analyzed, and recommended.

 EXAM TIP   OCTAVE is designed for larger organizations, while OCTAVE-S is intended for use by smaller organizations. OCTAVE Allegro is scalable for use by individuals or larger teams working in organizations of various sizes.

ISO/IEC Standards
ISO stands for the International Organization for Standardization, and IEC stands for the International Electrotechnical Commission. Together, these two organizations are responsible for a plethora of information technology and manufacturing standards used worldwide, including several that apply to information security and risk management.

ISO/IEC 27005:2018   Standards in the ISO/IEC 27000 series are all about information security, and the 27005:2018 standard ("Information technology – Security techniques –Information security risk management") supports the common ideas promulgated in both ISO/IEC 27001 and 27002. The standard defines the entire risk management life cycle, including detailed risk assessment principles. The standard doesn't offer specific risk management or assessment methodologies. However, it does serve to describe a formalized, structured risk management process, such as developing context, scope, methods, and so on. It also describes the two primary types of assessment methodologies: qualitative and quantitative. Additionally, it describes processes used to develop risk response strategies, communication with stakeholders, and continuous risk monitoring.

ISO/IEC 31010:2019   ISO/IEC 31010:2019 is where the meat of information regarding risk assessments is located for the ISO/IEC standards. This document, "Risk Management – Risk Assessment Techniques," articulates and extends the risk management principles of ISO/IEC 31000:2018 and provides a concrete overview of the risk assessment process. This standard describes risk assessment as the combination of risk identification, analysis, and evaluation, with a precursor step of establishing the risk context within the organization. The standard also addresses communication and consultation with various stakeholders and management, risk treatment (response), and monitoring risk.

    EXAM TIP   Of the ISO/IEC standards, ISO/IEC 31010:2019 is essential for the exam because it covers risk assessments in detail.

ISACA's Risk IT Framework

ISACA developed the Risk IT Framework to align with its COBIT framework. While COBIT is used to manage other aspects of business infrastructure and risk, the Risk IT Framework is explicitly used to allow organizations to identify and manage IT risk. The framework is broken down into three major process areas: Risk Governance (RG), Risk Evaluation (RE), and Risk Response (RR). We discussed this framework briefly in Chapter 1, but the focus of this chapter is on the assessment process, so we will cover the Risk Evaluation portion in more depth here.

The Risk Evaluation processes in the Risk IT Framework don't cover only assessment; they overlap with the risk identification areas. In RE processes, business impact is framed and described, and risk scenarios are also developed. Risks are assessed and analyzed as well as presented to the organization's management. The RE processes are further broken down into three areas (numbered RE1–RE3), which we will describe in more detail.

Collect Data (RE1)   The data collection process aligns with some of the risk identification processes we've previously described. During this process, risk management personnel develop a model for data collection, which provides for standardized data formats, measurements, and common data definitions. Data is collected on the various aspects of the organization and risk scenarios, including the business's operating environment, risk factors, threat sources and events, vulnerability data, and asset data. Data is also collected on the effectiveness of existing controls in the organization.

Analyze Risk (RE2)   In this part of the Risk IT Framework, the organization begins to assess and analyze risk. First, it defines the risk analysis scope. The scope determines how broad and deep the risk analysis efforts will be, what areas the risk analysis will cover, and which assets will be examined for risk. To complete this part of the process, you'll need to consider all the documentation assembled up to this point: risk scenarios, asset inventories, breakdowns of business processes, prioritization of assets, and so on. This will help frame the risk analysis as well as determine scope.

During this step, IT risk is also estimated. This involves determining likelihood and impact values associated with the developed risk scenarios. You will also consider existing controls and how effective they are as currently installed and functioning. Likelihood and impact values are considered after existing controls are considered.

Although risk response is the subject of Chapter 3, you also identify and consider possible risk response options during this step of the process. The person assessing the risk may recommend several different response options, based on the identified risk. What risk options an organization will use is determined later in the process and typically with the input and approval of senior management. Risk response options should be recommended that reduce risk to an acceptable level directly based on the risk appetite and tolerance of the organization. Finally, knowledgeable peers should review risk analyses to verify that the analysis process is sound and to validate the results.

Maintain Risk Profile (RE3)   A *risk profile* is a collection of detailed data on identified IT risks. Risk profiles can cover a single system or asset but are also often seen as describing risks on an organization-wide basis. During this risk evaluation step, a comprehensive document of identified risks and their characteristics, such as details regarding impact, likelihood, and contributing factors, is developed and maintained throughout the asset or system's life cycle. Remember that system or asset risk profiles are usually rolled up into a more comprehensive risk document that covers systems, assets, and business processes across the entire organization.

IT assets are also mapped to the business and organizational processes they support during this step; this helps translate IT risk to corresponding business risk and allows management to see how the organization would be affected if IT risk were realized on specific assets. This also enables the organization to develop criticality estimates of IT resources from a business perspective. It's worth noting that this is similar to the same process followed during a business impact assessment (BIA). The key to understanding how IT risk affects business operations at this point is in understanding how the capabilities of IT are provided to the business processes in question and how critical IT is to a particular business process or operation. Maintaining a risk profile also means monitoring and updating risk scenarios and analysis as conditions and risk factors change. This involves keeping the risk register up to date as well. Finally, the organization should develop key risk indicators (KRIs) during this step, specifically focusing on IT resources. While key risk indicators are discussed in Chapter 3, for now, you should know that they allow the organization to monitor changes in risk for given scenarios, enabling the organization to modify its risk profiles as these indicators change. Table 2-3 summarizes some of the different risk assessment methodologies available to you.

Methodology	Sponsor	Notes
NIST SP 800-30, "Guide for Conducting Risk Assessments"	National Institute of Standards and Technology	Part of the NIST Risk Management Framework
OCTAVE (OCTAVE, OCTAVE-S, and OCTAVE Allegro)	Software Engineering Institute, Carnegie Mellon University	Uses workgroups, is suited for any organization, and does not require extensive risk management experience or knowledge
ISO/IEC	ISO/IEC	Prescribes methods and processes for developing assessment programs as well as describes more than 30 different means to assess risk factors and elements
The ISACA Risk IT Framework	ISACA	Risk assessments covered in the Risk Evaluation (RE) phase

Table 2-3 Summary of Available Risk Assessment Methods and Frameworks

EXAM TIP Because this is an ISACA-sponsored exam, it is a good idea to understand risk assessment terms and processes from the perspective of the ISACA framework more so than any other. The ISACA Risk IT Framework directly aligns with ISO/IEC standards as well.

Risk Ranking

When risks have been identified in a risk assessment, it generally makes sense to display these risks in an ordered list. Most often, the highest risks will appear at the top of a list, indicating the nature of the sequencing. For instance, risks with the most significant impact may appear first, or perhaps a composite risk score will be calculated for each risk (based on probability, impact, and asset value) and risk items sorted by this overall risk calculation. Risk ranking, then, helps tell the story of the most critical risks that have been identified.

Risk ranking can be portrayed visually, which helps the reader better understand the universe of risks that have been identified. Figure 2-8 shows a risk map that visually indicates the nature and severity of risks.

Risk Ownership

To correctly manage and act on unacceptable risks, each risk is assigned a risk owner. Generally, the risk owner is the department head or business unit leader associated with the business process that is the focus of a risk. It is usually not appropriate to assign risk ownership to IT, as IT is the steward of information and information systems as well as provides services as directed by department heads and business unit leaders.

Similarly, the organization's cybersecurity leader (often a CISO) is not the assignee of risks. Instead, the cybersecurity leader facilitates risk conversations and decisions with

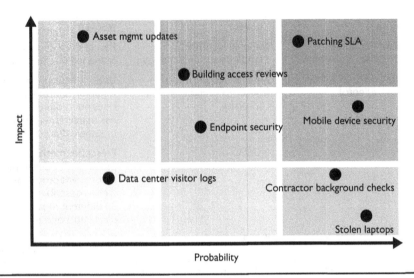

Figure 2-8 A risk map visually depicts the severity of risks.

department heads and business unit leaders, particularly those whose business processes are associated with individual risks.

In risk management, there are usually several different "owners" associated with each risk, including the following:

- **Risk owner** This is usually the department head or business unit leader associated with the business process where the risk resides. Even if a risk is related to an IT system, IT is generally not the risk owner. Rarely, if ever, is the cybersecurity leader assigned as a risk owner.

- **Risk treatment decision-maker** This person makes a business decision regarding the disposition (treatment) of an individual risk. Risk treatment is discussed fully in Chapter 3.

- **Risk remediation owner** This is the person responsible for any remediation that has been selected as a part of risk treatment.

An organization's risk management program charter (or other formal document) should define the roles and responsibilities of each type of risk owner.

These and other facets of risk ownership are generally indicated in the risk register, which is discussed next.

Risk Register

A *risk register* is a business record containing information about business risks and their origin, potential impact, affected assets, probability of occurrence, and treatment. A risk register is *the* central business record in an organization's risk management program (the set of activities used to identify and treat risks).

Together with other records, the risk register serves as the focal point of information that an organization is attempting to manage risk. Other records include information about risk treatment decisions and approvals, tracking projects linked to risks, risk assessments, and other activities that contribute to the risk register.

When new risks are identified, they are added to the risk register to be later analyzed, discussed, and decisions will be made about their disposition.

A risk register can be stored in a spreadsheet, database, or within an integrated risk management (IRM) tool—formerly known as a governance, risk, and compliance (GRC) tool—used to manage risk and other activities in the security program. Table 2-4 shows a typical risk register entry.

Item	Description
Entry number	A unique numeric value identifying the entry. This can be in the form of a date, such as 20210127a.
Status	Current status of the entry: • Open • Assigned • Closed
Date entered	The date the risk register entry was created.
Entered by	The person who created the risk register entry.
Source	The activity or event that compelled someone to create this entry. Sources include the following: • Risk assessment • Vulnerability assessment • Security incident • Threat intelligence • External party
Incident number	Reference to an incident record, if applicable.
Title	Short title describing the risk entry.
Description	Description of the risk.
Threat description	Description of the potential threat activity.
Threat actor	Description of the type of threat actor: • Worker • Former worker • Supplier, vendor, or partner • Cybercriminal • Nation-state
Vulnerability description	Description of one or more vulnerabilities that increases the probability or impact of threat realization.
Third-party organization	Name of the third-party organization where the risk is present, if applicable.

Table 2-4 Sample Risk Register Data Structure

Item	Description
Third-party classification	Classification level of the third-party organization, if applicable.
Business impact	Business language description of the impact of threat realization.
Technical impact	Technical language description of the impact of threat realization, if applicable.
Asset	The specific asset, asset group, or asset class affected by the risk.
Asset owner	The owner of the affected asset.
Risk owner	The owner of the risk.
Control group	A reference to the affected control group, if applicable.
Control	A reference to the affected control, if applicable.
Process	A reference to the affected process, if applicable.
Untreated probability of occurrence	An estimate of the probability of occurrence of the threat event associated with the risk. Usually expressed as high, medium, or low or as a number on a scale such as 1 to 5.
Untreated impact of occurrence	An estimate of the impact of occurrence of the threat event associated with the risk. Usually expressed as high, medium, or low or as a number on a scale such as 1 to 5.
Untreated risk score	An overall risk score that is generally a product of probability, impact, and asset value.
Treated probability of occurrence	An estimate of the probability of occurrence of the threat event associated with the risk after risk treatment. Usually expressed as high, medium, or low or as a number on a scale such as 1 to 5.
Treated impact of occurrence	An estimate of the impact of occurrence of the threat event associated with the risk after risk treatment. Usually expressed as high, medium, or low or as a number on a scale such as 1 to 5.
Treated risk score	An overall risk score that is generally a product of probability, impact, and asset value, after risk treatment.
Estimated cost of risk treatment	An estimated cost of risk treatment. This is expressed in dollars or the local currency.
Estimated level of effort of risk treatment	An estimated level of effort of risk treatment. This can be expressed as high, medium, or low, as a number on a scale such as 1 to 5, or as an estimate of range of man-hours, as follows: • Less than 1 hour • Less than 10 hours • Less than 100 hours • Less than 1,000 hours • Less than 10,000 hours
Risk treatment	The chosen method of risk treatment: • Accept • Mitigate • Transfer • Avoid

Table 2-4 Sample Risk Register Data Structure *(continued)*

Item	Description
Risk treatment approver	The person or body that approved the risk treatment method.
Risk treatment approval date	The date that the risk treatment method was approved.
Risk treatment owner	The person responsible for carrying out risk treatment.
Risk treatment description	A description of the risk treatment.
Risk treatment planned completion	The date when risk treatment is expected to be completed.
Actual cost of risk treatment	The actual cost of risk treatment, which would be known when risk treatment has been completed. This is expressed in dollars or the local currency.
Actual level of effort of risk treatment	The actual level of effort of risk treatment, which would be known when risk treatment has been completed. This is expressed in man-hours.
Risk treatment closure date	Date when risk treatment is completed.

Table 2-4 Sample Risk Register Data Structure *(continued)*

Sources of Information for the Risk Register

Awareness of risks can come from many places and through a variety of events. The information in Table 2-4 provides some hints about the potential sources of information that would lead to the creation of a risk register entry. These sources include the following:

- **Internal and external risk assessment**   A prime source for risk register entries, a risk assessment identifies risks in the organization's staff (for example, excessive workload, competency, and training issues), business processes, and technology.

- **Vulnerability assessment**   The high-level results of a vulnerability assessment (or penetration test, code review, social engineering assessment, and so on) may indicate overarching problems in staff, business processes, or technology at a strategic level.

- **Internal audit**   Internal audit and other internal control self-assessments can identify problems in staff, business processes, or technology.

- **External audits**   Audits performed by external parties can identify issues in business processes and information technology.

- **Security incident**   The occurrence of a security incident may reveal the presence of one or more risks that require attention. Note that a security incident in another organization may highlight risks in one's own organization.

- **Threat intelligence**   Formal and informal subscriptions or data feeds on threat intelligence may reveal risks that warrant attention.

- **Industry development**   Changes in the organization's industry sector, such as new business activities and techniques, may reveal or magnify risks that require attention.

- **New laws and regulations**   The passage of new laws, regulations, applicable standards, and private legal obligations may reveal the presence of risks that require attention. Also, note that compliance risk (that is, the possibility that regulators or others may impose fines or sanctions on the organization) may well be included in one or more risk register entries if the organization has identified such risks.

- **Consultants**   A visit by or conversation with an expert security consultant may reveal previously unknown risks. The consultant, who may be an auditor or assessor or may be working in the organization on a project, may or may not expect to find risks that the organization's security manager would want to be aware of.

Updating the Risk Register

Because the risk register is a living document, it should be periodically updated as risk conditions change. Risk assessments will provide updated information that should be included in the risk register and information about ongoing risk response actions applied to the risk. Whether the risk register is in the form of an electronic database, spreadsheet, or another type of document, it should be easy to read and readily accessible by risk managers and risk owners to stay updated on the current risk posture of the organization. As mentioned previously, it also should be considered a sensitive, access-controlled document. Table 2-5 shows a risk register and some sample entries.

Risk Analysis Methodologies

As stated earlier in this chapter, *risk analysis* is the detailed analysis of a risk identified in a risk assessment. In risk analysis, we examine a risk and apply techniques to better understand it from several perspectives:

- **Asset identification**   The asset(s) involved in a particular risk are identified. This could be an IT or IoT device, a business application, an entire IT environment (or specific parts therein), a database, a building, a procedure, or a business process.

- **Vulnerability**   Various weaknesses related to the asset are identified that could be exploited by a threat event.

- **Threat**   Various threat scenarios are considered, particularly those that are reasonably applicable to identified vulnerabilities.

- **Asset value**   The value of the asset is identified and considered. Various iterations of risk analysis may consider different types of asset value, including replacement cost, repair cost, lost revenue, and more. For various risk scenarios, it may be necessary to use and identify different types of asset value. For instance, one risk scenario may use replacement value while another might use repair cost.

- **Business context**   Because risk analysis is often an abstract mental exercise, it is necessary to define the business context for the risk. For example, risk analysis is performed on a database server; the business context is the organization's financial accounting system that supports all of the organization's accounting department's business processes. Without identifying business context, a risk remains abstract, and it is more difficult to apply risk treatment later on.

Risk Description	Likelihood	Impact	Risk Owner	Resources Required	Estimated Completion Date	Actual Completion Date	Current Status	Comments
Data theft from a malicious user (via risk assessment in April 2021)	Medium	High	Engineering department	$10,000 for new DLP system	January 2023		Assessing different DLP vendors	Purchase and implementation by December 2022
Loss of primary accounting server data	High	High	Accounting department	$15,000 for backup system	October 2021	September 2021	Vendor selected	Final purchase and installation in August 2022

Table 2-5   Sample Entries in a Risk Register

- **Business impact** To be relevant to the business, risk analysis needs to identify the impact of various threat scenarios on business processes and operations. For example, risk analysis focused on access controls on a database management system containing customer information would identify business interruption in scenarios involving data destruction and privacy breaches with reputation damage and fines in scenarios involving data theft.

- **Risk appetite and risk tolerance** The risk analyst should be familiar with the organization's stated risk appetite and risk tolerance to ensure that identified risks and subsequent risk analysis align with risk appetite and tolerance. Risk appetite and risk tolerance were discussed in more detail in Chapter 1.

- **Mitigation analysis** Once a specific risk is examined, various mitigation scenarios can be developed. For each, the risk manager would identify the time required to perform the mitigation, cost, the changes in the probability of various threat scenarios, the changes in impact for each, and the change in risk for each.

Asset Identification, Classification, and Valuation

Identifying the different elements of risk is a necessary precursor to assessing risk. One of the goals of the identification process is the development of risk scenarios. Risk scenarios require that you identify assets, vulnerabilities, and potential threat events.

Asset identification not only requires you to inventory all of your assets; you should also determine how critical they are to your business, decide how sensitive the data they process or produce is, and characterize or classify the system or asset in terms of confidentiality, integrity, and availability. Determining criticality is an essential aspect of the overall risk management process and typically is done before any assessment takes place. The NIST RMF process requires that you perform a system categorization on assets in the first step of that framework. This system categorization later helps you to assign controls to the asset based on its criticality factors. The set of controls you assign to each asset, based on its criticality, is assessed for effectiveness in mitigating risk and compliance.

Risk managers may also want to know the value of an asset. Quantifiable risk analysis requires that some value of an asset be identified, whether based on replacement cost, salvage cost, depreciated value, or another method of calculation that represents the expenditure of resources to return an asset to a pre-threat event state.

Likelihood Determination and Impact Analysis

Evaluation is the next step of the process. You must determine the likelihood of a given threat agent initiating a threat or of an identified threat exploiting a given vulnerability, as well as the level of impact or harm to the asset if a threat has successfully exploited a vulnerability. While threats and vulnerabilities in assets are necessary ingredients to determine risk, they are static ingredients; in other words, threats, vulnerabilities, and assets don't change much. On the other hand, likelihood and impact are variable and are the primary factors in measuring risk. People who don't understand how risk is framed often mistakenly state risk as a result of only one individual element. You could say that the risk to an asset is high, for example, simply because the likelihood of the adverse event occurring is high. You could also say that risk is high because the level of impact if an adverse event were to occur would be high. However, neither of these statements alone really captures the sense of risk. This is because they do not convey the other dimension of risk individually since risk is a product of *both* likelihood and impact. Additionally, you can't make these determinations without the background knowledge of the threat, the vulnerability, and the asset.

CAUTION Make sure you consider controls and their effectiveness when analyzing risk since controls can help decrease likelihood or reduce impact, thereby reducing the assessed risk for an asset and the organization.

Evaluation involves the measurement of these two primary factors: likelihood and impact. We've already discussed how there can be different ways to measure these factors based on subjectivity or concrete values. This is where the discussion on qualitative and quantitative techniques comes into play. We'll go into depth on those assessment techniques next.

EXAM TIP Remember that risk assessments are composed of the steps of risk identification, evaluation, and analysis. Identification produces threat–vulnerability pairs, asset inventories, and risk scenarios. Evaluation covers likelihood and impact calculations, resulting in risk values. Analysis looks at the overall application of these factors, as well as control analysis, to produce a comprehensive picture of risk.

Quantitative and Qualitative Analysis Techniques

You could take two different security professionals, both trained in the latest standards and practices associated with risk management, and have them both assess the same system, and, chances are, they would produce similar reports. However, they would not be the same. Why is that? It's because there are so many different methods of conducting risk assessment and analysis, depending on what governance the organization falls under, how the organization has framed its risk, and so on, that the risk would never be assessed the same; there are too many variables involved. Add to that complexity the natural subjectivity of human beings, and you may have very different risk reports. However, most risk assessment methodologies are still based fundamentally on the two primary ways to assess risk: qualitative and quantitative. Both methods have value, depending on the context of the situation, and often both methods can be combined. We discuss these techniques at length in the upcoming sections and how they can be used together.

Quantitative Quantitative risk analysis uses concrete (nonsubjective) numerical values and statistical analysis to calculate the likelihood and impact of risk. Quantitative methods use numerical values such as dollar figures, statistical numbers, and other hard-core numerical assignments. Quantitative risk assessments follow the same general pattern described previously; you must first list your assets (along with their replacement costs and exposure factors), calculate the impact of a full or partial loss of the asset, determine the likelihood of the adverse event, and come up with the overall risk to the organization.

This might be calculated in terms of dollars, for example. The following is a scenario that will help you better understand quantitative risk analysis and some of the factors that can be quantified and how.

Quantitative Risk Analysis: A Scenario Let's say you are a new employee in a small family-owned business that has no other security professionals employed. You've been tasked with developing a risk management strategy and program for the business. Suppose the business has a small server farm located in an older building on your small campus, with wooden walls, older wiring, no backup electrical power, and reasonably good fire detection and suppression systems. The server farm contains four servers, each performing a specific data-processing function. The data is backed up weekly, but it takes time to restore, and there is a good likelihood that some of the data would be lost because of the weekly backup schedule. Let's also say (just for the sake of illustration) that each of these servers costs $10,000 to replace with a new server (since they don't make your model any longer unless you were lucky enough to find a cheaper one on eBay). You've attempted to quantify factors for the owners, such as recovery time objective (RTO) and recovery point objective (RPO). These factors tell you how much data you could afford to lose if a disaster happened (such as a fire burning down that small wooden building) and how fast you would need to recover data to resume business operations to avoid suffering a significant loss of business.

Let's assume that the small business is in an area prone to thunderstorms, tornadoes, and hurricanes. One of the natural incidents that could occur in these areas is a lightning strike during a thunderstorm, where lightning strikes the metal roof of the building, and one of the servers suffers a power surge that completely renders it inoperable. If, after such an event, an assessment determines that the server can't be repaired, you decide to buy another one. The replacement cost of this server is $10,000. Let's do some simple quantitative analysis on this scenario:

Asset value (AV) = $10,000
Exposure factor (EF) = 1 (in this case, a 100 percent loss of the server and its data)
Single loss expectancy (SLE) = Asset value (AV) × Exposure factor (EF) = $10,000

With an SLE of $10,000, you must hope this scenario never happens. However, based on analysis of historical weather patterns in the area, and given the shoddy construction and limited electrical protections of the building the server farm sits in, this seems to be a likely possibility. So, you should determine how much the organization is likely to lose, per year, in such a scenario. You can calculate this if you know a couple of other pieces of information. First, you need to know how often to expect a severe storm in the area (say, on an annual basis). This annualized rate of occurrence (ARO) could be used with the SLE value given earlier to determine your loss expectancy for one year.

SLE × ARO = Annual loss expectancy (ALE)

So, given that severe thunderstorms are historically shown to occur 15 times per year in your area (likelihood), you could conclude the following:

$10,000 (SLE) × 15 (ARO) = $150,000 in *potential* loss per year (ALE)

Obviously, this is a bit of a stretch. Even if there are 15 severe lightning-producing storms per year, it's not likely that each one would produce a lightning strike on your server building every time. Even if that *could* happen, it's likely that after it happens the first time, your small business owners would invest in a new facility or relocate its servers, thus reducing the possibility of the other events. So, you might also do some statistical analysis to determine the likelihood of one or more of those 15 severe thunderstorms causing a lightning strike on the server farm building. This analysis might significantly reduce the likely number of events from 15 to, say, 3. Now your ALE would be a potential loss of only $30,000 per year. Keep in mind that the numbers show you the *potential* risk to the organization, which is expressed as lost dollars in terms of revenue and assets.

NOTE These formulas are based on standard basic risk analysis concepts taught in information security certification programs, such as CompTIA's Security+ and (ISC)²'s CISSP program.

Again, the previous scenario is a simplistic (but not too unrealistic) example. Other factors could come into play that are not considered in the previous simple analysis. For example, suppose the business is losing $1,000 per day in revenue for every day this server is out of commission, which the previous calculations do not consider. This consideration is not only related to the SLE value (since it increases the SLE over time) but also influences your RTO and RPO values. You should also realize that this scenario considers only one of the servers; a better risk assessment should include the possibility of *all* the assets being partially or completely lost.

Additionally, it's possible that a total loss of a server may not occur; let's say it's only a partial loss (say, 40 percent, or an EF of 0.4), which would reduce the SLE for that single asset ($10,000 [AV] × 0.4 [EF] = $4,000). So, you must take all of this into account when performing a quantitative risk analysis. There are so many other factors that we haven't mentioned here that could figure into your SLE values (asset depreciation, lost labor hours to repair or replace the server, and so on). However, you can see the basics based on this simple example.

EXAM TIP Be familiar with the elements of quantitative risk assessment techniques, such as asset value, exposure factor, single loss expectancy, annual rate of occurrence, and annualized loss expectancy.

The final piece of this puzzle is how much it would cost the organization to reduce this risk. Let's examine all of the factors that the organization could influence. First, it could not affect the weather, so the threat agent and threat can't be reduced or eliminated. However, the organization could address the vulnerability (the server building with its inadequate protection against bad weather, in this case), reducing it somewhat by relocating the server farm or even moving its applications and data to the cloud, for example. The organization could also reduce the likelihood for that particular threat-vulnerability pairing if it removed or changed the nature of the vulnerability itself, as described earlier.

The organization could also reduce the impact of this specific event in several ways. It could create a real-time failover cluster for the servers in another location that would instantly be available if said servers got struck by lightning, or it could at least have a hot spare server and a recent backup, if nothing else. The organization can affect the risk factors, but there is a cost for doing this. What is essential in developing risk responses is that the organization must balance the cost of mitigations (for example, acquiring another facility, moving to the cloud, using server clusters, or at least having hot spares and better backups) with how much it loses in terms of SLE and ALE and the added impact of lost revenue per day, as in this example. The bottom line is that you must find a solution that isn't more expensive or impacts the organization to a degree worse than the risk event itself. Risk responses are covered in more detail in Chapter 3.

Qualitative A *qualitative* risk analysis, on the other hand, involves using subjective scales. These scales could be numeric (a scale from 1 to 10) or have subjective labels (High, Medium, and Low, for instance). Qualitative risk analysis can come from historical trend analysis, experience, expert opinion, existing internal and external environmental factors, governance, and other inputs that are not always necessarily quantifiable but exist and are important nonetheless. Qualitative risk analysis is appropriate when you must evaluate risk based on factors that can be hard to quantify, such as those not typically measured with concrete, repeatable values. For example, what numerical value could you assign to a potential impact of the loss of consumer confidence or damage to reputation? You may attempt to frame it in terms of lost revenue (an educated guess at best) or loss of business. For example, you could also survey a sample population to determine how many people would or would not do business with the organization after a data breach. However, even that would be subjective and offer only a small statistical insight into a hard-to-define measurement.

That's not to say you couldn't assign numerical values to different risk factors, however. Instead of values such as Low, Medium, and High, you might assign numerical values that roughly correspond to those levels. For example, you might use a type of Likert scale, which may have values such as 1 (Very Low), 2 (Low), 3 (Medium), 4 (High), and 5 (Very High). This might characterize the subjective level of impact or likelihood the organization wants to assign to a particular risk event. In assigning these subjective values, you must also decide how they relate to each other, yielding an overall risk calculation. In other words, given likelihood values of 1 (Very Low), 2 (Low), 3 (Medium), 4 (High), and 5 (Very High), and identical values for impact, what would the overall risk level be when these two dimensions of risk are viewed together? How do their values affect each other? NIST Special Publication 800-30 offers an excellent example of how risk is calculated using qualitative analysis.

 NOTE NIST SP 800-30 refers to numerical scales as *semiquantitative* values since they are numerical values that can be used in calculations but are still subjective in nature (in other words, they cannot be independently derived or repeated and are based on informed opinion).

In Figure 2-9, taken from NIST SP 800-30, you can see how the relationships of likelihood and impact affect different risk levels. The values of each are correlated, and a qualitative risk determination results. For example, according to this figure, a *moderate*

Likelihood (Threat Event Occurs and Results in Adverse Impact)	Level of Impact				
	Very Low	**Low**	**Moderate**	**High**	**Very High**
Very High	Very Low	Low	Moderate	High	Very High
High	Very Low	Low	Moderate	High	Very High
Moderate	Very Low	Low	Moderate	Moderate	High
Low	Very Low	Low	Low	Low	Moderate
Very Low	Very Low	Very Low	Very Low	Low	Low

Figure 2-9   Qualitative assessment of risk (courtesy of NIST SP 800-30)

level of likelihood combined with a *very high* level of impact results in a level of risk determined as *high*. Determining what constitutes a likelihood of moderate and what is required for an impact level of very high is subjective. However, it should be defined within the organization for consistency and standardization.

Combining Quantitative and Qualitative Techniques   If you think that a qualitative or quantitative assessment alone may not be enough to adequately capture the different elements of risk and develop an overall risk determination, you're right. While there are instances where each of these techniques can be used alone, they are used together to varying degrees in most situations. Each technique is good at producing a valuable piece of the puzzle, but sometimes you need both a quantitative perspective and a qualitative perspective on risk. For example, in the scenario we described earlier for quantitative risk, say you have numerical values for AV, EF, SLE, and ALE. These values account primarily for impact. However, suppose you don't have enough solid information for a calculation of likelihood. You might have to give it a "best guess" that comes from a reasonably well-thought-out analysis, using anecdotal data or another type of data that can't necessarily be quantified but is a reasonably accurate predictor. You may have to assign likelihood values that are semiquantitative or the subjective High, Medium, and Low values. There might also be other subjective factors contributing to these values, so you would not have a purely quantitative assessment. Suppose you added "customer confidence" or "reputation" into the discussion on impact or loss to the company, for instance. Those would almost have to be qualitative values, so the assessment couldn't always be expressed in exact numerical terms that are easily repeatable or defendable.

In practice, most risk assessments are usually qualitative with some quantitative elements, or vice versa. There are usually few purely quantitative or entirely qualitative assessments performed. You should understand the elements and characteristics of both, however, for the exam and your profession.

Other Analysis Techniques

Now that you know the basics of qualitative and quantitative techniques, there are a few specific techniques, based on both of these methods, that we will discuss here so you are familiar with them for the exam. Note that professionals have developed dozens of different techniques over the years to assess risk; you'll find that most of them fall into either the qualitative or quantitative methodology. The ISO/IEC 31010:2019 standard we briefly described earlier lists more than 30 such techniques in its appendixes. Some of them approach assessments from different directions, but most of them have several things in common. We'll discuss just a few of these in the following sections.

Fault- and Event-Tree Analysis   A fault-tree analysis is a method where the analyst starts with a risk event and looks for all possible causes. This is diagrammed as a tree, with the risk event at the root and the causes extending away as branches. This analysis is used to discover all of the potential causes of the event (threats and threat actors in this case) to be further analyzed for likelihood. Like the fault tree, the event-tree analysis is also diagrammed as a tree structure but takes the opposite approach (bottom-up instead of top-down). In event-tree analysis, an initiating event is at the root of the tree, with all possible consequences (impacts) diagrammed from the root as branches (as opposed to causes of the event in fault-tree analysis). Both fault tree and event tree are predictive analysis tools; in other words, they seek to predict relationships between causes, events, and consequences. Figures 2-10 and 2-11 show examples of fault-tree and event-tree analysis diagrams, respectively.

Figure 2-10 shows a risk event (in this case, a firewall failure), with the potential causes shown as no rule configured, a firewall appliance failure, and unknown or unusual traffic. Note that the risk event itself is the root of the tree. Conversely, in Figure 2-11, an event-tree diagram, the risk event (in this case, a break-in to a corporate facility) is also at the root. However, the branches leading away are the potential consequences, not the causes.

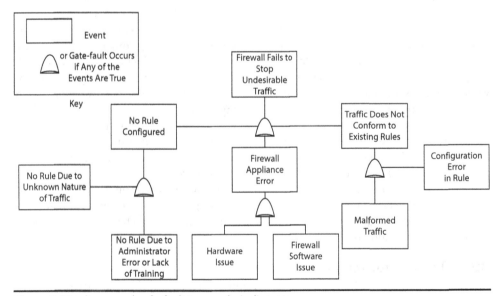

Figure 2-10   An example of a fault-tree analysis diagram

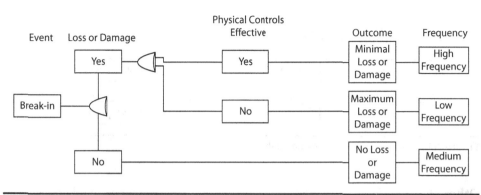

Figure 2-11 An example of an event-tree analysis diagram

Factor Analysis of Information Risk The Factor Analysis of Information Risk (FAIR) is a semiquantitative methodology used to determine the probable loss event frequency and magnitude for individual risks.

The FAIR methodology consists of four stages:

- **Identify scenario components** This step identifies the asset at risk, as well as the threat community being analyzed.

- **Evaluate loss event frequency** Activities in this stage include an estimation of threat event frequency, threat capability, protective control strength, vulnerabilities, and the frequency of loss events.

- **Evaluate probable loss magnitude** This stage is used to develop worst-case and most likely loss magnitude.

- **Derive and articulate risk** Derived from the values established in earlier steps, the level of risk is calculated and portrayed.

The FAIR methodology is presented in the book *Measuring and Managing Information Risk: A FAIR Approach*, by Jack Freund and Jack Jones. An organization known as the FAIR Institute offers membership, training, and events and is found at www .fairinstitute.org.

Bow-Tie Analysis A bow-tie analysis uses diagrams to analyze and explain relationships between various risk elements, from causes (threats) to events and then to impacts (consequences). It is similar to both the fault-tree analysis and the event-tree analysis. It looks at the various causes of a risk event (fault tree) and analyzes the consequences of the event (event tree). The difference, however, is that the bow-tie analysis looks at the intervening characteristics of the events and causes, such as the path by which the cause leads to the event and then the consequences. Figure 2-12 illustrates a bow-tie diagram. In this figure, the adverse event is shown as the center of the bow tie, with potential causes on the left and possible consequences on the right.

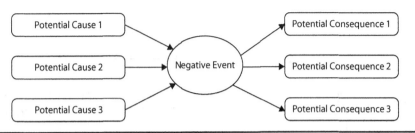

Figure 2-12 An example of a bow-tie analysis diagram

Other Methods As mentioned, there are too numerous other methods to perform the different types of assessments to discuss them all here. Some of these methods focus on data collection, while others emphasize different group analysis techniques. All are, again, some variation of either the qualitative or quantitative method and may require looking at specific aspects of data to determine various elements of risk. Other examples of these techniques include the Delphi method, which centers on expert opinion from questionnaires; the Bayesian analysis method, which uses data distribution and statistical inference to determine risk probability values, checklists, scenario analysis, and business impact analysis (described later in this chapter); root-cause analysis (discussed earlier in this chapter); and various collaborative techniques, such as brainstorming. You won't be expected to know all these methods for the exam, but you should be familiar with the concepts of qualitative and quantitative analysis and some of the techniques that use each. For further knowledge on various assessment and analysis techniques, consult with ISO/IEC 31010:2019.

EXAM TIP You will not have to know any particular risk analysis method in detail for the exam, but you should understand how the qualitative, quantitative, and semiquantitative methods work.

Business Impact Analysis

A *business impact analysis (BIA)* is used to identify an organization's business processes, the interdependencies between processes, the resources required for process operation, and the impact on the organization if any business process is incapacitated for a time for any reason.

While a BIA is considered a cornerstone of a business continuity and disaster recovery (BCDR) program, a BIA is also useful for risk analysis. The BIA reveals the most critical processes (and underlying resources such as information systems and other IT infrastructure), giving the risk manager a better idea of which business processes and systems warrant the most protection from an operational criticality point of view.

The presence of a BIA provides a strong indication of the organization's maturity through its intention to protect its most critical processes from disaster scenarios. Correspondingly, the absence of a BIA may suggest that the organization does not consider risk management as having strategic importance.

Inventory Key Processes and Systems

The first step in a BIA is the collection of key business processes and IT systems. Within the overall scope of the business continuity planning (BCP) project, the objective here is to establish a detailed list of all identifiable business processes and systems. The usual approach is developing a questionnaire or intake form that would be circulated to key personnel in end-user departments and IT. Figure 2-13 shows a sample intake form.

Typically, the information collected on intake forms is transferred to a multi-columned spreadsheet, where information on all of the organization's in-scope processes can be viewed together. This will become even more useful in subsequent phases of the BCP project, such as the criticality analysis.

 TIP The use of an intake form is not the only accepted approach when gathering information about critical processes and systems. It's also acceptable to conduct one-on-one or group interviews with key users and IT personnel to identify critical business processes and systems. We recommend using an intake form (whether paper-based or electronic), even if the interviewer uses it herself as a framework for note-taking.

Process or system name	
Interviewee	
Title	
Department	
Contact info	
Date	
Process owner	
Process operator(s)	
Process description	
Customer facing (Y or N)	
IT system(s) used	
Key suppliers	
Communications needed	
Assets needed	
Process dependencies	
Other dependencies	
Documentation location	
Records location	

Figure 2-13 BIA sample intake form for gathering data about key processes

> ## Planning Precedes Action
>
> IT personnel are often eager to get to the fun and meaty part of a project. Developers are anxious to begin coding before design, system administrators are eager to build systems before they are scoped and designed, and BCP personnel fervently desire to start designing more robust system architectures and tinker with replication and backup capabilities before key facts are known. In business continuity and disaster recovery planning, completing the BIA and other analyses is critical, as the analyses help define the systems and processes most needed before getting to the fun part.

Statements of Impact

When processes and systems are being inventoried and cataloged, it is also vitally important to obtain one or more statements of impact for each process and system. A *statement of impact* is a qualitative or quantitative description of the impact on the business if the process or system were incapacitated for a time.

For IT systems, you might capture the number of users and the names of departments or functions affected by the unavailability of a specific IT system. Include the geography of affected users and functions if that is appropriate. Here are some sample statements of impact for IT systems:

- *Three thousand users in France and Italy will be unable to access customer records, resulting in degraded customer service.*

- *All users in North America will be unable to read or send e-mail, resulting in productivity slowdowns and delays in some business processes.*

Statements of impact for business processes might cite the business functions that would be affected. Here are some sample statements of impact:

- *Accounts payable and accounts receivable functions will be unable to process, impacting the availability of services and supplies and reducing revenue.*

- *The legal department will be unable to access contracts and addendums, resulting in lost or delayed revenue.*

Statements of impact for revenue-generating and revenue-supporting business functions could quantify financial impact per unit of time (be sure to use the same units of time for all functions to be easily compared with one another). Here are some examples:

- *Inability to place orders for materials will cost at the rate of $12,000 per hour.*
- *Delays in payments will cost $45,000 per day in interest charges and late fees.*

As statements of impact are gathered, it might make sense to create several columns in the main worksheet so that like units (names of functions, numbers of users, financial figures) can be sorted and ranked later.

When the BIA is completed, you'll have the following information about each process and system:

- Name of the process or system
- Who is responsible for its operation
- A description of its function
- Dependencies on systems
- Dependencies on suppliers
- Dependencies on key employees
- Quantified statements of impact in terms of revenue, users affected, and/or functions impacted

Criticality Analysis

When all of the BIA information has been collected and charted, the criticality analysis (CA) can be performed.

Criticality analysis is a study of each system and process, a consideration of the impact on the organization if it is incapacitated, the likelihood of incapacitation, and the estimated cost of mitigating the risk or impact of incapacitation. In other words, it's a somewhat special type of risk analysis that focuses on key processes and systems.

The criticality analysis needs to include, or reference, a threat analysis. A *threat analysis* is a risk analysis that identifies every threat that has a reasonable probability of occurrence, plus one or more mitigating controls or compensating controls, and new probabilities of occurrence with those mitigating/compensating controls in place. To give you an idea of what this looks like, refer to Table 2-6, which provides a lightweight example of what we're talking about.

System: Application Server				
Threat	**Probability**	**Mitigating Control**	**Mitigation Cost**	**Mitigated Probability**
Denial of service	0.1%	High-performance filtering router	$60,000	0.01%
Malware	1%	Antivirus	$200	0.1%
Storage failure	2%	RAID 5	$20,000	0.01%
Administrator error	15%	Configuration management tools	$10,000	5%
Hardware CPU failure	5%	Server cluster	$15,000	1%
Application software bug	5%	Source code reviews	$10,000	2%
Extended power outage	25%	UPS Electric generator	$12,000 $40,000	2% 0.5%
Flood	2%	Relocate data center	$200,000	0.1%

Table 2-6 Sample Threat Analysis for Identifying Threats and Controls for Critical Systems and Processes

In the preceding threat analysis, notice the following:

- Multiple threats are listed for a single asset. In the preceding example, we mentioned just eight threats. For all the threats but one, we listed only a single mitigating control. For the extended power outage threat, we listed two mitigating controls.

- The cost of downtime wasn't listed. For systems or processes where you have a cost per unit of time for downtime, you'll need to include it here, along with some calculations to show the payback for each control.

- Some mitigating controls can benefit more than one system. That may not have been obvious in this example. However, in the case of an uninterruptible power supply (UPS) and an electric generator, many systems can benefit, so the cost for these mitigating controls can be allocated across many systems, thereby lowering the cost for each system. Another example is a high-availability storage area network (SAN) located in two different geographic areas; although it's initially expensive, many applications can use the SAN for storage, and all will benefit from replication to the counterpart storage system.

- Threat probabilities are arbitrary. In Table 2-6, the probabilities are for a single occurrence in an entire year (for example, 5 percent means the threat will be realized once every 20 years).

- The length of the outage was not included. You may need to include this also, particularly if you are quantifying downtime per hour or another unit of time.

It is probably becoming evident that a threat analysis and the corresponding criticality analysis can get complicated. The rule here should be as follows: the complexity of the threat and criticality analyses should be proportional to the value of the assets (or revenue, or both). For example, in a company where application downtime is measured in thousands of dollars per minute, it's probably worth taking a few weeks or even months to work out all of the likely scenarios and a variety of mitigating controls and then work out which ones are the most cost-effective. On the other hand, for a system or business process where the impact of an outage is far less costly, a good deal less time might be spent on the supporting threat and criticality analysis.

Recovery Objectives and Next Steps

After the criticality analysis is performed, business continuity planners will establish a metric known as *maximum tolerable downtime (MTD)*. This is the amount of time that the organization can tolerate a business process being nonfunctional before the ongoing viability of the business itself (or a major part of it) is at risk. Note that MTD is a theoretical figure that the organization will not attempt to verify.

Busines impact analysis is often used to establish recovery objectives that drive the development of disaster recovery plans. Recovery objectives and disaster recovery planning are discussed in more detail in Chapter 4.

Inherent and Residual Risk

Our coverage of the IT Risk Assessment domain in the CRISC certification concludes with a discussion of inherent and residual risk. These two concepts bring a small degree of added complication to the overall risk management and risk treatment concepts.

Risk treatment is discussed in full detail in Chapter 3.

Inherent Risk

No personal or business activity is entirely free of risk, and some activities are inherently more risky than others. The concept of *inherent risk* expresses the level of risk associated with a process or activity before applying any protections or safeguards. In the vernacular, some activities are just riskier than others.

Take, for example, two personal activities: gardening and hang gliding. We would state that the inherent risk associated with hang gliding is significantly higher than that of gardening. With hang gliding, any number of realistic scenarios can result in the death of the hang glider. At the same time, gardening is relatively safe, and death by gardening is highly unlikely. In both gardening and hang gliding, the probability of risk realization is relatively low, although the impact of risk realization is decidedly higher for hang gliding.

One approach to risk analysis is assigning inherent risk to a process or system, and then calculating changes to risk after protective controls and safeguards are applied. This helps a risk analyst understand the changes in risk when individual controls and safeguards are applied, and it better informs management of the full nature of risk for a given part of the organization.

Residual Risk

The risk management and risk treatment processes tend to reduce risk, but they rarely eliminate all risk. Instead, risk mitigation and risk transfer reduce risk to a lower level. This "leftover" risk is known as *residual risk*.

Residual risk is best explained with a real-world example. An organization's workforce is equipped with laptop computers running Windows or macOS, neither of which utilizes whole-disk encryption. Risk analysis suggests that the risks associated with the theft or disappearance of an unencrypted laptop computer are quite high, with potential for a significant security or privacy incident, depending on whose laptop computer is lost or stolen.

In this scenario, the organization decides to implement whole-disk encryption on all of its laptop computers. Note that this measure does nothing to change the probability of laptop computers being lost or stolen. However, this measure changes the impact significantly. While, with whole-disk encryption, the organization need no longer worry about the potential data compromise, the stolen laptop will still need to be replaced. The residual risk, in this example, is the financial risk associated with the funds required to purchase a new laptop computer, plus any labor needed to make it ready for employee use.

To continue this example further, this residual risk is one in which the residual risk may still be a risk that warrants further analysis and treatment. Analysis of the risks associated with the need to replace a lost or stolen laptop computer could result in a

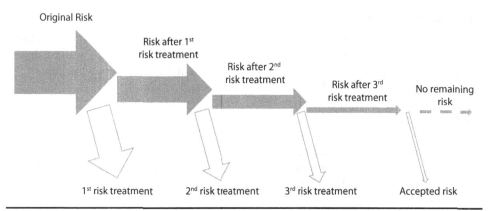

Figure 2-14 Risk reduction through multiple rounds of risk treatment

recommendation of the purchase of security cables that are issued to each employee, together with directives that laptop computers are to be locked to a piece of furniture (or locked in a safe) when not in the direct control of the employee. This measure reduces the probability of theft or loss, but not the impact: if the laptop computer is stolen, it must still be replaced, but theft is less likely to occur since, at least some of the time, employees will use those cable locks, reducing the number of opportunities for someone to steal them.

Larger and more complex risk scenarios may require multiple rounds of risk analysis and risk treatment. However, an organization will eventually reach the point where the residual risk is low enough that business leaders and department heads will accept the residual risk.

Often, risk analysis, risk treatment, and residual risk are more complicated than this. A risk assessment performed on a business process or information system is likely to identify multiple risks, which should be considered in whole as well as individually. It may be easier to understand all the risks together to compare various types of risks and risk treatment options when considered together. Sometimes, a single risk treatment measure may mitigate more than one of the identified risks. Figure 2-14 visually depicts multiple rounds of risk analysis and risk treatment until the final remaining risk is accepted.

Let's go back to our stolen laptop example for a moment. Imagine that multiple risks are identified in a stolen laptop scenario, all having to do with the compromise of different types of information: personally identifiable information (PII) such as human resource information, non-public financial information, intellectual property, and trade secrets. Whole-disk encryption will reduce the impact of all four of these scenarios to near zero.

Miscellaneous Risk Considerations

There may be other options to consider when performing risk assessments, which may or may not be applicable in an organization. Understanding industry and compliance models related to an organization's industry can be absolutely critical to using the risk assessment to pass an audit or ensure legal compliance. There may be unique methodologies used by the organization to illustrate different aspects of a cybersecurity program.

For companies that have *protected health information (PHI)*, there are extra considerations that should be followed related to the data from a legal standpoint because those companies should follow *Health Insurance Portability and Accountability Act (HIPAA)* regulations. In this case, tying in each risk to confidentiality, integrity, and availability is required by HIPAA. This can be as simple as creating a new column on a risk register that denotes if confidentiality, integrity, or availability is affected by the risk. It is a simple additional step that can help demonstrate not only compliance with HIPAA, but a deeper understanding of how the risks may affect an organization.

The enforcement arm of HIPAA is the Office of Civil Rights (OCR). Working with their regulations, they have risk requirements that need to be assessed for legal compliance reasons. The OCR does not expect companies to follow their exact risk methodology so long as the concerns are fully applied within the risk framework of the organization. If there ever is a HIPAA violation where the OCR becomes involved, considerations like this and assessing confidentiality, integrity, and availability can make regulators feel more at ease related to the violation and sometimes help reduce the overall penalties.

Stepping away from HIPAA considerations, sometimes organizations may choose to follow or report to others using frameworks such as NIST CSF (described previously). In this case, as with the confidentiality, integrity, and availability example, the NIST CSF functions (Identify, Protect, Detect, Respond, Recover) may be used in the same way. This can sometimes be useful to help business executives who do not understand the intricacies of cybersecurity to understand, at least at a high level, why certain risks are so important to consider.

Another option that may or may not be helpful depending on the organization is the concept of materiality. Materiality comes from the audit world and denotes a fundamental flaw in a specific program. For example, if there is no antivirus in an organization, that is a fundamental flaw and thus a material weakness. Adding a column like this into a risk register is yet another way that organizations can create extra emphasis around a risk management program.

It should be clear that there are a number of ways organizations can approach risk. In some instances, it is not so much about being right or wrong concerning a risk methodology but rather about working through the right flavor of risk within an organization.

Chapter Review

IT risk identification consists of activities performed to identify various types of risks associated with an organization's use of information technology, including strategic, operational, cybersecurity, privacy, supply chain, and compliance risks.

The types of activities where risks may be identified include risk assessments, audits, incidents, penetration tests, news and social media, advisories, threat modeling, word of mouth, whistleblowers, and passive observation.

Threat modeling is a risk identification technique that involves examining every possible threat agent, action or event, attack vector, and vulnerability for a given system, asset, or process, and then modeling or simulating how it could progress and the damage that could occur.

Vulnerability and control deficiency analysis are important parts of risk analysis, focusing on weaknesses in a system or process that could result in a potentially serious incident if exploited by a threat actor.

Root cause analysis, or RCA, is a method of problem-solving that seeks to identify the root cause of an event, situation, or problem.

A *risk scenario* is a potential real-world, business-impacting event that consists of a threat, threat actor, vulnerability, and asset.

Risk analysis is a detailed examination of a risk to better understand basic factors, including the likelihood and impact of risk occurrence, and the development of a measure that might be enacted to reduce likelihood or impact.

Several types of assessments can be used to identify risks, including a gap assessment, threat modeling, vulnerability assessment, maturity assessment, penetration test, data discovery, code review, architecture review, design review, code scan, audit, and risk assessment.

Several techniques are used in a risk assessment to identify risks, including interviews, documentation review, observation, and system testing.

Risk ranking is the process of sequencing risks, generally with the greatest risks appearing first.

A *risk owner* is the owner of a business process or system that focuses on an identified risk.

A *risk register* is a business record containing information about business risks and their origin, potential impact, affected assets, probability of occurrence, and treatment.

A *risk analysis* is the detailed analysis of a risk that has been identified in an activity, such as a risk assessment.

Quantitative risk analysis uses concrete (nonsubjective) numerical values and statistical analysis to calculate the likelihood and impact of risk. On the other hand, a *qualitative risk analysis* involves using subjective scales, such as a numeric scale from 1 to 10, or subjective values, such as High, Medium, and Low.

There are several risk analysis techniques, including fault- and event-tree analysis, factor analysis of information risk (FAIR), and bow-tie analysis.

A *business impact analysis (BIA)* is used to identify an organization's business processes, the interdependencies between processes, the resources required for process operation, and the impact on the organization if any business process is incapacitated for a time for any reason.

A *statement of impact* is a qualitative or quantitative description of the impact on the business if the process or system were incapacitated for a time.

A *criticality analysis* is a study of each system and process, a consideration of the impact on the organization if it is incapacitated, the likelihood of incapacitation, and the estimated cost of mitigating the risk or impact of incapacitation.

Inherent risk is the level of risk associated with a specific activity or function before applying any protective controls or safeguards.

Residual risk is the risk that remains after any risk transfer or risk mitigation that may have been performed.

The *materiality* of a risk may help to highlight its importance to management.

Quick Review

- CRISC candidates and risk managers must be familiar with the vocabulary of terms related to risk assessment and risk analysis, including *asset, vulnerability, threat, impact, attack,* and *risk.*

- CRISC and IT Risk Management consider cybersecurity risks and operational risk, workforce risk, privacy risk, and compliance risk.

- Appendixes D and E in NIST Special Publication 800-30, "Guide for Conducting Risk Assessments," offer a comprehensive list of threat agents and their related threats.

- Risk, asset, and control owners are not always the same person, functional area, department, or organization.

- *Risk analysis* is a detailed, focused examination of a risk performed as a part of an overall risk assessment.

- The *scope* of an assessment determines the boundaries of inquiry and analysis of a process or system.

- Well-known risk assessment standards include NIST SP 800-30 (Guide for Conducting Risk Assessments), OCTAVE, ISO/IEC 27005 (Information technology – Security techniques – Information security risk management), ISO/IEC 31010 (Risk Management – Risk Assessment Techniques), and ISACA's Risk IT Framework.

Questions

1. Awareness of new risks can be obtained through all of the following activities *except* which one?

   A. Security advisories

   B. Privacy incidents

   C. Budget reviews

   D. Audits

2. In a discussion about the security of endpoint devices, one security professional described that some endpoints' antivirus programs are not functioning correctly. What is this a description of?

   A. Threat

   B. Vulnerability

   C. Risk

   D. Threat model

3. A security specialist is examining a particular preventive control and has determined that the control is not operating as designed. What term describes the state of the control?

   A. Undocumented

   B. Inefficient

   C. Fail-open

   D. Ineffective

4. A risk analyst reviewing a business process has identified a control gap. What is the meaning of this conclusion?

   A. A control exists but is undocumented.

   B. A control does not exist.

   C. An earlier risk assessment determined that a control is not necessary.

   D. A new risk has been discovered.

5. Several security professionals are discussing a recent security incident. The discussion is proceeding through the phases of the incident and the conditions preceding the incident in order to understand why those conditions occurred. What are the security professionals performing?

   A. Root cause analysis

   B. Incident debrief

   C. Incident forensics

   D. Reverse engineering

6. What is the primary purpose for risk scenario development?

   A. To identify the highest rated risks

   B. To quantify the highest rated risks

   C. To prepare an executive briefing

   D. To associate risks with business objectives

7. A risk manager wants to better understand the factors in particular business processes that could lead to an incident. What activity should the risk manager perform?

   A. Risk analysis

   B. Threat modeling

   C. Vulnerability analysis

   D. Root cause analysis

8. Hackers, cybercriminal organizations, disgruntled employees, and hurricanes are known as what?

   A. Threat agents

   B. Threat actors

   C. Threats

   D. Attacks

9. An auditor has contacted an organization's data center security manager and has requested a walkthrough. What is the auditor asking for?

   A. A meeting to discuss one or more security controls

   B. A tour of the data center

   C. An explanation for a recent incident

   D. Interpretation of a security report

10. What does NIST Special Publication 800-30 describe?

   A. A risk management methodology

   B. A risk assessment methodology

   C. Security and privacy controls

   D. Audit procedures for security and privacy controls

11. A security analyst is finishing up a risk assessment and is about to identify the risk owner for each risk in the report. In general, who should be the risk owner for each risk?

   A. The board of directors

   B. The CISO or CIRO

   C. The CIO

   D. The related business process owner

12. Which of the following is the best description of a risk register?

   A. A list of threat agents and threat actors

   B. A list of identified risks

   C. The root cause analysis (RCA) for a security incident

   D. A list of likely risk scenarios

13. A risk manager is performing risk analysis on a specific risk to better understand the risk and to identify potential remedies. Various aspects of the initial risk and its potential remedies are scored on a scale of 1–10. What type of risk analysis is being performed?

   A. Qualitative risk analysis

   B. Quantitative risk analysis

   C. Semiquantitative risk analysis

   D. Factor Analysis of Information Risk (FAIR)

14. An organization has performed a risk analysis of a complex scenario. Two different mitigation strategies have been approved that will reduce the original risk to a much lower level. The risk that remains after these mitigation strategies have been completed is known as what?

A. Inherent risk

B. Leftover risk

C. Residual risk

D. Accepted risk

15. Which of the following is the best method for managing residual risk?

A. Subject it to risk analysis and risk treatment.

B. Retain it on the risk register and consider it as accepted.

C. Retain it on the risk register and label it as closed.

D. Add it to the cumulative total of risk tolerance.

Answers

1. C. Awareness of risks can be obtained through numerous sources and activities, such as audits, incidents, advisories, threat modeling, assessments, and news articles. Budget reviews are an unlikely source of information about new risks.

2. B. The matter of a failure of a protective control such as antivirus or a firewall is known as a vulnerability. The basic terms of risk, such as *vulnerability, threat, control,* and *risk,* are sometimes misused.

3. D. A control that is not operating as designed is considered ineffective. To reach this conclusion, an analyst or auditor needs to understand the objective of the control and determine whether the control as it is presently operating meets that objective.

4. B. A control gap is a situation where a control does not exist, but should exist. A control gap can also describe a situation where a control is not properly designed or implemented.

5. A. A root cause analysis (RCA) attempts to get to the ultimate explanation of an incident, by proceeding backward through time to ask "why" specific conditions or events occurred.

6. D. Risk scenario development is performed to associate specific risks with specific business objectives or business activities. Risk scenario development makes risks more tangible by describing their potential impact on the organization in business terms.

7. C. A vulnerability analysis is a detailed examination of a process or system to discover vulnerabilities that a credible threat agent could exploit.

8. A. Threat agents are the entities, human or not, that may perform actions that could cause harm to an organization, its processes, or its systems.

9. B. A walkthrough with an auditor is a discussion where a control owner describes the operation of one or more controls and answers specific questions about them.

10. B. NIST SP 800-30, "Guide for Conducting Risk Assessments," is a step-by-step guide to performing qualitative and quantitative risk assessments. The standard also briefly describes the overall risk management life-cycle process to provide context for individual risk assessments.

11. D. The owner of individual risks should be the business unit leader or department head that manages business processes most closely related to those risks. In rare circumstances, risks should be assigned to the CIO, CISO, or CIRO.

12. B. A risk register is a master list of all credible risks that have been identified and are awaiting further analysis, treatment, or follow-up.

13. A. Qualitative risk analysis uses a scoring scheme such as "high-medium-low" or a simple numeric scale such as 1–3, 1–5, or 1–10.

14. C. Residual risk is the risk that remains after risk treatment (whether mitigation, transfer, or avoidance) has been completed.

15. A. The best way to manage residual risk is to include it in the risk register and then subject it to the usual risk analysis, risk scenario development, and risk treatment.

Risk Response and Reporting

In this chapter, you will:

- Understand the concepts of risk and control ownership
- Understand the various risk treatment and response options
- Learn about the risk response process
- Understand risk response options and how to align choices with business objectives
- Understand how controls are designed, implemented, and evaluated
- Learn methods to document and assess risk responses
- Understand and define key performance indicators (KPIs)
- Understand and define key risk indicators (KRIs)

This chapter covers Certified in Risk and Information Systems Control Domain 3, "Risk Response and Reporting." This domain comprises 32 percent of the CRISC examination.

The CRISC Task Statements relevant to this domain address several key activities present in risk response and reporting, beginning with the collection of information about an organization's business and IT environments as well as identifying impacts to the organization's objectives and operations. This includes the identification and evaluation of threats and vulnerabilities and establishing accountability by assigning risk and control ownership. An IT risk register is used to document the risk profile. Identifying risk appetite and tolerance and conducting security awareness training help to promote a risk-aware culture. IT risk assessments and risk analysis help to identify control deficiencies that bring about risk responses, risk treatment plans, and the design and implementation of controls—all of which should be validated. Risk reporting includes the use and monitoring of key control indicators, key risk indicators, and key performance indicators. Assessments of controls and analysis of risks can help understand their maturity and effectiveness. New and emerging technologies should be evaluated to identify changes in risks. All of this should drive risk-driven decision-making.

In this chapter, we will review the concepts that comprise CRISC Domain 3, which is focused on risk response and reporting. There is a natural progression from the risk framing, analysis, and assessment discussions in the previous chapters, which covered

CRISC Domains 1 and 2, to the discussion of risk response in this chapter; you will see that many of the outputs from those processes lead directly to this chapter because an organization generally wants a meaningful response to any risk to itself and its systems and data. After discussing how risk responses are chosen, we will discuss how to implement those risk responses, including how to design, develop, and adjust controls, and then, finally, how to report on risk.

Risk Response

Every organization has risk. The leaders of smart organizations, however, have determined how they will deal with that risk appropriately for their business context. Will they accept all risks? Will they transfer some risks to a third party, such as an insurance company? These are some questions that need to be considered within the risk response process, as discussed in this chapter.

We will also discuss the major control frameworks within the field and how they are incorporated into risk response. You should note that risk is different for every organization; risk within an educational context is different from a financial context, which is different from a government context. Also keep in mind that IT risks are different from business or mission-oriented risks. It's important to note that the mission of the organization helps to shape risk responses as well. This is why it's so important that organizations conduct a thorough risk analysis and understand and prioritize the response options that are right for them. You should also remember that the risks to the business, the business goals and objectives, and the systems supporting those functions should all be considered throughout the risk response process. It's easy as an IT professional to forget that the business objectives are the top priority, but to maximize efficiency and effectiveness (and to pass the exam), you should keep that in mind.

Risk and Control Ownership

Risk and control ownership are issues that must be considered during a risk assessment and response. Depending on how the organization is structured and how the risk management strategy has been developed, risk ownership may be assigned to one or several different managers, spanning multiple functional areas. This is because the risk that affects one area likely affects other areas as well, so many different people may have responsibility over affected areas and be required to deal with and respond to risk.

Control ownership is also something that should be examined; often controls that provide protections for a given asset or a number of systems may not fall under the operational purview of the risk owner. Some controls span the entire organization and protect multiple assets, rather than only a specific system. These are referred to as *common controls*, and the responsible entity for these controls is the common controls' provider. For example, consider physical security controls. There may be a physical security officer for the organization who is in charge of guards, personnel security, and physical access to secured areas. They may also be responsible for locks, closed-circuit televisions (CCTVs), and physical intrusion detection systems and alarms. All of these controls serve to protect information systems and data assets that might be in a secure data center. Risks may be presented to the person who is responsible for information systems in the data center, but the controls that serve to protect them may belong to the physical security functional area. This would require some coordination between the different functional areas if controls managed by one functional area are insufficient to protect assets managed by another area. This may also affect organizational structures, budget, and allocation of resources.

It is normally important that risk and control owners be identified and documented on the risk register. This helps assign responsibility and accountability for risks, the responses, and the controls. Additionally, the risk and control owners should be given the authority to carry out responsibilities in reducing risk and implement controls as needed. Both risk and control owners, as part of this authority, should have some level of control over budgets, personnel, equipment, and other resources required under the purview of their responsibilities. If owners are given authority to carry out their responsibilities, they can be held accountable when risk is not properly responded to or when controls are ineffective in reducing risk.

 NOTE   Risk, asset, and control owners are not always the same person, functional area, or even organization. It's important that you identify these particular owners early in the assessment process and maintain careful coordination and communication between these and other relevant stakeholders, within the boundaries of your authority and assessment scope. Having different types of owners can result in politically sensitive issues that revolve around resourcing, responsibility, accountability, and sometimes even blame.

Risk Treatment/Risk Response Options

Having developed your understanding of risk, you should also develop an understanding of the corresponding risk response options. These options will help you bring your risk down to a level of risk tolerance your organization can accept. Understand that this is not just merely responding to risk; risk treatment and response options should also meet the needs of the mission, business goals and objectives, and overall organizational strategy. A risk response option whose focus is only to reduce risk in a vacuum may interfere with the normal business operations or reduce the effectiveness of the business when performing its mission. Therefore, you should consider risk responses not just within the context of simply reducing risk; they must also reduce risk and not adversely impact business processes at the same time. Within this context, consider how you would recommend your organization respond to risk effectively but with a balanced approach. We'll discuss the different risk response options in the next few sections.

Risk Mitigation

Risk mitigation generally involves the application of controls that lower the overall level of risk by reducing the vulnerability, the likelihood of a successful threat exploiting that vulnerability, or the impact to the asset if the risk were to be realized. Mitigation actions come in a number of forms; a policy requiring nightly offsite backups of critical data can mitigate the risk of data loss, for instance. Similarly, applying a newly released web browser patch can mitigate the risk of exploitation. The goal is to get the risk down to a level considered acceptable by the organization's leadership. We will discuss controls and their implementation a bit later in the chapter, but for now you should understand that you may have to add new controls; update, upgrade, or even change controls; or even in some cases change the way your business processes work. All of these actions are designed to mitigate or reduce risk.

Risk Sharing

Risk sharing (often referred to as risk transference) entails the use of a third party to offset part of the risk. Risk sharing can involve the outsourcing of some activities to a third party to reduce the financial impacts of a risk event in many cases. Sharing offsite (co-location) assets and contractual obligations with other entities is one way that organizations implement risk sharing; a cloud service provider can be used within this scenario. The cloud provider might be contractually obligated to assume part of the financial impact in the event of a breach, but be aware that there is a potential loss of brand goodwill or other intangible assets that can be difficult to offload. Another example of risk sharing is the use of an insurance service to cover the financial impacts (at least partially) of a breach; however, the intangible losses mentioned previously would still be present. The point is that risk sharing (or transference) typically only works with a portion of the risk; it does not reduce all of the risk. Therefore, multiple risk response options used concurrently will likely be needed.

 EXAM TIP Don't forget that use of a risk-sharing scheme does not totally absolve an organization of its responsibilities; organizations may still retain responsibility—and more importantly, accountability—if there is loss of data or revenue. Additionally, legal liabilities may also be involved.

Risk Acceptance

There will always be some level of residual risk, no matter how many controls you implement or the amount of insurance you purchase. Again, the goal is to get the risk down to a level considered acceptable by the leadership. Risk acceptance occurs when the active decision is made to assume the risk (either inherent or residual) and take no further action to reduce it. The word *active* is critical here; risk acceptance is different from being risk ignorant in that the risk is identified, alternatives are considered, and a conscious decision is made to accept it. A good example of this would be when you have taken all practical steps to reduce the risk of an attack from a malicious entity. Your organization may have installed perimeter security devices, strong authentication methods, and intrusion detection systems, which will reduce the risk significantly. However, since risk cannot be completely eliminated, there is always a chance that an attacker may enter the infrastructure through some other means. This residual risk may have to be accepted because it might be financially unwise to invest more resources into further mitigating the risk. Similarly, a company might choose to willfully ignore government-mandated control implementation that would incur fines or other financial penalties, assuming that the financial cost incurred would be less than the cost of implementing the controls. As we will also discuss, the value of the asset may be far less than the cost of implementing any mitigating controls, so in those cases risk acceptance may be the right choice.

Note that risk acceptance of any kind should be a formal management decision, and fully documented, along with provisions to monitor the risk, typically through the risk register. As with all risk response options, management should be cognizant of monitoring risk, since it frequently changes, and in turn make changes to the response as dictated by the changing operating environment, new technologies, and the threat landscape.

 EXAM TIP It's important to note that risk acceptance doesn't insinuate ignorance; it's an active acknowledgment and conscious decision to accept risk as it is, assuming it is at a level that is comfortably within risk appetite and tolerance ranges.

Risk Avoidance

Risk can be avoided through a number of methods. Sometimes risk can be avoided by simply choosing not to participate in the activity that incurs the risk. For example, an organization may decide that a particular business venture or entry into a new market would incur far more risk than it is willing to take on. Perhaps you don't need to conduct the activity at all. Avoiding risk can mean eliminating risk associated with a particular activity by not performing that planned activity. Risk avoidance is the option taken when, after all risk treatment options, including mitigating controls, have been considered, the level of risk is still not acceptable. An organization might choose not to take on a proposed project because of the probability of failure and subsequent loss of capital, for example. Another scenario might be the organization choosing to not adopt a cloud solution because of the level of sensitivity of information that would be stored within the cloud. In any event, risk avoidance does not simply mean ignoring the risk, as some people may be led to believe. Risk avoidance requires careful thought and planning as well as balancing the level of risk incurred in following a particular path versus eliminating the risk by not following that path at all.

Evaluating Risk Response Options

Risk mitigation, sharing, acceptance, and avoidance are all valid options you should consider using (sometimes at the same time) to lower the risk level you face. The key is to use these options together; you want to balance risk and reward to maximize the benefits. These benefits can be financial or some other, perhaps difficult to quantify, benefit (such as morale, partnerships, or long-term strategy).

One of the key considerations in balancing risk options is the cost and effectiveness of any response option. For example, as briefly mentioned, if the value of the asset to the organization is much lower than the security controls it would take to protect it, is risk mitigation or reduction the right option? You should also consider the effectiveness of the controls; if all possible controls you could implement still don't reduce the risk to an acceptable level, are they worth it?

Other factors that should be considered in risk response options include those inherent to the organization itself. Sometimes organizational design and layout is a factor because how different divisions and departments are structured within the organization and who they report to affect resource allocation, chain of command, and so on. Sometimes these factors have to be changed in order to implement a good risk response. Other considerations are governance, including legal and regulatory requirements, and organizational culture. An example of how organizational culture can affect a risk response is when an organization determines that it needs to pull back administrative privileges from ordinary users—something that is very much frowned upon in the security community. While this response may not be expensive in terms of any required equipment or additional controls, the cost here is the shock to and pushback from the organizational culture. People normally do not like giving up what they already have, and administrative rights is one of those things that all users seem to believe that they need. Organizational culture will definitely be an impediment to implementing this particular risk response.

In evaluating and selecting risk responses, you should consider all the factors we've discussed previously, such as the cost of the response (and of the potential cost of not responding), organizational context and associated missions, risk tolerance, governance, and the simple ease of implementation.

Third-Party Risk

In today's business world, an organization rarely functions independently from other entities. Most businesses are not entirely independent and self-sustaining; they depend on suppliers, service providers, and so on to help them bring their products and services to market. These third parties often perform services that are outsourced from the organization because of a lack of infrastructure or simply a desire to not perform these functions or services internally. A great example of a third-party service provider is one that provides cloud services to businesses, such as data storage, applications, and even entire infrastructures to organizations that don't have the means or the desire to create the internal structures needed to manage them internally. Sometimes it is more cost effective for an organization to simply hire a third party to perform a function or provide a service than it is to expend the resources to create and maintain all of the equipment and processes itself.

If you recall the risk treatment options discussed earlier, transferring (or sharing) risk includes the use of third parties to bear some of the risk in performing certain business functions. Insurance is the classic example of transferring risk used in most risk management training texts, but this instance usually only provides monetary funds in case of a disaster or liability scenario. Transferring risk to third parties also includes outsourcing certain functions and services to third parties, so this, too, is a standard risk treatment method. The organization, for example, can reduce its risk of accounting and budget errors with a small, untrained staff by outsourcing its accounting functions to a third-party accounting firm.

It's important to note that while this strategy of dealing with risk is effective and common, the organization is transferring only risk, not responsibility. The organization almost always retains final accountability and responsibility for functions and services outsourced to a third party. For example, transferring a business's accounting functions to an outside firm mitigates risk by transferring some of it to the third party, but the organization is still ultimately responsible to its stakeholders, government regulators, banks, and financial obligations, even if the accounting firm makes an error. As another example, an organization that makes use of cloud data storage services still maintains accountability and responsibility for any data stored with a cloud provider if that provider suffers a breach that results in the release of sensitive information. While third-party providers may still incur some level of liability in these cases, the final liability rests with the organization that contracted with them. Liability, accountability, and responsibility are also some of the key risk factors with third parties that we'll discuss next.

Third-Party Risk Factors

As indicated earlier, several risk factors relate to the legal aspects of dealing with third-party providers. Most of these risk factors deal with trust in the third-party provider or in dependencies the organization may have on the provider's services. For example, the organization must be able to trust that the third-party provider will provide adequate security for any data that is maintained in its infrastructure. In addition to trust, other risk factors include interoperability with existing systems in the organization, data protection and security, and legal liability. Remember we said earlier that an organization can outsource risk to third-party providers, but the organization typically retains accountability, responsibility, and legal liability. Some legal liability, however, is levied on the third-party provider since it usually has a duty to provide services as well as assurances that those services will meet certain legal standards, as written in the contract between the provider and the organization.

The risk factors relating to third-party providers depend on the types of services provided as well as how the contract agreements are set up between the organization and the provider. Some contracts have cybersecurity provisions built into them. A document known as a service level agreement (SLA) is the key to reducing risk factors when dealing with a third-party provider. The SLA stipulates what the third party must provide in terms of level of service, performance, and so on. Some of these contracts are specific to the data type involved. For example, third-party agreements that deal with protected health information, called business associate agreements (BAAs), have cybersecurity provisions built into them. Another common approach is to have companies that are performing business provide responses to security questionnaires. There are standardized formats available on the Internet, but many companies rely on answers from security frameworks or they design their own set of questions to assess the security/risk. Companies that are more mature may perform their own assessments of cybersecurity, including doing their own audits, penetration testing, evidence gathering, and so on. In some cases, these can be just as intensive as an actual audit. All of these methods can be used as minimal cybersecurity standards for the third-party providers. In many cases, they result in findings that need to be remediated in order to conduct business (meet minimal risk thresholds).

Third-Party Threats

Like the risk factors mentioned earlier, threats associated with dealing with third-party providers primarily relate to trust and the contractual and legal aspects of those arrangements. Threats include failure to provide services as specified in contracts, failure to meet performance or security levels, failure to protect data, and loss of availability for systems or data to an organization's users. Third-party providers can certainly succumb to some of the same threats the organization would, such as natural disasters and so forth. Therefore, some of the threats could also include loss of service or data for the business in some of these negative events. Third-party providers are also susceptible to hacking and malicious insiders, the same as any organization would be. Therefore, threats of data loss or disclosure are also present with third-party providers.

Third-Party Vulnerabilities

Vulnerabilities that result from associations or dealings with third-party providers include failure to adequately cover contingencies in contractual agreements, such as system or data availability or loss, lack of or inadequate security protections, and service levels that fall below an acceptable standard. Furthermore, any vulnerabilities that the third-party provider has inherent to its own organization are, unfortunately, indirectly incurred by any organization that deals with the third party, since those vulnerabilities could affect data in its custody or services provided to others. Examples of internal vulnerabilities that could affect organizations for whom the third party provides services include infrastructure vulnerabilities (such as patch or configuration management issues, loss of equipment, or malicious intrusion by hackers), organizational vulnerabilities (such as loss of revenue or bankruptcy), and even technological vulnerabilities (such as lack of sufficient encryption strengths or strong authentication methods). All these vulnerabilities could indirectly affect any organization that has a contractual agreement with a third-party provider.

 EXAM TIP Remember that even if risk is transferred to a third party, accountability and responsibility usually remain with the business.

Third-Party Risk Management

Managing third-party risk can be challenging and is an ongoing process. The initial risks may change due to a growing relationship with a business partner, additional data being sent to a third party, or the threat landscape affecting risks. Considerations for managing that risk may be performed yearly, as contracts change, as technology changes, and so on. As mentioned previously, some assessments are based purely on questionnaires, but there may be other tools that provide additional ongoing technical assessments of third parties. These can be used to help detect whether the effectiveness of a third party's security controls is trending in a negative direction, which in turn can be used as an additional set of information to more completely inform risk about third parties.

Issues, Findings, and Exceptions Management

Rarely do our security processes and risk response efforts go as smoothly as we would like. There are always things that don't go as planned. Sometimes there are contentions between security requirements, competition for resources within the organization, findings that cannot be easily mitigated, and other issues and exceptions that must be dealt with. These departures from planned activities, as well as from our established configuration baselines, are cause for concern, especially when we must implement solutions that are outside the normal security parameters we would like. Security and risk, like most things in life, involve compromise and balance. As security and risk practitioners, we are always trying to balance security, functionality, and resources, which always seem to be in conflict with each other. Security and functionality are almost always inversely proportional with each other; for example, typically the more secure a system is, the less functional it is for its users, and vice versa. Resources are always at a premium, and we never have enough money, qualified personnel, equipment, or facilities to achieve the level of security we would like. Additionally, risk itself is a give-and-take. We are often forced to accept a level of risk based on how cost-effective it is to implement controls to reduce the risk to a manageable level. In any case, how we deal with departures from the normal baselines, in the form of issues, findings, exceptions, and so on is critically important.

Change and Configuration Management

One of the primary sources of issues with our security posture, in the form of findings and exceptions, is our change and configuration management processes and status. Remember that change management is a formal management process designed to ensure that needed changes are carefully requested, considered, approved, tested, and implemented in a safe, secure, and predictable manner. The change management process, when implemented properly, should allow an organization to make major changes to the infrastructure without suffering unexpected or critical consequences. However, change management can cause issues if emergency changes must be made for security or other reasons, and there is simply not enough time to route the change through the organization's change control board (CCB). There are also issues if people do not follow the steps of a proper change management process, and simply implement changes on the fly without approval. Both of these issues should be carefully considered because they could incur additional risk, represent an undesirable departure from the normal change process, and must be minimized whenever possible.

Configuration management brings the same challenges. While change management applies to major infrastructure changes, configuration management is a subset of that process and is specific to individual systems. Arbitrarily changing configurations without careful planning and testing could result in unstable or unusable systems. If emergency configuration changes must be made, this represents additional risk because there may not always be time for the formal testing and approval process. Configuration management is also impacted by older or legacy systems that cannot be updated in the event a critical security issue is discovered, such as a zero-day vulnerability. These problems could crop up during a vulnerability scan, where a vulnerability finding is discovered and the patch for that vulnerability either does not exist or cannot be implemented on an older system, or on a system that, if patched, would break line-of-business systems.

This is where an exception would have to be considered: the company could either allow the system to operate under its current configuration, while acknowledging the security risk, or risk the impact of the update on the line-of-business systems, resulting in a loss of potential revenue. Even when the risk is considered and an exception must be made, this, again, is an undesirable departure from the normal process steps. We will discuss exception management in more detail in the next section.

Release management is also a subset of change management and, along the same lines, represents risks when software must be released ahead of its schedule or before it is adequately tested and considered for risk. The release management process must, as much as practical, adhere to scheduled releases that are tested as much as is practical and include risk-reduction measures. As discussed in the preceding paragraphs, emergency releases incur risk and should be avoided as much as is possible.

Exception Management

No matter how standardized security controls are, there are always exceptions, and you need to have a process in place to manage those exceptions and keep them minimized. Consider the example in the previous section where an operating system patch cannot be applied because of a legacy application that is critical to the organization's mission. This mitigation is important, but less important than the legacy application and its associated mission. Exception management, as mentioned earlier, comes into play here; you should evaluate the risk of implementing the patch and breaking the application, thus putting the organization's mission in jeopardy, versus the risk of not implementing the patch and dealing with the security ramifications that come with that decision. Management will have to make a decision regarding which is the riskier choice. If the choice is to make an exception and not implement the patch, you need to document this as an accepted exception to the policy and track it, usually in the risk register. Perhaps the patch can be implemented in the future, or another mitigation could come along and make the exception moot. This is another aspect of risk acceptance; you are asking management to accept an ongoing risk, as an exception, because the response cannot be implemented for whatever reason. Either way, keeping a close eye on the issue is key to not letting these exceptions slip through the cracks.

Regardless of where issues, security findings, and exceptions to normal processes, policies, or baselines occur, these departures should be avoided as much as possible, and when they cannot be avoided, they must be carefully considered, with great care taken to reduce the risks they present.

Management of Emerging Risk

Risk is not static; it is constantly changing. The dynamic nature of risk means that it must be constantly monitored, reassessed, and reevaluated, and risk responses will often need to change as risk changes. The components of risk, including threats and vulnerabilities, also change. The organization itself changes, as it is restructured, as its mission and goals change over time, as its place in the marketplace evolves, and of course as its risk appetite and tolerance change. Technologies also change, and organizations sometimes are in a hurry to adopt the latest and greatest technology because it becomes convinced that there is a need to do so; sometimes that need is indeed valid, but sometimes the technology marketing machine convinces an organization it has a need where before it did not. Emerging technologies, and their associated threats, vulnerabilities, risks, and, by extension, risk responses, must be constantly evaluated.

Emerging Technologies

New or emerging technologies can present risks to organizations simply because there are several different important considerations when integrating the latest technologies into the existing infrastructure. Many organizations have an unfortunate tendency to rush out, buy, and attempt to implement the latest (and often unproven) technologies on the market, without careful planning or consideration of the existing infrastructure and how it will react to the new technologies. One of the primary considerations organizations must look at is making a business case for a new technology, which may be to fill a gap that the older technology does not provide or to provide a capability that the organization must now have to compete in the market space. In other words, the company really must justify new technologies to make them worth the risk they could incur.

At the opposite end of the spectrum, many companies are averse to investing a great number of resources in new technologies, instead relying on older, tried-and-true technologies that have always worked in the past. These organizations fail to consider the changing threat landscape, and sometimes the need for maintaining a cutting edge in the marketplace. The threat landscape can render older technologies obsolete and ineffective in protecting the company's information assets. The market a particular organization participates in can also drive the need to update its older technologies to those that make it able to produce goods and services faster, more efficiently, and to better meet the needs of its customers.

In any event, emerging technologies present challenges to organizations that must be considered. These challenges include the emerging risk factors, vulnerabilities, and threats that go along with those technologies. We will discuss those in the next few sections.

Emerging Risk Factors

Emerging technologies have several risk factors inherent to their integration into the existing infrastructure. If the organization has been able to justify the implementation based on a true business need for the emerging technology, it must consider several risk factors. One of the major risk factors is interoperability with existing infrastructure. Frequently, newer technologies don't work properly with older systems right out of the box; adjustments might need to be made to the existing infrastructure to integrate the new technology, or bridging technologies may be needed to connect the two. Interoperability doesn't just involve the right connections; it can involve data formats and flows, security methods, and interfaces into other systems. These considerations, and many others, are risk factors that must be considered before acquiring and integrating new technologies.

Another risk factor is security. New technologies may have security mechanisms that are not necessarily backward compatible with existing ones. Examples include encryption algorithms and strengths, identification and authentication technologies, integrity mechanisms, and even redundant or backup systems. Additionally, the systems may involve a learning curve that might intimidate users who must now learn new security methods for the system. The human factor can be a weak link in the security chain, so either a lack of training or a lack of adaptability to the new security mechanisms can introduce risk.

Additionally, system updates and changes can be risky if not managed properly. Integrating new technologies into the environment with older ones can introduce both intentional and unintended changes into the environment, affecting the stability of the organization's implementation, operations, and maintenance of a particular system, so change is also a risk factor. Even in the disposal or replacement phase of a system's life cycle, introducing new technologies to replace older ones can be problematic if not planned and executed properly. New technologies that are not adequately tested for functionality, performance, integration, interoperability, and security may not be able to adequately replace older systems, resulting in extended costs and possibly even requiring the extension of the older systems' life cycle.

Emerging Threats

Threats resulting from the introduction of new and emerging technologies into the existing infrastructure are numerous. If the organization has failed to adequately plan for the new technology, these threats can become significant. These include untested or unproven technologies, non-interoperability, incompatible security mechanisms, and lack of suitability of the technology for use in the organization. The organization could also incur additional cost and require more resources because of a faulty implementation. These threats can be minimized by careful planning and integrating new technologies using a stable systems development life cycle (SDLC) model.

Additionally, organizations should implement both threat modeling and threat hunting processes into their security program when new technologies are considered. Threat modeling and threat hunting can help an organization identify not only the generic threats that affect all organizations, but those specific to its own business model, processes, assets, vulnerabilities, and risk scenarios involving the new technology.

Emerging Vulnerabilities

As with threats, vulnerabilities that go along with working with emerging technologies are numerous as well. General vulnerabilities could include a lack of trained staff committed to managing and implementing the new technology. Lack of adequate project planning is also a serious vulnerability that could affect the organization's ability to effectively integrate new technologies. Another vulnerability could be a weak support contract or other type of warranty, guarantee, or support for a new technology or system. Most of these vulnerabilities appear when new technologies are first implemented and tend to become mitigated or lessened as the technologies are integrated into the existing infrastructure, but they still exist.

Beyond general vulnerabilities, new technologies also have their own inherent technical vulnerabilities. Often these vulnerabilities are not discovered until long after a technology has been implemented. Although vendors are increasingly security conscious in implementing and designing technologies from a secure perspective, zero-day vulnerabilities are often discovered months or even years after those technologies are installed and operational.

To make matters more challenging, some vulnerabilities are not detectable by vulnerability management tools. They are only detailed by the vendor, and only if they happen to detail them. In some situations, this makes monitoring the updates for the applications all the more relevant to ensure, including in the vulnerability management process.

When implementing a new technology, organizations should make an extra effort toward vulnerability scanning and assessment, and they should pay particular attention to new vulnerabilities, even those that seem unrelated to the new technology. Often these vulnerabilities could be indirectly related and appear because of interoperability or integration issues with the infrastructure.

In some cases, it may make sense to perform other types of validations against new technology—especially if there are additional risk factors such as large amounts of sensitive data. Validations may include but are not limited to penetration testing, secure configuration reviews, and application security testing.

 EXAM TIP   The key areas of concern with emerging technologies are interoperability and compatibility. These two concerns affect the security, functionality, and performance of the new technologies when they are installed into an existing infrastructure.

Control Design and Implementation

A control is a measure or safeguard put into place to protect organizational assets (including systems, equipment, data, facilities, processes, and even people), ensure compliance with laws and regulations or other governance requirements, and reduce overall risk to the organization and its assets. Controls can help improve the overall security posture of your organization through correcting a gap or making up for a shortfall in another control. Controls can be technical solutions, such as firewalls or intrusion detection systems, but they can also be processes, procedures, policies, or physical controls.

In this part of the chapter we will discuss the various types and functions of controls as well as different control frameworks that can help an organization secure its assets. We will also discuss how an organization can design, select, and analyze its controls for effectiveness. Additionally, we will cover the particulars of implementing controls as well as control testing. So, how do you determine which controls to apply to your system or whether your existing controls are good enough? We will discuss this in more depth in the following sections.

Control Types and Functions

As you may have gathered by now, there are many types of controls to choose from. However, you can generally group these controls into a number of broad categories by their intended type and also by their function. Depending on which control framework you read, or which cybersecurity or risk expert you are talking to, these controls may be referred to differently, as some standards categorize them in different ways. However, for our purposes and for the CRISC exam, you need to understand three main types of controls: administrative (also sometimes referred to as managerial), technical (sometimes called logical), and physical (also called operational) controls. The following are examples of each.

Administrative (Managerial)

- Requiring an acceptable use policy to dictate IT usage within the organization
- Starting a risk management program to identify, lower, and monitor unacceptable risk levels within the organization
- Implementing additional policies and procedures within the organization to support external governance and the desires of management

Technical (Logical)

- Implementing additional firewalls to protect internal (non-public-facing) systems
- Adding 802.1X port-based network access control to deter unapproved assets being added to the network
- Installing an intrusion detection system/intrusion prevention system (IDS/IPS) to monitor for malicious activities or violations of policy

Physical (Operational)

- Implementing physical intrusion detection and alarm systems throughout the facility
- Deploying a human-based guard force to patrol sensitive areas
- Construction of fencing, bollards, and other physical obstacles to prevent unauthorized entry into an organization's campus

Controls are also categorized by function—that is, what purpose they serve and how they work. The most common control functions are deterrent, preventive, detective, corrective, and compensating. Table 3-1 lists each control type function, its definition, and an example of the control.

Control Function	Definition	Example
Deterrent	Deters individuals from performing policy violations or illegal acts	Video surveillance, guards, login warning banners, policies
Preventive	Prevents policy violations or illegal acts	Firewall rules, permission settings, perimeter fencing
Detective	Detects or discovers policy violations or illegal acts	Physical intrusion detection systems and alarms, system intrusion detection systems, integrity checks, audit logs, video surveillance
Corrective	Temporarily corrects an immediate security issue	Guards, systems configured to shut down when an attack occurs or logs are full, facility lockdowns
Compensating	Longer-term alternative solution when primary controls cannot be implemented for legitimate business reasons; used to reduce risk in lieu of a desired control	Cards, physical obstructions, signage, additional network security devices, encryption mechanisms

Table 3-1 Control Functions and Descriptions

EXAM TIP   Controls may be categorized by function, which includes preventative, deterrent, detective, corrective, and compensating controls. Often, controls can serve more than one function simultaneously, and it may be difficult to completely categorize them as one particular function or another.

Note that different control functions can fall within all three control types; there are deterrent, preventative, detective, corrective, and compensating controls that are technical, administrative, or physical. You will also notice some significant overlap between these types and functions. For example, video surveillance can be a deterrent control as well as a detective control. Also, since some experts do not distinguish between, for example, deterrent controls and preventative controls, it is important to point out their difference here.

A deterrent control must be known by an individual or entity in order for it to be effective since it dissuades them from committing a policy violation or an illegal act. For example, a video surveillance camera can be a deterrent control—if a person sees it in operation, they are less likely to commit a malicious act because they know they are being viewed and recorded. This deters them from that act. A preventative control, on the other hand, does not have to be known by an individual for it to be effective. An example of this would be a firewall rule that prevents a user from surfing to a malicious site. The user doesn't have to know that the firewall rule exists in order for it to still be effective and prevent them from committing this policy violation.

Another difference worth pointing out is the one between corrective and compensating controls. As indicated in Table 3-1, compensating controls are implemented to take the place of a more desired or primary control, which can't be implemented for various legitimate business reasons (for example, lack of resources). Even if the primary control can't be implemented, the risk must still be reduced, so a control (or sometimes multiple controls) is implemented in its place. Compensating controls are longer-term controls, which are not likely to be changed anytime in the immediate future.

Corrective controls, however, are temporary, short-term duration controls. They are designed to correct an immediate security issue. For example, let's say that a storm comes through your area and destroys a section of strong concrete wall surrounding your facility. Now there is a huge hole in the perimeter, which could allow an unauthorized person to enter at the facility grounds. To immediately mitigate this risk, you may post a guard to patrol that particular area for a few days until you can come up with something better. Obviously, keeping a guard there on a long-term basis is not wise financially or from a resource usage perspective. After a few days, you might be able to fix the wall, if possible, which restores the primary control to its operational state. If for some reason that portion of the wall can't be fixed, however, you may install temporary fencing or another physical obstruction in its place, and supplement it with surveillance cameras, an intrusion detection system, and additional alarms so that it would reduce the risk of an intruder entering the area, without having to keep a guard there all the time. These might be considered compensating controls since the primary control (the strong concrete wall) can't be immediately addressed.

As mentioned previously, control types and functions can overlap. They can also complement each other. For a given administrative control (for example, a policy that dictates that all sensitive data must be encrypted), there is usually a technical control, such as the encryption mechanism, and possibly even a physical control, such as hardware encryption devices being locked in a secure area, to back it up. Again, it should be pointed out that the various standards and frameworks, which we'll discuss in a moment, often categorized these types and functions of controls differently, so don't be surprised if sometimes you see them referred to in a different manner.

 NOTE Some professionals, texts, and frameworks also include *recovery controls* as a control function. These controls could include safeguards such as backups, redundant systems, and so on. While you likely won't see this control function called out on the CRISC exam, simply be aware that sometimes you will see other control functions, as well as other control types, such as operational controls, in other contexts.

Figure 3-1 summarizes some of the key characteristics of controls and their implementation, with regard to types and functions. Note that, as depicted in the figure, controls that are designed to prevent a malicious act or policy violation are generally known as *safeguards*, whereas controls that come into play after a violation has occurred, and must be used to respond to the event, are called *countermeasures*.

Control Standards and Frameworks

Control standards and frameworks are defined sets of controls that can be used in a given set of circumstances, market, or area. Controls are often tied to governance directives and regulations, but this isn't always the case. Sometimes different regulations or even process frameworks reference controls only to the extent that a control framework is required, but not to specify which control standard must be used. The Health Insurance Portability and Accountability Act (HIPAA) is good example of this scenario because HIPAA requires security and risk controls, but it does not specify which control set must be used (although HIPAA guidance does recommend the NIST control catalog). As another example, while references to controls are specifically called out in the ISACA Risk IT Framework (RR 2.1, "Inventory Controls," and RR 2.4, "Implement Controls"), the framework itself does not give any clear guidance on how controls are defined, selected,

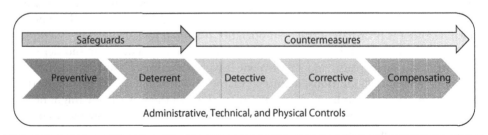

Figure 3-1 Control characteristics and their implementation

or implemented; however, the assumption is that implementing the framework will show you how to use and evaluate whichever control set you choose. The NIST Risk Management Framework (RMF), in contrast, does provide guidance on how its controls are constructed, used, and assessed, devoting several publications to this subject.

Specific industry or market environments may require the use of specific, context-related controls, as indicated in Table 3-2.

Controls in a given framework are often organized according to a particular area or context, usually by functionality or relevance. For instance, the CIS and NIST control standards (discussed shortly) are broken down into areas, or *families,* which are categories that apply to a specific context. As an example, the NIST Physical and Environmental Protection (PE) controls address physical and environmental concerns such as physical access control and environmental factors (lighting, humidity, and temperature), whereas the NIST Program Management (PM) control family addresses management processes that often appear as administrative controls, such as formally appointing a responsible information security officer. Most other control frameworks discussed in this chapter similarly categorize controls, usually by process area or other relevant aspect of context.

 TIP You'll find that most control libraries similarly group controls into specific categories based on function or context, and most use specific identifiers for each control.

Which controls from the various frameworks are used by an organization depends on several factors, including governance, market segment or area, level of regulation, and internal factors such as risk tolerance, risk appetite, and maturity of the risk management processes. We cover more of how controls are selected, designed, implemented, and used later in this chapter and in the other chapters, but suffice it to say for now that controls are usually developed and applied to specific risk scenarios. These risk scenarios are developed by the organization or industry as part of their risk identification process.

Area or Environment	Corresponding Control Set
U.S. federal government	FISMA, which is based on NIST Special Publication 800-53, revision 4, but is transitioning to revision 5
U.S. federal government related	FedRAMP or CMMC, which is based on NIST Special Publication 800-171
Aggregated healthcare	HIPAA, HITECH, or MARS-E
Healthcare	HIPAA or HITECH, although HITRUST is sufficient from a legal perspective
Finance	FFIEC, SWIFT, or relevant international controls
Credit cards	PCI DSS
Publicly traded	Sarbanes-Oxley (SOX)
Private/commercial	Center for Internet Security (CIS) controls, NIST Special Publication CSF, ISO/IEC 27001, or AICPA's SOC2

Table 3-2 Examples of Areas Requiring Control Standards

They describe threats, threat actors, events, time, and other circumstances, but of course control assignment and use may be required by legal or regulatory governance, as well as the needs of the organization that intends to employ them. It's also fairly common for an organization to use more than one control set or framework because it may apply differently to various aspects of the business or mission areas in an organization. For example, a hospital may use NIST controls for some areas but may also be required to use PCI DSS controls since it may process payments from credit cards as patients pay for medical services. Oftentimes, controls from more than one source are applied against one or more areas of the business.

In examining the various control frameworks, you'll also find that there are many similarities between controls in some instances; often a control in one framework has a close equivalent in another framework. For example, CIS Control 10, "Malware Defenses," loosely maps to the corresponding NIST control, SI-3, "Malicious Code Protection," but describes a more generic process than the equivalent NIST control. There will also be controls that have no matching control or even context in another framework; these are often controls that deal with specific instances of risk or security requirements unique to a particular environment.

NOTE Most control catalogs have controls that can be easily mapped to controls in other catalogs, although in some cases, this mapping may be imprecise, may not be as detailed, or may even map to multiple controls in another control library.

Control Frameworks

Now that we've covered some generalities about controls, it's time to look at various control frameworks you might use in your professional career. Keep in mind that some control frameworks go into more depth than others on their controls; some controls in a given framework may treat a particular subject area lightly, whereas others may go into detail on a particular subject area. Also keep in mind that some control frameworks are geared toward specific environments or areas, and not all frameworks are necessarily geared toward security specifically; some frameworks apply to a broad general business or risk management area but may have security controls built into them for specific needs or direct security actions from a higher level. Not all control frameworks are technical in nature either; some frameworks apply to security and risk from a business process perspective rather than a technical perspective. Some control frameworks are privacy oriented and provide a different set of controls. The control frameworks described in the following sections are just some of the more popular ones you may encounter in your professional career as a risk practitioner.

NIST The U.S. Department of Commerce's National Institute of Standards and Technology (NIST) has produced several documents—some of which we have already mentioned—that relate to risk management. The entire Risk Management Framework (RMF), and all of its different components, spans several documents. We're not going to provide a comprehensive review of the framework and its related documents here, but we will examine a particular piece of the framework: the controls catalog. NIST Special

Publication (SP) 800-53, revision 5, "Security and Privacy Controls for Information Systems and Organizations," is the control catalog supporting NIST's RMF. The NIST controls are a comprehensive set of security measures and processes intended to mitigate and reduce risk from an IT security perspective. The NIST control catalog is divided up into 20 separate control groups, called *families,* each related to a particular aspect of IT security.

The NIST control families span a great deal of subject areas. Each family has several controls in it; there are smaller families (such as the Awareness and Training family) that may have as few as six controls, but there are others that have many different controls that go into great detail on security measures. An example is the System and Communications Protection (SC) family, with 51 controls.

 EXAM TIP You will likely not be tested on any specific NIST controls; however, it's a good idea to have this knowledge in order to differentiate among the different control frameworks you may see on the exam, as well as for real life.

PCI DSS The Payment Card Industry Data Security Standard (PCI DSS) is a set of security requirements levied on merchants that process credit card transactions. The standard was developed jointly by the major payment card industry players, including Discover, Visa, MasterCard, and American Express. The standard was developed in an effort to impose security requirements and controls on retailers (merchants and service providers) to reduce credit card fraud and identity theft. Note that PCI DSS is not a law; rather, it is an effort by the credit card industry to self-regulate. Although not a law, it does have the effect of being mandatory in terms of governance requirements; retailers must comply with PCI DSS to be allowed to process credit cards from the major industry brands. A few U.S. states, however, have codified into their laws the use of PCI DSS standards.

The PCI DSS (currently in version 3.2.1 as of this writing) is a set of six control objectives, broken down into 12 major requirements, which are further broken down into sub-requirements. Table 3-3 lists the basic PCI DSS requirements.

On the surface, these objectives and requirements don't seem to go into much depth. Understand, however, that PCI DSS further decomposes the requirements into detailed processes and procedures. The standard also provides guidance for testing at the control level. For example, requirement 5, "Protect all systems against malware and regularly update antivirus software or programs," breaks down into four sub-requirements, some of which break down even further. Requirement 5.1.2, continuing the example, specifies continuous monitoring and evaluation of hosts for malware threats. Overall, there are actually more than 200 sub-requirements, which are the equivalent of controls.

 EXAM TIP You likely won't be asked any PCI DSS control–specific questions on the exam, but you should keep in mind its applicability to merchants and retailers that process credit card transactions. You can find more detailed information on the PCI DSS standards at the website of the PCI Security Standards Council at https://www.pcisecuritystandards.org/security_standards/.

Control Objective	Requirement
Build and Maintain a Secure Network and Systems	1. Install and maintain a firewall configuration to protect cardholder data. 2. Do not use vendor-supplied defaults for system passwords and other security parameters.
Protect Cardholder Data	3. Protect stored cardholder data. 4. Encrypt transmission of cardholder data across open, public networks.
Maintain a Vulnerability Management Program	5. Protect all systems against malware and regularly update antivirus software or programs. 6. Develop and maintain secure systems and applications.
Implement Strong Access Control Measures	7. Restrict access to cardholder data by business need to know. 8. Identify and authenticate access to system components. 9. Restrict physical access to cardholder data.
Regularly Monitor and Test Networks	10. Track and monitor all access to network resources and cardholder data. 11. Regularly test security systems and processes.
Maintain an Information Security Policy	12. Maintain a policy that addresses information security for all personnel.

Table 3-3 PCI DSS Control Objectives and Requirements

CIS Controls The Center for Internet Security (CIS) publishes 18 critical security controls, which are essentially areas or families that decompose into 153 individual safeguards, spanning three implementation groups. These 18 areas are similar to other control sets in that they cover areas of common security concern, including malware, penetration testing, inventory of software assets, account management, access control, and so on. The three Implementation Groups (IGs) are designed to provide a path for progressively implementing safeguards, with prioritization and scalability in mind, to help smaller organizations, or those that have limited resources, implement a minimum of 56 core security controls that are absolutely necessary to secure systems and data.

The CIS controls were formally known as the SANS Top 20 Critical Security Controls, before the CIS took responsibility for them in 2015. They were originally developed by an effort led by the National Security Agency (NSA) and many other government and industry partners. The most current version of the CIS controls is version 8, published in May 2021.

ISO/IEC 27001 Although we've primarily discussed different control sets that originate in the United States (such as PCI DSS and NIST), most of the various control frameworks map to, and in some cases originate from, standards used worldwide and developed by internationally respected governing bodies. In Chapter 1, we briefly mentioned some of these standards, including those from ISO and IEC. The ISO and IEC produce information technology standards used internationally, including several that apply to information security and risk management. You may see individual standards prepared by each of these organizations, but you may also see combined standards, usually indicated as ISO/IEC for those standards that are jointly developed. We discussed standards that applied more specifically to risk assessments in Chapter 1, but there are also ISO/IEC standards that are essentially control requirements. Two examples are ISO/IEC 27001:2013, "Information technology – Security techniques – Information security management systems – Requirements," and its companion guide, ISO/IEC 27002:2022, "Information security, cybersecurity and privacy protection – Information security controls." These two standards, like the ones discussed previously, break down their controls into different areas or categories and include areas such as information security policies, human resource security, asset management, access control, cryptography, and so on. Since the ISO/IEC 27001 and 27002 standards are developed by an international standards organization, they can be used across the globe.

As mentioned earlier, most of the control standards we have discussed have built-in mappings to help facilitate their implementation where organizations may have multiple governance requirements to which they are required to adhere. Both the NIST and CIS controls have mappings to the ISO/IEC standards, for example. In examining these control mappings, a couple points should stand out. First, there's not necessarily a straight one-to-one mapping of controls. In some cases, the requirements for a given control in a control set may map to one, many, or even none of the other control set's controls. Second, controls tend to follow similar patterns and requirements, such as acceptable use, password requirements, media and storage, encryption, and so on. Most controls from the various control sets have these commonalities because all of them in some way trace back to the three goals of security (confidentiality, integrity, and availability) as well as the supporting elements of identification, authentication, and authorization. This is generally true regardless of which security control framework you examine.

 NOTE You'll find that many control frameworks are derived from and map to the ISO/IEC standards. They are international standards and can be applied across most industries and market spaces.

Control Design, Selection, and Analysis

The importance of designing, selecting, maintaining, and monitoring the right controls cannot be understated. Remember that controls serve three primary purposes: protecting assets, ensuring compliance, and reducing risk. If controls are not adequately planned for and implemented, they will fail to meet any or all three of these purposes. In the next few sections of this chapter, we will discuss the critical elements of control design, selection, and analysis.

Control Design

Controls are designed and applied to a system, data, process, or even organizational element to address a weakness or vulnerability or to counter a specific threat. Often, controls are designed to address a specific risk response strategy, such as risk reduction/mitigation, sharing, avoidance, and acceptance. Controls are applied to reduce the impact and likelihood elements of risk, as follows:

- Reduce the likelihood of a threat agent initiating a threat (deterrence, preventative, and detection controls are examples).
- Reduce the likelihood of a threat exploiting a vulnerability (preventative and detection controls).
- Reduce the impact to the organization or asset if a threat exploits a vulnerability (corrective, compensating, and recovery controls).
- Reduce the vulnerability (deterrent, preventative, corrective, and compensating controls all could perform this action).

Note that none of the scenarios listed earlier describes a case where a control prevents a threat or a threat actor. Threats and threat actors exist, and controls can't really prevent their existence. Controls can, however, affect how they interact with vulnerabilities and assets. Also note that all these strategies may be pursued simultaneously in the case of controls that are well designed and effective, using the concept of economy of scale and multiple use of controls.

 EXAM TIP Remember that controls can affect the likelihood or impact of risk elements only by reducing vulnerabilities or protecting assets. They cannot eliminate or reduce threats or threat actors; they only serve to reduce the likelihood or impact resulting from an attempted or successful exploitation of a vulnerability by a threat.

Control Selection

When an organization selects controls to be applied to protect systems and minimize risk, several considerations come to mind. First, the organization should look at its governance requirements and ensure that its controls meet those requirements, particularly where specific data protection requirements are indicated. This may include level of performance or function of a control (encryption strength, for instance). The organization also has to look at its existing infrastructure. It is likely to already have some level of controls in place, although the controls might not be applied directly to the system in question. Take, for example, an organization that has industrial control systems and other types of operational technologies present. Many of these devices cannot support basic security measures, such as authentication or encryption; however, as compensating controls, the organization could implement network segmentation by putting them in their own physically or logically separated subnets and install authentication and encryption mechanisms specifically for those devices, since they do not have their own built-in capabilities. If there are existing controls that can already fulfill the requirements for a control, those should be used to the maximum extent possible.

Second, controls should be selected also based on their level of effectiveness, as indicated by the design parameters we discussed earlier. A control that is minimally effective, and perhaps meets governance requirements, may still not be desirable if it does not provide the level of security the organization needs. Effectiveness also may mean how good the control is at reducing risk or ensuring compliance. If either of these levels of functionality or performance are not met by the control, the organization should consider strengthening or changing the control.

Third, cost is also an issue with control selection. A control that costs $10,000 to implement but only protects a single system that is valued at $2000 is not cost-effective. However, a control that costs $10,000 and protects several systems, even if individually they are not high-value systems, but collectively generate $100,000 in revenue for the organization per year, is likely more cost-effective. Control selection with regard to cost should include the cost of the control as well as the cost to maintain it. This includes spare parts and components, service contracts, and the cost of qualified personnel to maintain the control. This is where quantitative data elements, such as asset value (AV), exposure factor (EF), single loss expectancy (SLE), and annualized loss expectancy (ALE), which you learned about in earlier chapters, come into play, since they affect whether a control is worth it financially to implement.

Ultimately, security and risk practitioners recommend controls based on their effectiveness and cost to management, who must make the decision regarding their implementation. If the desired controls cannot be implemented, for whatever reason, both the practitioners and management must consider selecting appropriate compensating controls, which must be approved and documented.

Control Analysis

Controls are analyzed at several different points in their life cycle. They are looked at to ensure they fulfill their basic functions of asset protection, compliance with governance, and risk reduction. They're examined for not only effectiveness (how well they do their job) but also efficiency (meaning that they do their job with as little additional effort, resources, and management as possible). Even if a control is performing its job functions wonderfully, if the cost to maintain it is prohibitive, the organization may need to look at changing the control or its implementation in some fashion.

The most common way to analyze controls is through controls assessment, where controls are evaluated for their effectiveness. A control can be evaluated using various methods, such as interviewing key personnel responsible for managing and maintaining the control, reviewing the documentation associated with the control, observing the control in action, and testing the control through technical means. These different assessment methods will give a risk practitioner an idea of how effective the control is in meeting its primary functions.

Risk assessments for the specific system under review, as well as the entire organization, will also indicate how well a control is performing its function. Even if a risk practitioner is not examining a particular control, levels of increased or decreased risk for the system itself or the entire organization would indicate whether or not one or more controls are effective. Historical and trend analysis methods tell a risk practitioner how risk has changed over time. They also help the practitioner predict how risk will change, given changes in the environment, technology, the threat landscape, and how effective the control will be. If risk has increased inexplicably, the practitioner must analyze the different controls designed and implemented to mitigate that risk.

After controls have been tested and analyzed, results from those analyses should be recorded on the overall risk register, particularly with regard to risk the control is supposed to mitigate. Obviously, management must be informed of any changes in risk caused by control effectiveness issues.

Control Implementation

Controls aren't simply installed in infrastructures, even in the event there is urgency to do so. As we have previously discussed, some planning goes into control implementation. Most of this planning focuses on determining the effectiveness of the control and ensuring it is designed to protect assets, assist in compliance, and reduce risk. There are also other considerations when implementing controls, including the change management process, configuration management, and testing.

Change and Configuration Management

Change and configuration management processes are critical during control implementation because, in actuality, implementing new controls is a change that occurs in the infrastructure and must therefore be part of the formal change control process. This involves requesting the change and presenting a justification as to why it is necessary. In this case, the change is necessary to fill a gap or need that an existing control (or the absence of a control) does not fill. Compliance may also drive the need for the change, since governance may require that the control be implemented. Risk reduction is also valid justification for implementing a control in the change management process. Once the change is requested as part of the formal process, it is reviewed by the change control board and approved or returned for amendments to the request. After it has been approved, it must go through the testing process. Once it clears the implementation testing process, discussed in the next section, the change is formally approved and implemented. If, for some reason, it does not pass the different types of tests it must go through before implementation, the change is returned to the requester so that any test failures can be addressed.

Control implementations may go through different types of implementation strategies, such as parallel installation and implementation with like systems, a gradual update to the system, a phased implementation, or even a clean cut-over with the system using the new controls. Since the installation may incur unacceptable downtime for critical systems, this must be carefully considered. The organization must decide the appropriate strategy, based on its resiliency, system and data criticality, and tolerance for any risks that always come with implementing a significant change in the infrastructure.

Implementation Testing

Although controls undergo testing at various points in their life cycle, testing before implementation is critical because often it is difficult to go back to a previous control or a point in time before the control is implemented. This is especially true if the infrastructure is significantly altered to accommodate the new control. Consider a network infrastructure that has a new firewall or other network security device installed. The network may have to be rerouted and reconfigured and new rules configured on the network security device. If for some reason it is installed without testing and then fails, it may cause serious impact to business operations if users cannot use the network, get on the Internet, or otherwise are unable to perform their duties.

Several types of implementation testing should occur on new controls before they are implemented. One of the first is interoperability testing. Interoperability is critical since the new control must work with existing technologies and infrastructure. If for some reason they do not work together, this can cause work stoppages or outages and will impact business operations. A risk analysis conducted before implementing a new control should take this into account, and the organization should be reasonably informed about how the new technology or control will interact with the existing infrastructure before it is tested and implemented. Another type of testing involves testing security mechanisms that are inherent to the new control, such as authentication and encryption mechanisms. Not only should they be interoperable with existing infrastructure, but they should also be tested for function and performance as well as compliance with any governance. It would not do to install a security control that has legacy authentication or encryption mechanisms that do not meet governance requirements, for example, and therefore fails to protect systems and data.

Testing a control, especially a complex one, before implementation ensures that it is interoperable, satisfies technical requirements, meets governance requirements, and performs and functions as it should. Understanding the limitations and operating parameters of a complex control through testing before implementation is in itself a method of risk reduction.

Other Implementation Considerations

It goes without saying that implementation of a complex control has many more aspects to it than are discussed here. Some of these are resource considerations, such as having enough money in the budget, having enough qualified people to install, manage, and monitor the control, not to mention political considerations within the organization. Consider the implementation of a relatively "easy" control, such as revoking administrative rights on user workstations. Not only will users typically revolt, but managers who are used to having administrative rights over their own workstations will complain and likely go to upper management, who may cave in to those complaints, effectively rendering the control useless. Users also typically balk at having their systems offline for any amount of time since it may interrupt their work. All these issues should all be carefully considered and decided upon by management, or at the very least kept in mind by the risk practitioner.

Another aspect of control implementation is documentation. All steps of the implementation should be thoroughly documented, as well as any exception items, such as configuration or interoperability issues that may need to be addressed later. Documentation also includes policies and procedures to support the control, change management records, implementation test results, operator training materials, schedules for maintenance, and any other information relevant to the control.

Control Testing and Effectiveness Evaluation

Control testing and evaluation, as well as analysis, were discussed earlier in the chapter, but they bear repeating here. Controls must be tested and evaluated not only prior to implementation, but also at various points during their life cycle. Controls should be tested and assessed as part of routine risk assessments, controls testing, vulnerability and penetration testing, and so on. Controls are tested not only for their effectiveness in protecting assets, but also their compliance with governance and their ability to reduce risk to acceptable levels. Remember that earlier we discussed four methods for testing a control:

- Interviews with key personnel, such as operators, security analysts, engineers, and even managers
- Observation of the control in operation to ensure it does what it is supposed to do
- Review of any documentation supporting the control, such as policies, procedures, maintenance records, architectural diagrams, exceptions, and so on
- Technical testing, such as that conducted during vulnerability assessments and penetration testing

All of these different types of tests are critical in getting the complete picture of how well a control is functioning and performing. The results of control testing should be documented and reported on in various circumstances as part of different assessments and tests.

Controls that fail testing or do not perform or function as expected should be further evaluated in more detail for any possible changes and any additional increase in risk. A control may need to be reinstalled, replaced, or upgraded, or compensating controls may need to be added to strengthen the function the control is meant to perform.

Risk Monitoring and Reporting

What are the reporting requirements for your organization? Are they dictated by government regulations, international business partnerships, or other binding agreements? Understanding what is required of your organization in terms of reporting risk is absolutely critical in fulfilling governance requirements, whether they are imposed by external sources, such as laws and regulations, or by internal governance, such as policies published by executive management. You also need to understand what you should report in any of these contexts. For example, it is a good idea to report any ongoing risk issues you have, the status of any ongoing remediation actions, how your controls are performing, any incidents, and how your overall risk response activities are performing.

Along with understanding the organization's risk environment, it is important to understand your stakeholders and what their reporting needs are. For example, your board of directors will likely want a high-level, quarterly presentation on compliance levels relative to the previously discussed risk and control environment, as well as security performance relative to business goals and objectives. Business process owners, conversely, may want a much more detailed report about the individual risks identified previously, the new risks that could potentially come to the forefront, and how different business units are supporting the risk management program across the entire organization. It's important that you understand how these different stakeholders need different reporting mechanisms and tools and that you identify clearly how they expect you to support them through timely and relevant risk reporting.

When reporting, you can include a few standard items, such as measured control effectiveness (which can be rolled up to a higher level, as necessary, for management), any ongoing issues, any perceived gaps, the status of any remediation actions, any incidents or risk events that have occurred since the last report, and the overall trending status of the effectiveness of the risk management process. Also, identify ahead of time whether your report will be included as an input to a greater enterprise report and work to include any appropriate information needed to facilitate that enterprise-level view. This will help garner support for the risk program supporting the business goals and objectives.

You should review the results of any third-party analysis or audit that has taken place and incorporate the findings into your understanding of the organization's risk posture. Has your organization conducted any type of internal audit or self-assessment? These will be important to review to see how they affect the risk profile and where they will need to be included. We've discussed the organization's tolerance for risk in many places throughout this book, so suffice it to say that the risk tolerance should be considered throughout the reporting process as a key input.

In the end, in order to develop a report that is valuable to management, a risk professional needs to make sure they have a clear understanding of the exposures their organization faces, the active mitigations for those exposures, and the indicators being used to measure the success or failure of the organization's implemented control set, as well as the current risk posture as measured against the risk appetite. This all needs to be communicated to the stakeholders. The importance of articulating risk should not be underestimated; this is a critical task that ensures management receives accurate and unbiased information that is both actionable and supports the overall organizational risk strategy.

Responsible reporting involves helping leadership understand the risks to the organization and how critical it is to support its reduction through implementing appropriate controls, as well as monitoring and managing risk. This needs to be done in the most clear and concise manner possible, understanding the concepts of risk, the indicators that have been chosen, and the current statuses that allow leadership to make the best-informed decisions possible. Without the best possible information, we cannot expect organizational leadership to make informed decisions. You will also need to interpret technical findings and perhaps portray information in a manner that is less technical and more business-focused. By doing this, you will not only make the point that the risk program is useful, worthwhile, and supports business goals and objectives, but you will also identify opportunities for the risk program (and associated reporting) to integrate throughout the enterprise more cleanly.

No communication is complete without thoroughly understanding and depicting both the worst-case and most probable scenarios involved with a risk event. A risk event could mean many potential losses take place, and not only those affecting the company's financial bottom line. There could be losses to the company's goodwill, including any associated brands. Think about major security breaches in previous years, such as Target, T.J. Maxx, and Sony. The result of their losses was both tangible (financial) and intangible (brands associated with a major breach), which is difficult to quantify. This is also the time to include any other information pertinent to supporting the recommendations you've made, such as situations where a financial gain could be made (through exploiting an opportunity), or any outlying legal or regulatory concerns you might have.

Risk Treatment Plans

While reporting may at first seem to be only an occasional aspect of risk management, it actually takes place on a continual basis. Obviously, risk assessments, control assessments, and different types of tests have their own reporting requirements that will be accomplished when those test events are completed. However, reporting can also take place as continual information is sent to management on a regular basis.

Some of the most critical pieces of information that should be reported to management, regardless of a point-in-time test event, are risk response and treatment options and any plans used to implement those options. Management should always have the opportunity to review risk treatment options as they are developed, and risk practitioners have a responsibility to make those recommendations formally to management so that leadership can make the appropriate decisions regarding those particular treatment options. Understand that simply because a risk practitioner recommends specific treatments or responses, this does not necessarily mean that management will approve those options. Alternative risk treatment responses may be approved instead, based on information the risk practitioner doesn't necessarily have or the priorities of management. This is particularly true when risk treatment options are expensive and management is seeking to reduce cost, but balance that with effective risk response at the same time. It is also true if management needs to make a broader decision, such as one that may involve risk avoidance, for example, by taking an entirely different strategic path within the business. When reporting on risk treatment options, you should always present the best recommendation, but also always have alternatives developed for management to consider. In any event, it's important to convey risk treatment options, as well as their progress, to management on a continual basis, not merely after they have been implemented.

Data Collection, Aggregation, Analysis, and Validation

In order to make recommendations on risk treatment, risk practitioners must have a wide variety of data at their disposal. The data must be trustworthy and accurate as well as complete. A risk practitioner can take advantage of multiple sources of data. Technical data, such as logs, can show how a control is operating. Real-time data regarding intrusion detection alerts, user behaviors, and so on is also helpful. Other data, in the form of risk reports, incident reports, change and configuration management documentation, as well as information derived from control assessments should be used to help inform risk management decisions. The vast multitude of data available to the risk practitioner, however, might not be useful to an executive manager. It's the job of the risk practitioner to take all this data and distill it down into useful, actionable information that clearly and concisely conveys how effective a control is, how it is meeting compliance requirements, and how it reduces risk. This information should also convey particulars about changes in risk and how these changes impact the organization.

Regardless of the source of the data risk practitioners use to perform risk management activities, the data must be collected in a sound and verifiable manner and validated as true and accurate. This is where formalized and documented data collection and analysis processes can assist. Some data may be collected in an ad hoc manner, but for the most part, data should be collected on a regular basis, from verified sources, and validated using various integrity-checking methods. The data must also completely describe the situation in the proper context and, of course, be analyzed by qualified risk practitioners and cybersecurity personnel. Data may be synthesized into useful information by reducing it, clarifying it, and performing trend or historical analysis on it. In any event, information supplied to management needs to present a clear, concise, and accurate picture.

Risk and Control Monitoring Techniques

The techniques used to monitor and assess risk, as well as control effectiveness, should be part of a formalized methodology adopted by the organization. This is where the overall risk strategy and associated policies and procedures come in. The risk strategy is management's commitment to risk management and provides an overall long-term direction for where the organization wants to be in terms of managing its risk. The risk strategy is a high-level document and does not necessarily go into detail on the day-to-day risk management activities in which an organization must engage. The risk management policy, on the other hand, should go into further detail on the overall risk management program. This policy should be handed down by management, with consultation from the risk practitioner. It should assign roles and responsibilities as well as dictate what risk management, assessment, and analysis methodologies the organization officially uses. The policy can also define risk treatment options and how they should be considered. Most of the details required to implement the policy and, in turn, the strategy will typically be included in various lower-level risk management procedures, such as procedures used for risk assessment. In any case, the organization's risk management and monitoring processes should be standardized and approved by management for consistency, reliability, and predictability.

Risk and Control Reporting Techniques

Reporting on risk and controls may use various techniques to convey data in a clear, accurate, and complete manner. Some techniques lend themselves to reporting better than others; narrative reports may often be undesirable except where a great deal of technical data is needed to support a recommendation or decision. Graphics and charts, on the other hand, are sometimes better suited to convey the bottom line to management, without all the unnecessary details involved in a technical explanation. Other data presentation techniques, such as statistical, historical and trend analysis, in the form of graphs or bar charts, may be useful to present data in the right way so that management can make an informed decision.

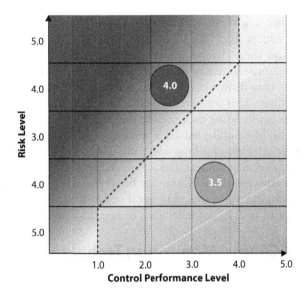

Figure 3-2
An example of a
heat map

Some of these data reporting techniques include heat maps, scorecards, centralized dashboards, and real-time information feeds. Heat maps focus on data that shows areas of red, yellow, and green, for example, with data points in red (darker) being the obvious areas of concern, and data points in the green (lighter) areas being of lesser concern. Figure 3-2 shows an example of a heat map.

Scorecards are used to collect pieces of data and offer a comparison with other pieces of data, showing a relative performance or effectiveness increase, compared to previously collected data. Centralized dashboards, along with real-time information feeds, have the goal of showing a one-stop single view of all the necessary data points risk practitioners and managers need to view, often in real time, the status of control effectiveness, compliance, or risk. Often, however, these dashboards can seem to be very complex and "busy" with information, so extra effort must be taken to ensure they only display critical information, in the most simplistic manner possible, while allowing a risk practitioner or manager to "drill down" further to obtain more details about a piece of data in the dashboard.

Regardless of the data presentation technique used, reporting must be clear, accurate, and complete, and it must convey the critical information needed for managers to make meaningful risk-based decisions.

Key Performance Indicators

We have discussed the necessity to test, assess, and evaluate controls as well as risk itself. Remember that we're trying to ensure that controls are effective, meet compliance requirements, and reduce risk. In order to determine those things, we have to measure different aspects of the control's performance characteristics, both positive and negative. For this we use various pieces of information, called *indicators,* to help us measure these items. Once we identify these indicators, we can move toward the indicators associated with measuring and reporting that performance, and current risk levels, accurately and efficiently.

You will often hear indicators referred to as *metrics,* and in this text, those terms are interchangeable for our purposes. However, the types of indicators, and what they measure, differ. *Key performance indicators (KPIs)* are used to understand and enable the measurement of control performance. Control performance can be anything from how often your firewall blocks malicious incoming traffic to how often your continuity of operations plan is exercised. The level of "performance" can be different for each organization; it's important that you determine performance goals unique to your organization, based on its own performance goals as well as its risk appetite and tolerance levels.

So why do you need indicators? How do you know if you're doing well (or poorly)? Do you trust your risk team, hoping that they have some sort of reporting mechanism that will present stakeholders the correct information? At the end of the day, you want to be able to monitor and analyze those indicators to track trends and determine the effectiveness and efficiency of the controls, and to make decisions for creating new controls, ditching others, and sounding the alarm when risk has passed a predefined threshold.

Understanding what a KPI means to your organization requires you to ask yourself a few questions. What is your organization's mission? Are you a research organization attempting to develop a new cryptographic algorithm? What things are important to your organization? Does it value availability above all other attributes (that is, the ability to conduct business through any fire, storm, hacking attempt, or any other scenario it may encounter)? Or does your organization value data privacy and security above any other consideration? These are questions you need to ask yourself when developing KPIs. Remember that these KPIs help you understand how controls are performing to enable all these attributes. You want to make sure the controls are performing at the level you expect.

Ideally, KPIs should be "S.M.A.R.T." in order to be most effective. In other words, KPIs should be

- **S**pecific
- **M**easurable
- **A**ttainable
- **R**elevant
- **T**imely

When a KPI is S.M.A.R.T., it is tailored to the organization and the area being measured. The first question you need to answer is, what are you trying to measure? You should be, according to the S.M.A.R.T. methodology, *specific.* Are you attempting to measure availability? Then you may want to look at a metric that measures how often your systems go down—or, conversely, what is the percentage of time your systems are up?

A KPI also needs to be *measurable,* in a way that is ensured to be accurate. In the case of the availability, how would you measure it accurately? Perhaps you could determine how often the systems went down based on the "uptime" command in the UNIX operating system.

When a KPI is *attainable*, it is readily achievable. For example, you wouldn't want to set a performance goal of 100 percent uptime in a situation where you have an entirely new staff, new equipment, new management, and so on. Perhaps 85 percent is more achievable, and then you can work toward a higher goal.

KPIs that are *relevant* matter to your organization. If you're in a situation where time is of the essence, such as stock trading, then availability is essential. Without availability, your systems cannot buy or sell stocks, and your user base will quickly move on to another organization that values availability as much as they do. However, other contexts, such as educational institutions, may not care so much about availability. Usability might be of more concern, or the ability to access content via mobile applications or other cutting-edge technologies. Take the time to consider what's important or relevant to your organization when determining your KPIs.

Finally, *timely* KPIs allow the data to be collected when needed to quickly determine the performance of your measured initiative. You should be able to obtain data for the metric relatively easily from existing sources and repositories.

In some instances, a KPI may not meet all the criteria of S.M.A.R.T. For example, a firewall may block a number of external attacks per month. Depending on the organization, there may be nothing to attain, but most of the S.M.A.R.T. criteria is still met. This is perfectly fine in some circumstances.

Key Risk Indicators

Risk indicators are metrics, much like KPIs, used to determine if and when the organization has a high probability of risk that exceeds the defined risk appetite. Not all risk indicators, however, are key. *Key risk indicators (KRIs)* are considered to be highly probable indicators designed to accurately predict important levels of risk based on defined thresholds.

Along with determining the level of performance for our controls, we need to determine ways to indicate the risk that our organization is subject to. KRIs are related to, but separate from, KPIs, in that KRIs are all about how the metric predicts current and future risk rather than past performance of a specific control or set of controls. KRIs are linked to specific risks and provide an early warning alarm that a risk is emerging, allowing leadership to be proactive and deal with that risk sooner rather than later.

ISACA's Risk IT Framework includes the following criteria to select KRIs:

- **Impact** When a risk indicator has a high impact, it is likely to be a KRI.
- **Effort to implement, measure, and report** When all else is equal, the easiest indicator to measure from is the best.
- **Reliability** The indicator reliably predicts an outcome.
- **Sensitivity** The indicator accurately indicates variances in the risk.

Similarly to the determination of KPIs discussed earlier, KRIs should be S.M.A.R.T., and they should drill down to the root cause and not just focus on the symptoms that are immediately evident. KRIs should include lagging indicators (indicators that determine current risk after an event has occurred), leading indicators (which indicate the controls in place to prevent an event from occurring), and trends (which consider patterns in the data that indicate risk). Root cause analysis is also important here in order to determine the root cause for any risk, not just the symptoms. This is where risk assessments and analysis, control evaluations, and other types of data collection and tests come into play, to give you this information.

Key Control Indicators

As discussed previously, KPIs are used to understand and enable the measurement of control performance. *Key control indicators (KCIs)* are often used interchangeably with KPIs, but they are really a subset of KPIs, since some KPIs don't necessarily relate to controls. KCIs are those specific indicators that show the relative effectiveness of controls. This effectiveness, as mentioned before, can be in how well a control protects an asset, how well a control helps with compliance with governance (for example, the number of compliant versus noncompliant controls), and, probably most importantly in our context, how well the control reduces or mitigates related risk. It is important that the control indicator focus on the specific control as well as the particular risk that the control is meant to mitigate. Associating a KCI with a broad spectrum of risk is not effective; it should be associated with a very specific risk scenario. For example, a KCI could indicate effectiveness of the control in terms of risk reduction, by showing how it reduces the impact of a particular risk scenario for a given asset, the likelihood that a threat will exercise a particular vulnerability, or the vulnerability itself.

KCIs should be developed based on the known performance tolerances of the control. You should determine what the normal operating parameters for the control are and what should be expected based on how the control is configured and implemented. Baselining control performance is important so that you understand what normal operation looks like. Abnormal or anomalous operation, such as a sudden spike in unknown network traffic, may indicate that the control is not operating within its normal range. This, in turn, shows the control may not be as effective as it should be.

Examples of key control indicators might include, but are definitely not limited to, the following:

- Bandwidth utilization
- Number of false positives or false negatives detected
- Number of instances of malware detected
- Number of incidences per month attributable to user complacency or policy violations
- Number of vulnerabilities discovered during a scan

Additionally, not all KCIs have to be technical in nature, although those likely are the majority of the ones many organizations concern themselves with. KCIs can be developed for not only technical controls but also administrative and physical controls as well.

Chapter Review

Once an organization has assessed and analyzed its risk, it must respond accordingly. In this chapter we discussed several key areas of risk response, including the different risk treatment and response options. Risk and control ownership are key to responsibility and accountability for risk response. Risk and control owners are not always business process owners, although they could be. Sometimes controls are dispersed across an organization and protect multiple assets in several areas at once. These are called *common controls*, and the control owners are common control providers. These entities are responsible and accountable for risk and its mitigation, respectively, and must be given the authority to carry out their responsibilities.

Risk treatment and response options include risk mitigation, risk sharing or transference, risk acceptance, and risk avoidance. Risk mitigation involves the reduction of risk through the implementation of adequate security controls. Risk sharing involves transferring risk to a third party, such as a cloud services provider, or through insurance. Note that even if risk is shared, responsibility and accountability are retained with the organization. Risk sharing usually involves offsetting financial responsibility or liability in the event of an incident or disaster. Risk acceptance means that the organization must accept any remaining or residual risk after all other risk response options have been implemented. Risk must be formally accepted and documented as well as monitored through the risk register. Risk avoidance does not mean simply ignoring risk; it means that an organization has chosen a different path or solution that eliminates a particular risk associated with an activity. Evaluating risk response options involves considering many factors, including the cost effectiveness of controls and how much they reduce risk versus the cost of the control and the asset's value, organizational structure, governance, and other factors. More often than not, more than one risk response is necessary.

Third-party risk management involves considering all the different threats, vulnerabilities, and other risk factors inherent to engaging with third-party providers. Third parties incur many of the same vulnerabilities and threats that other organizations do, including external attack, infrastructure and system vulnerabilities, governance issues, and so on. Key considerations with third parties include contractual obligations to protect data, division of legal liability, data ownership, and so on.

Issues, findings, and exceptions management means the organization must have proactive measures in place to reduce risk when situations or events occur that are out of the normal processing parameters or configuration baselines. Examples of these cases include vulnerabilities that cannot be easily remediated, exceptions to security policies, and compliance findings. Each of these types of events should be considered carefully for risk and mitigated as much as practical by the organization. In the end, exceptions may have to be made, but they must be formally approved by management after due risk consideration, thoroughly documented, and monitored through the risk register.

Risk is dynamic; it changes according to the operating environment, new technologies, the threat landscape, and organizational changes. These emergent risks must be considered, since they may present unknown vulnerabilities that might not surface for a long time after new technologies have been implemented or the environment has changed. Emerging technologies are a key source of emergent risk, and organizations must be careful about the rush to implement those technologies. The implementation of emerging or new technologies should justify a valid business need, and appropriate risk assessment and analysis should take place before their implementation. Risk responses should be changed based on those emergent risks.

Security controls are measures or safeguards implemented to protect organizational assets and reduce risk. The three general types of controls you must understand are administrative, technical, and physical. Administrative controls usually involve policies and procedures, technical controls involve equipment and software, and physical controls involve physical barriers used to protect people, equipment, and facilities. Control functions are divided into five general categories: deterrent, preventive, detective, corrective, and compensating. Deterrent controls must be known in order to be effective. Preventive controls do not have to be known in order to prevent a violation of policy or illegal act. Detective controls are used to discover a violation of policy or malicious act. Corrective controls are temporary in nature and are used to solve an immediate security issue. Compensating controls are more longer-term controls and are used when a primary or desired control is unavailable. There are several control frameworks published by various entities, including government and professional frameworks. Examples of these include the ISO/IEC 27001 controls, the NIST controls, and the PCI DSS control set.

Controls are evaluated and selected based on their effectiveness in protecting assets, the level of risk they help to reduce, and compliance with governance. Controls are also evaluated based on cost-effectiveness. If the cost of an asset and its continued maintenance versus the revenue it produces or its value to the organization compared to the cost of the controls used to protect it do not correspond, a decision must be made whether to implement the controls for the asset.

Several considerations go into control design, including reducing risk elements such as the likelihood of an event occurring, the impact to an asset, and the severity of the vulnerability. Threats cannot normally be reduced through controls, but their interactions with the organization can be mitigated through properly designed controls. Controls are selected based on several factors, which include the cost to acquire and maintain, the level of risk they reduce, and the amount of protection they offer. Existing controls in an organization can be leveraged if they provide the proper security protections and are interoperable with all systems. If desired controls cannot be implemented, compensating controls must be considered. Controls are analyzed at different points in their life cycle, particularly during installation and periodically to ensure they are still effective, comply with governance, and reduce risk. Controls may need to be updated or changed periodically when technology changes, the controls become outdated, threats to the organization increase, and the operating environment changes.

Control implementation must consider how the control will interact with the infrastructure. Change and configuration management processes are critical to ensuring the safe, secure, and stable implementation of new security controls. Both before and after controls have been installed, they should be tested to ensure they meet functional and performance requirements and are interoperable with the existing infrastructure. Controls must also be documented thoroughly and any risks should be included in the risk register. Controls must be periodically tested during various assessments by interviewing those responsible for maintaining the controls, reviewing all documentation related to the controls, observing the controls in operation to ensure they fulfill their security functions, and testing the controls through technical means.

Risk monitoring and reporting are necessary to conveying control and risk information to management. Internal management policy as well as external governance will drive reporting requirements. Risk practitioners should understand reporting requirements as well as stakeholder needs so that they will be able to report data with clarity, accuracy, completeness, and timeliness. Risk treatment options and plans should be conveyed to management through reporting channels on a periodic and as-needed basis, rather than after the risk response is complete. Data used to create information for consumption by managers should be accurate, complete, and trustworthy. Risk practitioners must determine, based on their audience, how the information is presented using various techniques. Risk control and monitoring techniques should be part of a formally approved risk management methodology and promulgated in the risk strategy, policy, and procedures. Various risk reporting techniques exist, including narrative reports, scorecards, graphs, and real-time information feeds such as those that are part of a centralized management dashboard.

Key performance indicators are pieces of information that measure and show performance levels of different aspects of the security and risk management programs. Key risk indicators show how risk has changed. Key control indicators show how effective controls are functioning and performing as well as ensure compliance and reduce risk.

Quick Review

- Risk response is what is needed after risk has been appropriately assessed and analyzed.
- Risk and control ownership must be carefully considered as part of risk response.
- Business process owners are not necessarily risk or control owners.
- Controls that span the entire organization are called common controls.
- There are four generally accepted risk responses: mitigation, sharing or transference, acceptance, and avoidance.
- Risk mitigation means to reduce risk through the implementation of controls.
- Risk sharing allows an organization to transfer some of the risk to a third-party provider or through insurance.
- Risk sharing does not absolve an organization of its responsibility, accountability, or legal liability.
- Risk acceptance means to take on any leftover risk after all other risk treatment options have been implemented.
- Risk avoidance does not mean to ignore risk; it simply means to avoid actions that result in the risk.

- Evaluating risk response options involves considering several factors, including cost, effectiveness, value of the asset, the organization, and governance, as well as other external factors.

- Third-party risk management means that the organization must manage any risk inherent to third-party risk sharing, contracts, and so on.

- Third-party risk factors include the same vulnerabilities and threats that other organizations encounter.

- Considerations with third-party risk include protection of controls, responsibility, accountability, legal liability, and data ownership.

- Issues, findings, and exceptions management helps to manage risk when there are departures from normal processes, security controls, or baselines.

- Exceptions must be approved by management, thoroughly documented, and tracked in the risk register.

- Emerging risk must be managed due to a changing operating environment, emerging technologies, or a changing threat landscape.

- Emerging technologies should not be immediately adopted until they have been evaluated for risk.

- The primary risks of emerging technologies include interoperability and compatibility with existing systems as well as security mechanisms.

- Controls are security measures or safeguards implemented to protect systems and data, ensure compliance with governance, and reduce risk.

- The three types of controls are administrative, technical, and physical.

- Administrative (managerial) controls are implemented through policies and procedures.

- Technical (logical) controls are implemented through hardware and software.

- Physical (operational) controls are implemented through physical barriers and systems used to protect people, equipment, data, and facilities.

- The five control functions are deterrent, preventative, detective, corrective, and compensating.

- Deterrent controls must be known in order to be effective.

- Preventative controls do not have to be known; they serve to prevent malicious actions or policy violations.

- Detective controls are used to discover or detect malicious actions or policy violations.

- Corrective controls are used to remedy an immediate security issue and are temporary in nature.

- Compensating controls are used in place of a preferred primary control and are generally longer-term in nature.

- Control frameworks are available to assist organizations in implementing controls to protect their systems, meet governance requirements, and reduce risk.

- Which control framework an organization selects may be based on governance. Some governance vehicles require specific controls, but others are more flexible.

- Control frameworks include the NIST controls, CIS controls, PCI DSS, and the ISO/IEC 27001/27002 control catalogs.

- Controls are designed and selected based on their cost effectiveness, how well they perform and function, how well they protect assets, how they assist in meeting compliance requirements, and how well they reduce risk.

- Controls are tested and evaluated during various points in their life cycle, including before and after implementation and during security assessments such as vulnerability assessments, risk assessments, and penetration testing.

- Controls can be tested using four primary methods: interviews with key personnel, documentation reviews, control observation, and technical testing.

- Change and configuration management are key processes involved in control implementation.

- Interoperability with the existing infrastructure is a key concern while implementing a new control.

- Controls must be thoroughly documented in the risk register.

- Risk responses and risk treatment options should be reported to management on both a periodic and as-needed basis.

- Risk practitioners should understand reporting requirements levied on the organization by both internal management and external governance.

- Risk practitioners should ensure that all data collected to form reports and give information to management must be complete, accurate, and trustworthy.

- Risk and control monitoring techniques should be part of the formally adopted risk management methodology and included in various documents, including risk strategy, policy, and procedures.

- Risk reporting techniques include narrative reports, charts, and graphs such as heat maps, scorecards, and centralized dashboards, among other techniques.

- The risk reporting technique used, as well as the complexity of the data and the goal of the report, should be tailored to the audience.

- Key performance indicators are pieces of information that help measure the performance of controls and other aspects of the security program as well as show progress toward the organization's goals in those areas.

- Key risk indicators show how risk has increased or been reduced.

- Key control indicators show how controls are performing and functioning in terms of effectiveness, compliance, or risk reduction.

Questions

1. You are the business process owner for the manufacturing department of your company. After a risk assessment, several key risks have been identified that directly involve the protection of data within your department. Both the IT security and physical security departments have security safeguards in place, or planned for implementation, to help reduce those risks. Which of the following most accurately describes ownership in this scenario?

    A. You are the risk owner, and the IT and physical security departments are the control owners.

    B. As the business process owner, you are both the risk and control owner.

    C. The IT and physical security departments own both the risk and the controls.

    D. Executive management owns both the risk and controls; neither you nor the IT and security department have any responsibility for that ownership.

2. As a risk practitioner in a larger organization, you have been asked to review the company's risk response options for a particular risk and make recommendations to the company's executive management. For some of the risk, there are obvious controls that could be implemented, but this will not completely eliminate all of the risk. None of the risk can be borne by any third party, and the business processes involved with the risk are extremely critical. Which of the following risk treatment options would you recommend after all possible mitigations have been put in place?

    A. Risk avoidance

    B. Risk mitigation

    C. Risk acceptance

    D. Risk sharing

3. Your company has just established a contract with a third-party cloud services provider. Based on the contract language, in the event of a breach, the provider must disclose details of the event as well as allow an audit of the security controls that should have protected any data disclosed during the breach. The contract language as well as laws and regulations also stipulate that the third-party provider retains some legal liability for the loss. Which of the following accurately describes the responsibility and accountability borne by both your organization and the third-party provider during this event?

    A. All the responsibility and accountability are placed on the third-party provider.

    B. All of the responsibility and accountability are placed on the organization.

    C. The third-party provider has the responsibility for protecting the data, but the organization retains accountability.

    D. Both the third-party provider and the organization bear responsibility and accountability for the loss of the data as well as legal liability.

4. Which of the following is the major risk factor associated with integrating new or emerging technologies into an existing IT infrastructure?

   A. Security mechanisms

   B. Data format

   C. Vendor supportability

   D. Interoperability

5. During a vulnerability scan of its systems, your organization discovers findings that cannot be remediated without breaking several critical line-of-business applications. Which of the following should be the path forward in determining a solution to this problem?

   A. You should patch the systems regardless of the impact of the line-of-business applications since security is far more critical to the organization. Business process owners must accept this and configure their line-of-business applications accordingly.

   B. You must not patch a system that would affect the line-of-business applications, since this affects the mission and bottom line of the organization, which is far more important to the organization than its security posture.

   C. You should employ the risk avoidance response by not worrying about the security or business ramifications of the problem, since it is beyond your control and will waste critical resources in addressing it.

   D. You should evaluate the risk of patching systems and suffering the impact to the line-of-business applications versus the security risk if the systems are not patched and then allow management to make a decision based on that risk. Any exceptions should be formally approved and documented.

6. Your company has implemented several new controls to strengthen security inside its facility. These controls include stronger steel doors, with new cipher locks, and two more guard stations to keep unauthorized personnel from entering sensitive areas. Which of the following types and functions would those new controls be considered?

   A. Physical, detective

   B. Physical, preventive

   C. Administrative, preventive

   D. Administrative, deterrent

7. Your company is now doing business internationally, and as a result, one of its key business partners overseas requires that it adopt international security standards. You examine several different standards, and you are already using internally developed controls that may be mapped to a new standard. Which of the following control standards is the most appropriate to use when working with international partners?

A. NIST SP 800-53

B. CIS controls

C. ISO/IEC 27001/27002

D. HIPAA controls

8. Your company is concerned about implementing controls for a new sensitive system it is about to install. Some existing controls can be easily used, but the new system will require more advanced network security devices since the data sensitivity requirements are much higher under laws and regulations imposed on the company. These laws and regulations mandate a higher level of protection because of the sensitivity of that system and data. Which of the following is the most important concern the company must consider when implementing the new security devices?

A. Cost

B. Compliance

C. Risk reduction

D. Interoperability

9. Your company has installed a new network security device and is testing it in parallel with the rest of the infrastructure before cutting over all systems on the infrastructure to rely on the device. Security mechanisms within the device meet your strict governance compliance requirements, and risk analysis shows that it can reduce risk of an external attack significantly. However, some but not all critical systems on the network refuse to communicate with the device, making it difficult to troubleshoot any issues and stopping critical data from transiting the network. Which of the following is the most likely issue you should examine?

A. Interoperability

B. Authentication mechanisms

C. Encryption mechanisms

D. Network protocol issues

10. Your organization is preparing to implement many new security controls, including upgrading legacy network security devices. While a thorough risk analysis has been performed, there is still uncertainty about how the network devices will interact with the rest of the infrastructure. Management is concerned with interoperability issues and the ability to monitor the installation carefully. Which of the following will assist in helping the implementation go smoothly?

   A. Vulnerability assessment prior to installation

   B. Parallel cutover

   C. Risk analysis

   D. Change and configuration management processes

11. You are collecting data for your annual risk and control effectiveness report to the company's board of directors. You're gathering data from multiple sources, but you are concerned about the usefulness of the data used to create a report. Which of the following is not a concern regarding the data you're collecting?

   A. Completeness

   B. Accuracy

   C. Trustworthiness

   D. Complexity

12. You are creating a schedule for risk reporting for various managers and events. Which of the following strategies should you employ regarding reporting of risk treatment options and plans?

   A. Report on their progress periodically and as needed.

   B. Report annually to senior management and quarterly to middle management.

   C. Report results only when the risk treatment options have been implemented and are complete.

   D. Do not report on risk treatment options; only report on increases or decreases in risk as required by governance.

13. Which of the following documents should describe the risk management methodology, to improve risk assessment and analysis methodologies, adopted by the organization?

   A. Risk management policy

   B. Risk management strategy

   C. Risk assessment procedures

   D. Organizational strategy

14. You are implementing a new method to quickly inform management of any changes in the overall control effectiveness or risk posture of the organization. You want it to be in near real time but only include the critical information necessary that managers need to make informed decisions. You also want management to have the ability to drill down into more detailed information if needed. Which of the following reporting techniques would fill these requirements?

    A. Heat map

    B. Narrative report

    C. Centralized dashboard

    D. Scorecard

15. You are developing metrics for senior management regarding control effectiveness and the risk posture of the organization. You need to create a metric that shows managers how potential risk has been reduced due to implementing several new controls over the past six months. You want to aggregate this measurement into one indicator. Which of the following would be the most effective indicator to show this reduction?

    A. Key performance indicator

    B. Key risk indicator

    C. Key management indicator

    D. Key control indicator

Answers

    1. **A.** As the business process owner, you have responsibility and accountability for the risk, while the IT and physical security departments are the control owners.

    2. **C.** After all other risk reductions and mitigation actions have been implemented, any residual risk must be accepted. Risk mitigation has already occurred, and the scenario states that risk cannot be shared with any third party. Since these are critical business processes, the risk cannot be avoided.

    3. **D.** Both the third-party provider and the organization bear some level of responsibility, accountability, and legal liability for the data loss since both the contract language and laws address this situation. However, it is likely that the organization will ultimately bear the most responsibility and accountability for the data loss to its customers.

    4. **D.** Interoperability is the major risk factor associated with integrating new or emerging technologies into an existing IT infrastructure. It covers a wide range of factors, typically including backward compatibility, data format, security mechanisms, and other aspects of system integration.

5. **D.** You should evaluate the risk of patching systems and suffering the impact to the line-of-business applications versus the security risk if the systems are not patched and then allow management to decide based on that risk. Any exceptions should be formally approved and documented. You cannot simply ignore the risk, and taking any action without carefully considering the risk would be detrimental to the organization, whether it is making the choice to break the line-of-business applications or ignoring the security ramifications of the problem.

6. **B.** The controls are *physical* because they involve using physical barriers to secure the interior of the facility. The controls are also *preventive* because they prevent people from entering sensitive, restricted areas. The controls are not administrative because they do not involve written policy or procedures established by management.

7. **C.** ISO/IEC 27001 and 27002 are international standards developed to ensure interoperability and translation of security controls across international boundaries. The other control sets, while they may possibly be used in areas outside the United States, are unique to the U.S.

8. **B.** Compliance is actually the most important consideration in this scenario because the company is installing a system that is considered sensitive enough to be regulated by laws and regulations. Since the data sensitivity requirements under those laws and regulations require that level of protection, the company has no choice but to implement those advanced network security devices, regardless of cost, interoperability, or any other consideration.

9. **A.** Interoperability seems to be the issue here. Since authentication and encryption mechanisms meet compliance standards, it may be that they are not interoperable with existing infrastructures. Network protocols aren't likely an issue since some devices on the network can communicate with the new device. All indications are that the new device may not be interoperable with some of the other devices, security mechanisms, or protocols on the network.

10. **D.** Proper change and configuration management processes will assist in an orderly implementation and changeover to the needed network security devices. Management has the ability to carefully consider, prove, and monitor changes to the infrastructure, with the ability to back out the changes according to defined processes if something goes wrong.

11. **D.** Data complexity is not an issue since it will be your job as risk practitioner to distill the data into understandable information for the board of directors. You are most concerned with the completeness of the data, how accurate it is, and whether it comes from a trustworthy source.

12. **A.** You should report the progress of risk treatment options both periodically, as determined by organizational policy, and as needed, depending on the criticality or importance of the information and the desires of management.

13. A. The risk management policy, which supports external and internal governance, should dictate the risk management methodology used by the organization. Often this methodology will include any risk assessment or analysis methods mandated for use. Both the risk management strategy and the overall organizational strategy are long-term, higher-level documents that do not go into this level of detail. Risk assessment procedures are step-by-step processes, activities, and tasks used to perform a risk assessment, but they do not direct overall risk management methodologies.

14. C. A centralized dashboard can supply all the necessary critical information managers need to view control effectiveness and risk posture, all in one location. Information can be fed to the dashboard in real time, and managers would have the ability to drill down on particular data elements to gain more details if needed.

15. B. In this scenario, a key risk indicator (KRI) could be developed to show the reduction in risk. A key performance indicator (KPI) would show the level of performance of a control or other aspect of organizational security, not necessarily the reduction in risk. A key control indicator (KCI) would show the effectiveness of a particular control, not the reduction in risk. Key management indicators are published by executive management and cover various metrics they are concerned with regarding the overall performance of organizational objectives. They do not indicate a reduction in risk.

Information Technology and Security

In this chapter, you will:

- Learn to describe how business goals, information criteria, and organizational structures affect risk
- Determine how enterprise architecture presents risk to the organization
- Analyze factors of enterprise risk, including areas such as data lifecycle management, hardware and software, third-party relationships, the system development life cycle, project management, business continuity and disaster recovery, IT operations management, and implementation of new technologies
- Learn basic information security concepts
- Examine different frameworks and standards

This chapter covers Certified in Risk and Information Systems Control Domain 4, "Information Technology and Security." The domain represents 22 percent of the CRISC examination.

The CRISC Task Statements relevant to this domain focus on several key activities found in an information security program, including identifying threats and vulnerabilities, establishing accountability through the assignment of risks and control ownership, creating a risk-aware culture through security awareness training, reviewing risk analyses, developing remediation plans to fill gaps, collaborating on the development of risk treatment plans and on the selection and design of controls, and ensuring that business practices align with risk management, risk appetite, and risk tolerance, and selected security frameworks.

Information is a commodity. Even if an organization is in the business of producing goods to bring to market, it still relies on its information and its technology as enablers to produce those goods and deliver them to the market and consumers. Without the ability to generate, process, and otherwise use information, modern businesses would not be able to produce goods or services and compete in market spaces. Therefore, any negative events that affect the organization's ability to process information directly affect the ability of the organization to survive. Information technology directly supports business goals, objectives, and strategies. All elements of a business endeavor depend on IT, including the organization's information (or data), its people, its line-of-business applications and systems, and its overall infrastructure, including all of its equipment and processes.

Information technology affects risks to the business enterprise in two different ways. First, information technology is used to help *protect* the enterprise from risk; in other words, it serves to protect the information the business generates and relies on. That's the purpose of having high-capacity storage, faster networking equipment, redundant systems, and security devices sprinkled throughout the infrastructure. The second way that IT affects risk is that it helps the organization to *produce* the information needed to fulfill its business goals and objectives in the first place. Without IT, there would be no information processed, no systems designed, and no advanced technologies developed for a business to take to market and compete with. Therefore, IT serves to both protect information and generate it to advance business goals.

The information the business generates and uses has several key characteristics. First, the information should be relevant to the processes that the business supports. It should also be timely; stale information can prevent a business from fulfilling its functions in both short-term and long-term time frames. It should also be accurate and complete. This is where information integrity comes in, which is one of the goals of information security. Anything that affects the accuracy and completeness of information is a risk. Information should also be controlled for access. Confidentiality is one of the goals of information security, and controlled access to information and the systems that process it is a must to maintain business function. As you might guess, another characteristic of business information is its availability to the users who need it whenever and however they need it. This means that authorized users should have business information, again, on a timely basis, but also in a format that suits their needs. Risk factors that affect any of these information characteristics, such as relevance, timeliness, integrity, confidentiality, and availability, must be considered in the overall risk management process for the organization. Any detrimental impact on these characteristics presents a risk to the business mission.

Enterprise Architecture

The enterprise architecture within an organization affects the business's risk in several different ways. Aspects of enterprise architecture risk include interoperability, supportability, security, maintenance, and how the different pieces and parts of the infrastructure fit into the systems development life cycle. The business views IT as an investment of capital funds, much like it does facilities and other equipment: as a means of supporting the business mission. Information systems represent a risk to the business because of interoperability, supportability, security, and other issues. It costs the organization money to maintain and support all the IT assets within the organization, in the form of parts, software licenses, training for administrators and users, and upgrades. There are also the intangible aspects of IT, such as business value and liability. IT systems affect the bottom line of the organization, so a lot of thought is put into managing risk for them. Additionally, you should take care to remember that information technology risk is only a piece of the entire enterprise risk picture. In the next few sections, we're going to talk about different aspects of the information systems architecture and how they contribute to the overall enterprise risk in the organization.

Platforms

Platforms are an element of the enterprise infrastructure that contributes to information security and business risk for several reasons. First, it costs to field and simultaneously maintain different operating systems and environments that come in different platforms. Platforms also introduce risk into the environment in the form of interoperability, security, and supportability. A diverse platform environment (with mixed platforms, such as Windows, Linux, Macs, Unix, and so on) can affect interoperability with other systems due to different versions of software, different network protocols, security methods, and so on. A diverse environment can also affect supportability because the organization must maintain different skillsets and a wide knowledge base to support the diverse platforms.

On the other hand, maintaining a homogeneous environment can reduce costs, ensure interoperability, and allow a more common set of security controls and mechanisms, such as patch management and configuration management. However, there is even risk involved in a homogeneous platform environment because of the likelihood that a vulnerability discovered in one system would also be shared in many others, offering a wider attack vector for a potential malicious actor. It is really a matter of the systems development life cycle as to how and when platforms are developed, introduced into the infrastructure, implemented, maintained, and, eventually, disposed of, and there is risk inherent in all of these different phases, as we'll discuss in more detail later.

Software

Software introduces risk simply because, today, it's so critical to business operations. Businesses need not only basic word processing and spreadsheet software but also complex databases, line-of-business applications, specialized software, security software, and other types of applications. Software must be managed within its own life cycle as well; it is constantly being patched, upgraded, superseded, and replaced by better, faster software with more features that usually costs more. Risks that are inherent to managing applications within an organization include supportability, backward compatibility, data format compatibility, licensing, and proper use.

Adding to this complexity are the decisions an organization makes in terms of the selection of proprietary software, open-source software, general-purpose commercial software, or highly specialized software. All these different categories incur different levels of cost, supportability, licensing, and feature sets. Interoperability also plays a part in application risk, as it does with other infrastructure components. Applications that do not use common data formats or produce usable output for the organization create the risk of expense or additional work that goes into transforming data between incompatible applications. Applications also introduce risk into the business environment with the level of security mechanisms built into them and how effective those security mechanisms are in protecting data residing in the application.

It's worth mentioning here that web-based applications, in addition to presenting the same risks as normal client-server apps, also have their own unique risks. Security is a definite risk imposed by web-based applications since they often directly connect to unprotected networks such as the Internet. Other risks include those that come from the wide variety of web programming languages and standards available for developers to use.

Databases

Databases, as a subset of applications, impose some of the same risks that applications and other software do. Additionally, databases incur risks associated with data aggregation, compatibility, privacy, and security. Aggregation and inference are risks associated with database systems. Unauthorized access and data loss are also huge risks that databases introduce into the enterprise environment.

Operating Systems

Although we discussed platforms in a previous section, it's also worth mentioning operating systems as their own separate risk element in the enterprise infrastructure. The terms *platform* and *operating system* are sometimes used interchangeably, but, truthfully, a platform is more a hardware architecture than an operating system categorization. A platform could be an Intel PC or a tablet chipset, for example, which are designed and architected differently and run totally different operating systems. Different operating systems, on the other hand, could run on the same platform but still introduce risk into the organization for the same reasons discussed previously with applications. For example, there are interoperability and supportability risks and all the other issues that go hand in hand with the normal operating system life cycle, such as patch and vulnerability management. Licensing, standardization, level of user control, and configuration are also issues that introduce risk into the organizational computing environment.

 EXAM TIP Although information security professions tend to focus more on the technical aspects of IT risks, for the exam, keep in mind that all IT risks also contribute to the overall business risks in the enterprise. Make sure you look at the larger picture beyond the IT realm.

Networks

Networks are another aspect of enterprise infrastructure that is absolutely critical to protecting data. They are most effective when they are implemented in a way that not only incorporates the business logic of the organization but also follows the data flow—taking into account how the software is most implemented and integrated with other systems such as databases.

Let's first take a step back to understand what a network is. At its most basic level, a network is a mechanism that allows systems to communicate with each other. The components are often devices such as switches (for local network communication) and routers (for communications between networks). There are a number of protection mechanisms on networks such as firewalls (which regulate network traffic), intrusion protection systems (which protect traffic at a deeper level than firewalls), threat intelligence gateways (which are designed to protect external networks prior to connecting to firewalls), and so on. This is only a sampling of the protective technologies that are network based. The deeper the understanding of the technologies, the more granular a risk assessor may be.

The philosophy one uses to set up the location of protective network devices can be referred to as the architecture. For example, for sensitive data, most compliance frameworks require that the data not be stored in the database on the same local network segment as a web server. This way, if the web server is compromised, attackers will not have immediate access to the data. If they sit on the same network, that may be considered a higher risk in a risk assessment—the recommendation being to move the database to another network behind the web server, with firewalls and intrusion detection systems being the intermediary between the two local networks.

Another factor to consider is encryption of data in motion. If a legacy system does not have encryption and it is sending data to another location on the Internet, there is a risk to anyone between the networks for an on-path attack (formerly known as a "man-in-the-middle attack"). A VPN tunnel can be set up between the two networks to ensure that at least the traffic is encrypted as it traverses the networks (or Internet).

In the end, networks and networking can be extremely challenging and detailed. What we have covered here only scratches the surface of what is entailed by networks and networking. It is worth your time to explore this topic in depth to help create a better network and ultimately add to a risk assessment.

Cloud

No book on risk would be complete without considering cloud-based risks. The concept of "Anything as a Service" (XaaS) means that, for a price, nearly anything a user or company would use a computing system for can be delivered to them by a cloud service provider through the cloud infrastructure—typically through a thin client or web interface. In such a serverless architecture, a cloud provider manages the server and associated architecture and allocates resources as necessary to the end users. This requires less upfront investment in hardware and software by the customer, greater scalability, and centralized management for administration and security concerns. Each cloud infrastructure is a little different, but there are three main types of cloud infrastructure to consider when looking at risk:

- *Software as a Service (SaaS)* allows a customer to essentially lease software, such as applications and databases, thus enabling rapid rollout to the greater user community.

- *Platform as a Service (PaaS)* provides the framework of an operating system and associated software required to perform a function (for example, the Linux operating system and components needed to run a web server).

- *Infrastructure as a Service (IaaS)* provides the ability to quickly stand up virtual machines, storage devices, and other infrastructure that would otherwise require the purchase of physical devices.

Gateways

A number of other technologies that can be used to protect organizations can be factored into a risk assessment. For example, secure e-mail gateways and secure web gateways are a must-have to protect organizations from web-based threats. These technologies can help to filter malware, block malicious links or websites, help prevent phishing, or a host of other tasks. Technically, they do not fit into the category of other technologies so they deserve special mention. A good risk assessor will learn about these technologies and how they can help reduce the risks related to the organization. That knowledge can be applied to the risk assessment process.

Enterprise Architecture Frameworks

Another facet to consider is enterprise architecture (EA). This is different from network architecture, presented earlier. EA focuses on the relationship between business and technology. In most cases, this includes the relationship between security and technology. It is very important because it provides a view into the governance of an organization, which can provide insight into some core problems that cause risks within the organization.

Two frameworks for enterprise architecture are discussed in this book: The Open Group Architecture Framework (TOGAF) and the Zachman framework.

 NOTE TOGAF and the Zachman framework are enterprise architecture models, not enterprise *security* architecture models.

The Open Group Architecture Framework

TOGAF is a lifecycle enterprise architecture framework used for designing, planning, implementing, and governing an enterprise technology architecture. TOGAF could be considered a high-level approach for designing enterprise infrastructure.

The phases used in TOGAF are as follows:

- Preliminary
- Architecture vision
- Business architecture
- Information systems architecture
- Technology architecture
- Opportunities and solutions
- Migration planning
- Implementation governance
- Architecture change management
- Requirements management

Figure 4-1
TOGAF
components

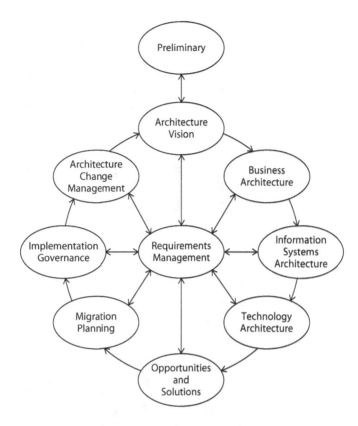

TOGAF is a business-driven, lifecycle management framework for enterprise architecture overall, and it certainly can be used for information security architecture as well. Figure 4-1 depicts TOGAF visually.

You can find information on TOGAF at https://www.opengroup.org/togaf.

The Zachman Framework

The Zachman enterprise architecture framework, established in the late 1980s, continues to be a dominant EA standard today. Zachman likens IT enterprise architecture to the construction and maintenance of an office building: at an abstract level, the office building performs functions such as containing office space. As you look into increasing levels of detail in the building, you encounter various trades (steel, concrete, drywall, electrical, plumbing, telephone, fire control, elevators, and so on), each of which has its own specifications, standards, regulations, construction and maintenance methods, and so on. Zachman can easily be used to develop an enterprise security architecture as part of the enterprise architecture.

In the Zachman framework, IT systems and environments are described at a high, functional level and then in increasing detail, encompassing systems, databases, applications, networks, and so on. Table 4-1 illustrates the Zachman framework.

	Data	Functional (Application)	Network (Technology)	People (Organization)	Time	Strategy
Scope	List of data sets important in the business	List of business processes	List of business locations	List of organizations	List of events	List of business goals and strategy
Enterprise Model	Conceptual data/ object model	Business process model	Business logistics	Workflow	Master schedule	Business plan
Systems Model	Logical data model	System architecture	Detailed system architecture	Human interface architecture	Processing structure	Business rule model
Technology Model	Physical data/ class model	Technology design	Technology architecture	Presentation architecture	Control structure	Rule design
Detailed Representation	Data definition	Program	Network architecture	Security architecture	Time definition	Rule speculation
Function Enterprise	Usable data	Working function	Usable network	Functioning organization	Implemented schedule	Working strategy

Table 4-1 Zachman Framework Showing IT Systems in Increasing Levels of Detail

While the Zachman framework allows an organization to peer into cross-sections of an IT environment that supports business processes, the model does not convey the relationships between IT systems. Data flow diagrams are used instead to depict information flows.

Information about the Zachman framework is available at https://www.zachman.com/about-the-zachman-framework.

Implementing a Security Architecture

Organizations use different means for implementing a security architecture. Because security architecture is both a big-picture pursuit and a detailed plan, different decision makers may be involved, and different business processes are used.

At the enterprise level, the organization will use its policy and governance functions to make decisions about major aspects of security architecture, such as decisions about the brands of servers, workstations, and network devices to be used.

At the detail level, processes such as configuration management and change management are used to implement device characteristics on individual devices or groups of devices. For instance, an upgrade to an organization's Domain Name System (DNS) infrastructure might result in an increase in the number of name servers in use, necessitating that most or all devices in the organization be updated accordingly.

Over time, organizations will make changes to their architecture models (both at the macro level and micro level). For instance, changes and advances in technologies such as software-defined networking (SDN), virtualization, and microservices architectures will compel organizations to revise their enterprise security architecture. However, updating architecture documents is only the beginning. Organizations will also initiate tasks or projects to implement these improvements in their environment. Some of these changes, such as updates to industry device-hardening standards, may result in little more than change management to update a few configuration settings, but other changes may involve multiyear projects to modernize some aspect of an organization's environment.

IT Operations Management

Managing the enterprise infrastructure is one of the most work-intensive efforts in an organization, especially in a larger business. The enterprise infrastructure in an organization covers a broad scope of areas. Infrastructure, of course, covers workstations, printers, and other end-user devices. It also covers the major pieces needed to conduct business, such as servers, cabling, switches, routers, and a variety of other network and security devices. Most organizations also include wireless networks in their supporting equipment. Additionally, the infiltration of mobile devices into businesses makes this a new and sometimes difficult area to bring under the organization's infrastructure umbrella. Challenges with the enterprise infrastructure include not only maintenance, upgrades, updates, and implementing new technologies but also includes some of the more typical traditional management challenges, such as budgeting, project management, and staffing.

Key areas in IT operations management include server and infrastructure management, end-user support, help desk, problem escalation management, and, of course, cybersecurity. IT managers must maintain and meet any internal agreements that cover guaranteed service delivery in support of the different divisions within the organization, as well as service level agreements (SLAs) with other organizations. While information security personnel tend to focus more on IT risk, we find that most of the risk factors, threats, and vulnerabilities affecting IT also affect all the operations within the business. In the next few paragraphs, however, we'll focus on those that directly affect managing the IT operations in an organization.

Management of IT operations incurs risk factors such as the size and complexity of the organization and its IT infrastructure, the criticality and priority of the different systems that make up the infrastructure, and the internal management processes of the organization. Resourcing issues also affect the management piece of IT operations; staffing the right people who have trained on the various technologies the organization needs as well as creating a budget that helps maintain the current level of support and future growth for IT are examples of resource-related risk factors. Additionally, compliance with legal and governance requirements in the face of increased regulation are also risk factors the IT managers must deal with.

Organizational structure also affects IT operations because the IT infrastructure may be managed on either a centralized or a decentralized basis—sometimes by one centralized IT shop, or in the case of larger organizations, by multiple areas within other divisions that are delegated the task of managing their own piece of the infrastructure. IT might also be managed on a functional basis; the accounting and human resources divisions may have the responsibility for managing the systems that support their mission. Additionally, the IT infrastructure may be managed on a geographical basis, in the case of physically separated locations in large organizations. All these structural considerations are factors that contribute to risk in managing IT operations.

Also directly affecting IT operations risk are two key processes: the change and configuration management processes. We've already discussed risk factors that affect the SDLC model in an organization, as well as how new and emerging technologies can affect the existing infrastructure. These same risk factors also directly affect the daily management of IT operations simply because they introduce change into the network. Some of this change can be planned and carefully introduced, but often there is change—from the large-scale network side, all the way down to individual configuration items on hosts—that may have unforeseen consequences and affect the network in different ways. How the organization deals with change and configuration management is a risk factor that affects not only the SDLC but also the management of day-to-day operations.

Threats that affect the IT operations are like those that affect other areas of the business and could be external or internal threats from a variety of sources. Some of these threats have a ripple effect in that they may first affect other areas of business and, in turn, affect IT. For example, the threat of a poor economy may affect the profitability and sustainment of the business, resulting in cuts, which often include IT personnel or equipment. Obviously, there are also direct threats to the daily management of the IT infrastructure. These include external threats such as hackers, of course, but also more commonly come as increases in cost to maintain operations, issues with external service providers, and disaster-related events (weather, fire, and so on). Internal threats could include those carried out by malicious insiders or even careless workers, such as theft, sabotage, accidental equipment breakage, and so on. Internal threats could also come from management processes and include budget cuts, loss of trained personnel, shifts in organizational priorities, and transitioning from one market segment to another.

Technical vulnerabilities are beyond the scope and purpose of this book; our focus here is on those associated with the IT management aspect of the organization. Vulnerabilities affecting IT management include faulty processes and procedures, lack of resources, and lack of trained technical personnel. An end-user population that has not been trained or held accountable for proper care and treatment of the infrastructure could also be a vulnerability. Other vulnerabilities might include a lack of infrastructure monitoring, a lack of control of sensitive information in IT systems, and a failure to maintain a stable SDLC throughout the entire infrastructure.

Project Management

Organizations use project, program, and portfolio management to oversee and sustain both short- and long-term aspects of systems and processes. These categories apply to the scope and scale of different sets of activities or processes within an organization. *Projects* are limited duration sets of activities geared toward a particular goal; *programs* are ongoing, longer term, and may also encompass several individual projects as well as other activities specific to processes that may have an indefinite duration. *Portfolio* management is the oversight of several different programs by a senior person in the organization. Keep in mind that the major difference between a project and a program is duration; a project has a definite beginning and ending, whereas a program is indefinite.

At the core of a project are three primary drivers: the scope (the amount or range of work), schedule (when work is to be done and its completion date), and cost (including all the resources expended toward the completion of the project). All projects depend on these three elements to ensure success. Any shortfalls in cost, delays in schedule, or out-of-scope work (also called *scope creep)* affect the ability of the project to succeed, on time, within budget, and all the agreed-upon work completed. We'll discuss the risk factors that can affect all three of these elements next.

Since the three major elements of a project or program are scope, schedule, and cost, risk factors associated with projects and programs primarily affect each of these elements. Factors that affect scope often come from disagreement on exactly what work must be accomplished, in what order, and who will do it. These factors should be examined and agreed upon during the requirements process, where the project is formally scoped.

In complex projects, factors that may affect scope include the necessity to task workers from different sections or departments, the exact amount of work to be done, in what order it will be done, and the priority of each task and subtask. The political culture within the organization can adversely affect scope as well since there may be disagreement between departments or executives on what work is required and whose responsibility it is to accomplish it.

The scheduling component of a project has several risk factors as well. The amount of work to be done (scope) affects the schedule as a risk factor because of the time given to accomplish a specific amount of work and the resources allocated to this work. Lack of workers or materials adversely affects the schedule, as does the availability of equipment, work location or site, and external factors such as contract negotiations, government shutdowns, and so on, as examples.

Cost risk factors stem from lack of budget control during the project, including an inaccurate budget or estimation of cost, unexpected expenditures, a weak economy, and so on. Project costs are affected by the cost of labor (to include wages, insurance, and benefits) as well as the cost of supplies or materials needed to complete the project. Additionally, since all three of the elements of scope, schedule, and cost are also risk factors for each other, a delay in schedule or any extra, out-of-scope work impacts the project budget and costs as well.

Other risk factors for projects include training, staffing the project with the right mixture of personnel who have the right skill sets, attitudes, and focus on making the project or program a success. A manager without the right project management skill set is a risk factor that can affect scope, schedule, and cost if they do not manage those three critical elements properly. A technician without the right technical skills may cost the project more money in training or delay work unnecessarily due to rework or slow production.

In addition to factors such as scope, cost, and schedule, adding an indefinite or longer-term duration affects programs as a risk factor because you must project how they will be staffed, funded, equipped, and otherwise managed in the future, over a longer, indeterminate period. Therefore, risk factors could be long term and fluctuate over that time. Factors such as market, economy, and technology changes will influence risk in a program much more so than a project, affecting its scope, schedule, and cost over a longer period.

The threats to a project or program are similar; the major difference is the duration of the time that the threat represents potential harm to a project or program. Keep in mind that threats for a project or program aren't those you might traditionally think of as threat sources; they are rarely malicious in nature and usually come from the business environment itself. For example, threats to cost are usually those that involve money or resource issues, such as price increases, currency value fluctuation, stock market variations, and so on. These are usually external threats; internal threats to costs might include a sudden budget restructuring, cutting funds for a project, bankruptcy, and so on. Threats to the schedule might include worker shortage, strikes, inadequate training, delays in contract negotiations, delays from suppliers, and so on. Scope threats usually involve extra or additional work due to faulty requirements gathering and decisions about what falls into the project's scope and scale.

 NOTE Sometimes it's difficult to distinguish between threats to each of these elements individually and threats that affect all three project elements simultaneously, as it is more often the case that any threat affecting one element will usually, even indirectly, affect all three.

Since vulnerabilities are weaknesses or a lack of protective controls, the vulnerabilities found in project and program management are inherent to weaknesses in their critical elements and processes. For example, a weakness often found in the cost element of a project or program is a failure of the organization to adequately budget for all the resources it requires for the project. The organization might not list every piece of equipment or every major supply it needs or consider labor costs such as overtime in the event of schedule slippage. It may not adequately negotiate firm prices with a supplier, who then may raise prices on critical parts or equipment. These are all vulnerabilities inherent to the budgeting and cost elements of a project.

Scheduling also has some common vulnerabilities associated with it. If an organization fails to build in potential scheduling delays, such as work stoppages, dependencies on other organizations to fulfill parts of the schedule or even holidays, this can lead to problems with getting the project completed on time. Another scheduling vulnerability is to incorrectly estimate the amount of time it takes to perform a task or get a piece of work accomplished.

Vulnerabilities inherent to the scope element of a project affect how much work must be done, in what order, and by whom. A *work breakdown structure (WBS)* is a document that the project manager develops that covers exactly all this information and more. The WBS describes, in excruciating detail, the work, its subcomponent parts and tasks, what skill sets are needed, and what resources are required to do the job. Other documents may break down individual tasks into much more detail, even describing step by step how a task is accomplished. If the project manager and team do not create these documents, this is a weakness in that the work may not be performed exactly as needed. Resources may not be adequately allocated for the work, or the work may be performed by unskilled persons. Additionally, the amount and quality of work may not be performed to requirements. Failure to set requirements initially in the project and periodically check and track the work against those requirements are also vulnerabilities associated with scope since they can affect whether or not the work meets the established requirements.

An additional vulnerability that simultaneously affects all three project elements is the failure to monitor or control all these elements on an ongoing basis throughout the life of the project or program. Scope, schedule, and cost must be monitored on a continuing basis to ensure that they meet the original requirements set forth in the project's charter.

Risk Factor	Threat	Threat Agent	Vulnerability	Affects
Unstable economy	Cost increases for critical parts	Supplier	Tight budget or inexact budget estimates	Cost
Inability to accurately define scope during requirements meetings	Scope creep; inexact work specifications	Different department managers and supervisors	Lack of defined scope or work specifications	Scope
Manufacturing expensive parts for sensitive components	Delays due to inability to receive spare or replacement parts	Supplier	Lack of critical parts	Schedule
Training levels/ skill sets	Incomplete or shoddy work	Untrained worker	Precision or delicate work required	All

Table 4-2   Examples of Project Risk Factors, Threats, and Vulnerabilities

The project or program manager must monitor and control these things to prevent cost overruns, schedule slippage, and scope creep. Failure to monitor or control these elements is a serious vulnerability and could jeopardize the success of the entire project or program. Table 4-2 gives examples of some of the risk factors, threats, and vulnerabilities related to project and program management.

Business Continuity and Disaster Recovery Management

Business continuity and disaster recovery management are necessary parts of running a business, regardless of its market area. This is because incidents, disasters, and other negative events happen to all organizations eventually, despite the most favorable conditions and the most careful planning. Business continuity and disaster recovery are primarily concerned with the goal of business resilience. An entire area of expertise is dedicated to this goal with these processes in mind; sometimes, it's referred to as *continuity management.*

One thing to keep in mind is the difference between business continuity and disaster recovery. Business continuity is concerned with the careful planning and deployment of resources involved in keeping the mission of the business going (that is, keeping the business functioning regardless of negative events). This process is more long term and requires continual commitment from the organization. Disaster recovery, on the other hand, is primarily concerned with the quick reaction involved with preserving lives, equipment, and data immediately following a serious negative event. Disaster recovery is (hopefully) a short duration process and does not concern itself with conducting the daily mission of the business. Business continuity is more concerned with the long-term survival of the business, while disaster recovery is more concerned with the short-term process of reacting to a disaster. While closely related, these two efforts are not the same thing; in fact, disaster recovery could be viewed as a subset of the activities that go on during the overall continuity management strategy.

Business Impact Analysis

Business continuity planning involves several steps. Since the focus of this domain isn't solely on business continuity and disaster recovery, we're not going to go into an in-depth treatment of these processes. However, we will discuss some of the basic concepts of business continuity and disaster recovery as they relate to risk. Two of the key processes involved in business continuity planning are conducting a *business impact assessment (BIA)* and determining a recovery strategy. A business impact assessment closely resembles some of the steps you would take during a risk assessment, simply because you are identifying assets (which include, of course, people, equipment, facilities, and processes) and prioritizing those assets. The reason they are prioritized is that in the event a disaster was to occur, the business would have to rely on certain assets or processes more so than others to get back in business. These critical assets or processes should be brought back online and recovered first, but to accomplish this, they must be identified by the organization, and plans have to be made for their recovery. That's where the business impact assessment comes in. The organization must identify critical processes and assets, prioritize them for recovery, and, additionally, measure the impact on the business if those assets or processes were lost for any given amount of time due to an incident or negative event. Business impact analysis was described in more detail in Chapter 2.

Recovery Objectives

Two key areas of concern in business continuity are the *recovery point objective (RPO)* and the *recovery time objective (RTO)*. Both areas can be measured in the context of time. The recovery point objective is the amount of data that can be lost based on a time measurement. In other words, if the recovery point objective is two days, the most amount of data that can be lost without a serious effect on the organization's ability to function would be two days' worth of data. Note that this measurement isn't concerned with the actual amount of data in terms of quantity, such as gigabytes, for example; instead, it's concerned with measuring how many days or hours' worth of data can be lost, at most, without impeding the function of the business. The recovery time objective, also measured in terms of time, is the maximum amount of time the organization can afford to lose before it starts recovery. This measurement of time could be days, hours, minutes, or even seconds.

Recovery Strategies

The recovery strategy developed by the organization is a result of careful planning, as well as budgeting and allocating resources to the continuity management efforts. The recovery strategy should address the most efficient methods of getting the business back online and functioning after properly responding to the critical needs of protecting people and equipment during the disaster itself. Keep in mind that recovering the business to an operational state does not necessarily mean it will be working at 100 percent of its previous operational capacity; the business may only be able to get a few key services up immediately following a disaster. The organization should take a realistic look at the degree of continuity possible, given the seriousness and scope of the disaster, its resources, the environment it is working with after the disaster, and the availability of people, supplies, infrastructure, facilities, and equipment. All of this should be considered in the recovery strategy planning.

Plan Testing

Testing the disaster recovery plan is of critical importance; without testing the plan, the organization won't really know whether it's effective until a disaster occurs. Normally, that's a bit too late to find out that you haven't carefully considered all the different events that could occur during a disaster and how you will deal with them. Testing the plan involves making sure that people know what their responsibilities are, that they are well-trained, that they have all the equipment and resources needed to adequately respond to disaster, and that they practice these responses. Testing the disaster recovery plan will point out deficiencies in training, equipment, resources, and response activities.

NOTE Much more information on business continuity and disaster recovery planning can be found in National Institute of Standards and Technology (NIST) Special Publication 800-34, "Contingency Planning Guide for Federal Information Systems," which was written for use by government agencies but can be used by anyone or any business to help in understanding and planning for business continuity.

Resilience and Risk Factors

Resilience is a term that refers to the ability of the business to survive negative events and continue with its mission and function. In other words, it could be said that resilience is the ability of an organization to resist the effects of negative events and its ability to bounce back after one of these events. Resilience can affect to what degree different risk factors, as well as threats and vulnerabilities, have on impacting the normal business operations of the organization. A more resilient organization can better tolerate risk factors and the effects they have on the organization's ability to prepare for and respond to negative events.

Various risk factors can affect the organization's ability to respond to disasters as well as to continue the business and mission functions after it has recovered from a disaster. Some of these risk factors are inherent to the organization itself; these include the size of the organization, its facilities, its people, and how well it has performed business continuity and disaster recovery planning. A higher level of management commitment to business continuity planning reduces the effect of risk factors on the business; less commitment may render the organization more susceptible to these risk factors. A larger organization may have more complexity in terms of the number of people to take care of during a disaster, as well as the number of critical assets or processes that must be planned for. Small organizations don't necessarily have an advantage; however, a small organization may have fewer resources to adequately plan for and address business continuity and disaster recovery.

Another risk factor that an organization could face is physical location and geography. For example, a business situated on the U.S. Gulf Coast is probably more susceptible to adverse weather, such as hurricanes and tornadoes, than a business located inland. Businesses that are in areas prone to heavy flooding or have forest fires or extreme snowstorms at various times of the year should plan for these weather conditions appropriately. Distance could also be a risk factor; if the organization is located farther away from population centers or infrastructure services (such as fire departments, police, hospitals, telecommunications providers, and so on), there is a greater risk that the organization could not adequately respond to a disaster.

There are also risks associated with third-party providers, and these providers can affect business continuity and disaster recovery as well. Yet another risk factor could be the degree of outsourcing the organization is involved with. A business that outsources some of its processes or key functions may have less control over those functions or processes during an incident or disaster. The business may be at the mercy of the third party with whom they are contracted and subject to the third party's disaster recovery strategies (or lack thereof). Business continuity and disaster recovery are two areas that should be carefully considered when engaging in business with any external provider, usually through a service level agreement or another method.

In addition to the factors we discussed previously, the very nature of the organization's mission or business could be a risk factor. Organizations that have critical processes or produce critical goods and services that are time-sensitive, for example, may incur more risk than an organization that can afford to be down or out of service for a few days. Time sensitivity can increase the impact of a disaster on an organization, so it should be considered when developing continuity and recovery strategies. Market factors, such as the perishability of goods, for example, can become risk factors that an organization must deal with as well.

Most people associate the threats involved with business continuity and disaster recovery with natural disasters. Obviously, natural threats exist: severe weather, earthquakes, fires, and so on. These are threats that can't be typically prevented or neutralized, but they can be planned for. Hardened facilities, adequate ventilation, fire suppression systems, and other physical or environmental controls can mitigate the damage from these threats. On the other hand, man-made threats can also affect the ability of an organization to recover from an incident or continue to function. These can be broken down into unintentional and intentional threats. Intentional threats include those associated with hackers, terrorists, theft, and other malicious actors and activities. Unintentional threats may be attributed to accidents that are caused by carelessness, lack of training, and so on. All of these threats, both natural and man-made, are usually the types that cause incidents or disasters. However, there are also threats to the continuity management process itself.

Threats to the business's ability to manage its continuity and disaster recovery include incomplete or inadequate planning as well as limited resources to carry out any BCP/DRP activities. Because of regulatory considerations in many cases, a business usually must have some degree of business continuity planning accomplished; the real threat centers on whether it is enough and adequately covers the different facets of recovery and continuity that the business must consider. Usually, inadequate planning and insufficient resources committed to this area are a result of shortsightedness on the part of the organization's leadership and management.

A wide variety of vulnerabilities can affect the ability of an organization to respond to and recover from an incident or disaster. The same vulnerabilities can also, in turn, affect the organization's ability to continue to function at some level or degree after the disaster. Some of these vulnerabilities involve the lack of resources, such as a lack of personnel, equipment or facilities, or dedicated recovery resources. For instance, if the organization has not acquired an alternate processing site, there may be no way it can quickly recover its operations back to a functional state. Other vulnerabilities include the lack of training for personnel tasked with disaster recovery or business continuity responsibilities. Additionally, there are also process vulnerabilities. Process vulnerabilities are those that result from a failure of the organization's management to adequately plan for, staff, and equip continuity management efforts. For example, a lack of management commitment is a vulnerability that will certainly lead to a lack of training, resources, and personnel dedicated to continuity management. An inadequate or nonexistent business impact assessment is a vulnerability because an organization won't be able to adequately identify its critical processes or assets and determine how the loss of those critical items impacts the organization. Another critical vulnerability could be faced if the organization has failed to adequately test the response plan.

 EXAM TIP Be familiar with the different business process areas and their respective risk factors, threats, and vulnerabilities. Remember that risk factors, while not a threat or a vulnerability, contribute to the overall risk of the organization by increasing or decreasing the likelihood or impact of threats exploiting vulnerabilities or the organization's resilience to negative events.

Data Lifecycle Management

Most organizations produce a wide variety of documentation—from publications for internal use, to confidential papers for senior management, to publicly available documents. Without proper controls, such documentation could be used to compromise an organization's security. Every organization should have guidelines that ensure all documents produced by the organization are classified, organized, and stored securely to prevent their loss, damage, or theft.

As part of its governance and risk management programs, an organization should develop data lifecycle management programs. This process also contributes to the business continuity planning we previously discussed. The organization takes a good look at all its data, categorizes it in terms of sensitivity and type (PII, proprietary, government classified, and so on), and assigns classification values to it. To ensure control over the protection and distribution of data, it needs to be classified with a certain designation.

This data classification indicates what type of document it is, whether the information it contains is confidential or can be made public, and to whom it can be distributed. The classification also defines what levels of data retention and storage are needed for that document. Finally, policies must exist concerning the legal status of data and what can be destroyed and what needs to be retained.

Standards and Guidelines

To ensure the continuity of documentation across the organization, a set of documentation standards and guidelines should be introduced. These standards and guidelines can serve as templates for all documentation to guarantee that documents have the same look and feel and to ensure they'll all be distributed and stored securely, according to their scope or sensitivity.

The standards and guidelines should address the following topics, at a minimum:

- Data classification
- Document handling, retention, and storage
- Document disposal

Data Classification

An organization's documentation can be voluminous, comprising a variety of documents of varying levels of value and importance. Depending on the type of document, the amount of security and types of procedures used in storing and distributing that document can greatly vary. Some documents might be considered public, so they can be posted in a public forum or distributed freely to anyone. Other documents might be highly confidential and contain information that only certain individuals should be allowed to see.

To aid in the document management effort, documents need to be assigned security classifications to indicate their level of confidentiality and then labeled appropriately. Each classification requires different standards and procedures of access, distribution, and storage. The classification also sets a minimum standard of privileges required by a user to access that data. If a user doesn't have the necessary access privileges for that classification of data, the user won't be able to access it. Typically, access is delineated using subjective levels such as high, medium, and low. These should be agreed upon by management based on the data's sensitivity and the damage to the organization if the data is subjected to unauthorized access.

Several levels of classification can be assigned, depending on the type of organization and its activities. A typical organization might have only two classifications: private and public. *Private classified documents* are intended only for the internal use of the organization and can't be distributed to anyone outside the organization. *Public documents*, however, would be available to anyone. Government and military institutions might have several levels of confidentiality, such as Unclassified, Confidential, Secret, Top Secret, and so on. Each level of classification represents the level of severity if that information is leaked. For example, the lowest level (Unclassified) means that the document is not considered confidential or damaging to security and can be more freely distributed (though not necessarily releasable publicly). At the highest level (Top Secret), documents are highly restricted and would be severely damaging to national security if they were to fall into the wrong hands. Each document needs to be assigned a classification depending on the sensitivity of its data, its value to the organization, its value to other organizations in terms of business competition, the importance of its integrity, and the legal aspects of storing and distributing that data.

 EXAM TIP The type of security protections, access controls, data retention, and storage and disposal policies to be used all depend on a document's security classification.

Document Handling, Retention, and Storage

Depending on the classification of a document, the procedures and policies for handling and storing that document can be quite different. For example, a document might incur certain legal liabilities if it isn't properly stored, distributed, or destroyed. To ensure proper document management, organizations have implemented data retention policies to help reduce the possibility of legal issues.

Certain documents are required to be archived, stored, and protected, while others should be disposed of after a certain period. These policies must be created by senior management and the legal department, which can define what retention policies apply to different classifications of documents. The data retention policy needs to be specific to your organization's data. It also needs to consider items that could be legally damaging and information that could be damaging to the business if it were lost, leaked, or stolen.

To protect documentation properly, it should be kept offsite at a special document storage facility. In case of a disaster, such as a fire at the organization facility, this will ensure that all important documentation is secure and can be recovered.

Document Disposal

Document disposal can often be a tricky issue. In some cases, a document needs to be destroyed to avoid future legal or confidentiality ramifications. In other cases, it's illegal to destroy certain documents that are required by law as evidence for court proceedings. Only your organization's legal department can decide on retention and disposal policies for documents. Once decided on, these policies need to be communicated to workers to ensure that sensitive documents are either destroyed or retained as per their classification. Without proper disposal techniques, the organization is susceptible to dumpster diving attacks.

Data Retention Policies

Many organizations have been affected legally by archived e-mail or data that offers evidence against them during court proceedings. To prevent legal liabilities, organizations have implemented *data retention policies* to help reduce the possibility of legal problems arising from past messaging communications and data.

Data retention policies should apply to electronic information, such as files, e-mails, instant messages, and traditional paper documentation. Some clashes might occur between data retention policies and backup policies, where certain files are required to be archived, while others should be disposed of after a certain period. Only management and the legal department can define which data is covered under either policy. The data retention policy needs to be specific to your organization's information and consider items that could be damaging legally, as well as information that can be damaging to the business if lost. In the case of e-mail, the concept of data retention becomes complicated because e-mail can contain file attachments. Part of your policy might require that e-mail be retained for a certain amount of time before deletion, while the policy for actual electronic files could be different.

Hardware Disposal and Data Destruction Policies

Any policies must also include guidance for the disposal of old hardware that might contain data. As the lifetime of computers is very low (three to five years), older equipment is constantly swapped out for newer, faster machines with more capabilities and resources. However, a critical security issue is apparent regarding the proper disposal of these systems. Servers and personal computers are typically returned with their original hard drives, which could contain sensitive and classified data. System administrators must follow a specific policy for the removal and disposal of hardware to ensure that any media containing data is completely erased or overwritten.

For electronic files, this process is more complicated. Merely deleting a file or e-mail from a hard drive doesn't necessarily delete the data. Many operating systems use a special recovery method that enables you to recover deleted files easily. When a file is deleted, only the locator for the file in the hard drive directory has been removed; the data itself usually still exists in its original location. To ensure complete destruction of data on magnetic media such as hard drives, the media should be overwritten, or the drive physically destroyed. Many "shredder" utilities are available that can overwrite the contents of a hard drive with random data to ensure that any information on the drive is unrecoverable. Also, many high-security organizations, such as the military and national security agencies, opt to destroy the drives physically instead of using a shredding machine.

Systems Development Life Cycle

The *systems development life cycle* (sometimes known as the SDLC, which confusingly is used as the acronym for software as well) is essentially the entire life of a system, product, or piece of software. The life cycle covers every single aspect of a system or product, from the concept to development, from implementation to disposal. There are several popular system development life cycle models, including waterfall, iterative, and Agile. We won't cover any of these models here, as an in-depth discussion on any one of them would fill an entire book. However, we will mention some of the more generic parts or phases of the SDLC and briefly describe them so that we can put them in the context of risk factors, threats, and vulnerabilities.

NOTE Some models are linear, in that they progress in a sequential manner only, and some are cyclic in some way (repetitive, recursive, or iterative), where a system can be re-introduced into an earlier phase for updates or upgrades or to fix problems or issues.

At the basic level, the SDLC consists of several phases that include conceptualizing the system, discovering the requirements for a system, designing its architecture, developing the system, testing it as both a single unit and as integrated with larger systems in its environment, implementing the system, and, finally, disposing of the system after it has reached the end of its useful life. Each of these different phases of the life cycle has different aspects that include planning, management, resourcing, and so on. Each also has inherent risks. We'll discuss these phases generically in the next few paragraphs.

NOTE Some of the names we give to the different lifecycle phases may vary among different lifecycle models, but in general, the concepts are the same.

Software Development Life Cycle

It should be noted that in most organizations, the skills to properly set up computers and develop software are completely separate from one another. In fact, many compliance frameworks consider it a serious risk to have the software coders (often called developers) have access to a live production environment—some focusing on the ability of the software coders to implement their code in production. This need to prevent this is called *separation of duties* (sometimes *segregation of duties*). This came down from the banking industry in that two people were required to perform a task, which means that the likelihood of abuse is drastically reduced. This is another critical factor for risk assessors to take into account.

As a result of the differentiation, a *software development life cycle (SDLC)* is often used as a separate term from system development life cycle—two completely different groups and sets of governance are part of the organization. Typically, the CIO oversees an IT organization while a CTO would oversee the software development within an organization. As a result, for many organizations, SDLC typically refers to the former and not the latter interpretation. Both are extremely critical for many organizations, but the approach is different even though the goals may be the same.

Another factor today would be that with many cloud technologies, the software development life cycle is resting on cloud systems and system development is entirely up to the cloud provider and not as much on the organization. Cloud changes the whole relationship of systems development life cycle to software development life cycle.

Planning

The first phase of the SDLC normally involves some type of conceptual planning process, where the need for the system is determined and a general idea is developed of what the system needs to do and what purpose it will serve. Some models refer to this as the *initiation phase*. During this phase, the feasibility of developing or acquiring a system is studied and includes considerations such as when the system is needed, how much it might cost, what type of staffing it might need to develop, implement, maintain it, what other systems it might need to connect to or interface with, and so on. Security and privacy professionals want to be involved in this phase of the life cycle so that they can understand the basic concepts of the system and provide feedback on any potential security or privacy risks.

Often, it is the planning phase where a business case is developed, to help the organization determine whether the system (or changes to an existing system) is justifiable. A business case describes the resources required to build (or change) the system and the economic benefits expected to be derived from the system.

The phrase *move to the left* or *shift left* describes the desire for security and privacy professionals to be involved as early as possible (as far to the left on a timeline) in the conceptualization, requirements, and design of a system, in order to help avoid situations where basic concept or design of a system may be deeply flawed from a security or privacy perspective.

Requirements

The next phase of the SDLC is generally the *requirements phase*, and this phase is typically named as such in most models. During this phase, different sets of requirements are developed. These requirements might include functional requirements, performance requirements, security requirements, and business requirements. Requirements dictate concrete terms, such as what a system is exactly supposed to do, how it will do it, to what degree, and what standards it must meet. Without a clear set of requirements, there can't be any good traceability back to what the system was supposed to do in the first place. That's why it's very important to try to accurately cover all the possible requirements and needs the system may have to meet. This is also where the scope of the development process is established. Security and privacy professionals should be invited to develop security and privacy requirements for the system, to ensure that later phases of the project will include all required characteristics.

Design

The next few phases can be a bit different based on the model under discussion and whether the product being developed is a system or software. System developers would move from the requirements phase into designing the architecture in terms of developing a general high-level design of how the system is supposed to work, what major components it might have, and what other systems it might interface with. Software developers similarly might design software architecture at a higher level during this phase.

As the SDLC development process moves forward, this overall architecture is decomposed down into smaller pieces until finally individual components or pieces of code can be developed. Again, how this design process progresses depends on which model is being used. Security and privacy professionals should be asked to review the design of the system to ensure that requirements were properly represented.

Development

After the design phase, decisions must be made as to whether to build a system or software or simply acquire it from a third party. Some systems and software can be bought from other developers, but some must be developed specifically for the end application or end use. If the system is to be acquired from some other source, and the design specifications are provided to the best source, then a system or software that meets the requirements and design will be provided. If the system is to be developed, the next phase of the SDLC comes into play. During this phase, the software is written, and systems are assembled from individual components. Organizations can use tools to examine a system's source and object code to identify any security-related defects that could be exploited by an attacker.

Testing

Following the development phase, many SDLC models include a test phase. In the test phase, different aspects of the software and systems are tested. Many different tests can take place during this phase. Some of these tests might involve *unit testing,* which simply means to test an individual component or unit of software at its most basic level for functionality and performance. *Integration testing,* another type of testing, usually involves testing the overall function and performance of all the components of the system or piece of software working together, as they would when assembled. During this phase, other types of testing could take place, including *interface testing* (testing different aspects of the system when it interfaces with other separate systems in its environment) and *security testing* (which may include compliance testing, vulnerability testing, and even penetration testing). *User acceptance testing* involves end users of the system performing various functions to determine whether they will accept the system in its current, developed state.

Implementation and Operation

Once a system has been tested and accepted, the implementation phase usually follows. In this phase, systems or software are put into production and used for their originally intended purpose. Some development models describe an overall implementation phase that includes the day-to-day maintenance and operations of the system. Other models move from the implementation phase to a more long-term maintenance or sustainment phase for the product. Regardless of how the phase is described in the model, during these phases, the system is used, undergoes minor maintenance and upgrades, and is periodically tested to make sure it still meets its original design and requirements.

Disposal

Once a system has been in operation for a while, it may eventually be superseded or replaced by a more efficient or updated system. When the system is replaced or removed from the environment, it is said to have entered the *disposal phase*. Some models refer to this also as the *retirement phase*. During this phase, the system is taken out of production, dismantled, and is no longer used. Its components may be reused, or they may be disposed of.

EXAM TIP While you will likely not be expected to know the details of any specific SDLC model, be familiar with the generic phases of the SDLC: Initiation, Requirements, Design, Development, Testing, Implementation, and Disposal. Also, keep in mind that different models may refer to these phases by different names or even combine or separate phases out to some degree.

SDLC Risks

Most of the risk factors inherent to the SDLC affect both the entire model and each of the different phases separately. Since the SDLC could be considered to have several different facets, including a management process, an engineering framework, and even a methodology, you could say that risk factors that affect the SDLC are also common to other types of processes. For instance, earlier, we discussed risk factors that affect project and program management. These risk factors affect scope, schedule, and cost. The SDLC suffers from similar risk factors because each of the phases, as well as the SDLC, have different scope, schedule, and cost elements. Each of these phases can also be affected by risk factors that impact the availability of resources (manpower, funding, equipment, facilities, and so on), such as management commitment and organizational structure.

Unique risk factors that affect the SDLC include those that affect system changes, system configuration throughout the life cycle, and those that affect releasing different versions of the system as updates take place. Most of these elements occur during implementation, maintenance, and sustainment of a system but also can occur in other phases of the SDLC where multiple versions of a system are fielded simultaneously, as well as in models where there is a continuous iterative process of updating and upgrading a system or software. Risk factors that affect system changes include how well the change and configuration management processes work and how changes are implemented into the system. Change and configuration management processes that are not well managed are risk factors, because this could cause changes that are not documented or not tested for security, functionality, or performance. Additionally, factors such as the complexity of the system, how the organization is structured to manage the systems development process, and how rapid system changes occur are also potential risk factors.

Threats to the SDLC manifest themselves when systems are produced that are not interoperable or compatible with other systems and their environment or systems are not secure. Other threats might include systems that do not meet the requirements they were originally intended to meet. These threats would affect both the functionality and performance of the system as well. Threats to the design process include faulty design specifications as well as faulty requirements input from the previous requirements phase. Most of the threats to the SDLC come in the form of mismanagement, miscommunication, incorrect expectations, and lack of a commitment of resources or expertise.

Many different vulnerabilities can affect the SDLC; again, a great many of them have been previously discussed as also affecting the project or program management process. These vulnerabilities affect scope, schedule, and cost, of course, but can also affect the quality of the system or product. In addition, the system's security, functionality, and performance are also affected by these different vulnerabilities. While probably too many to list here, examples of vulnerabilities that affect the SDLC start with a lack of firm requirements and mixed expectations from the different system stakeholders. A lack of documentation in all phases is also a significant vulnerability to the entire SDLC, but particularly to the requirements and design phases. Failure to develop solid design specifications and systems architecture is a vulnerability that can result in a faulty design that does not meet system requirements. In the development phase, lack of adequate consideration for system interfaces, as well as how subcomponents fail to support higher-level components or meet technical requirements, can result in a shoddy system or software. Failure to test systems properly and thoroughly, as well as their interaction with their environment, may mean that serious functional or performance issues with the system are not discovered until well after it is put into production. Vulnerabilities in the implementation phase include faulty implementation, lack of traceability to original requirements, and failure to properly maintain a sustained system after it has been put into production. And lastly, vulnerabilities associated with the disposal or retirement phase of the SDLC can result in systems that are not properly replaced or not securely disposed of. This can cost the organization money and potential liability.

Emerging Technologies

New or emerging technologies can present risks to organizations simply because there are several different important considerations when integrating the latest technologies into the existing infrastructure. Many organizations have an unfortunate tendency to rush out, buy, and attempt to implement the latest and greatest technologies on the market without careful planning or consideration of the existing infrastructure and how it will react to the new technologies. One of the primary considerations organizations must look at is making a business case for the new technology, which may be to fill a gap that the older technology does not provide or to provide a capability that the organization must now have to compete in the market space. In other words, the organization really must justify new technologies to make them worth the risk they could incur.

Emerging technologies have several risk factors inherent to their integration into the existing infrastructure. If the organization has been able to justify the implementation based on a true business need for the emerging technology, it must consider several risk factors. One of the major risk factors is interoperability with existing infrastructure. Frequently, newer technologies don't always work properly with older systems right out of the box; adjustments may need to be made to the existing infrastructure to integrate the new technology, or even bridging technologies may be needed to connect the two together. Interoperability doesn't just involve the right connections; it can involve data formats and flows, security methods, interfaces into other systems, and changes to business processes. These considerations, and many others, are risk factors that must be considered before acquiring and integrating new technologies.

Another risk factor is security. New technologies may have security mechanisms that are not necessarily backward compatible with existing ones. Examples include encryption algorithms and strengths, identification and authentication technologies, integrity mechanisms, and even redundant or backup systems. Additionally, the systems may involve a learning curve that may intimidate users who must now learn new security methods for the system. The human factor can be a weak link in the security chain, so either lack of training or a lack of adaptability to the new security mechanisms can introduce risk.

Earlier, when we discussed the SDLC model, we pointed out that system updates and changes can be risky if not managed properly. Integrating new technologies into the environment with older ones can introduce both intentional and unintended changes into the environment as well, affecting the stability of the organization's SDLC with a particular system. Therefore, change is also a risk factor. Even in the disposal or replacement phase of the SDLC, introducing new technologies to replace older ones can be problematic if not planned and executed properly. New technologies that are not adequately tested for functionality, performance, integration, interoperability, and security may not be able to adequately replace older systems, resulting in extended costs and possibly even requiring an extension of the older systems' life cycle.

Threats resulting from the introduction of new and emerging technologies into the existing infrastructure are numerous. If the organization has failed to adequately plan for the new technology, these threats can become significant. Some of these threats include untested or unproven technologies, non-interoperability, incompatible security mechanisms, and suitability of the technology for use in the organization. The organization could also incur additional costs and require more resources due to faulty implementation. These threats can be minimized through careful planning and by integrating new technologies using a stable SDLC model.

As with threats, vulnerabilities associated with emerging technologies are numerous as well. Vulnerabilities could include a lack of trained staff committed to managing and implementing the new technology. Lack of adequate project planning is also a serious vulnerability that could affect the organization's ability to effectively integrate new technologies. Another vulnerability could be a weak support contract or another type of warranty, guarantee, or support for a new technology or system. Most of these vulnerabilities appear when a new technology is first implemented and tend to become mitigated or lessened as the technology is integrated into the existing infrastructure, but they still exist.

 EXAM TIP The key areas of concern with emerging technologies are interoperability and compatibility. These two concerns affect the security, functionality, and performance of new technologies when they are installed into an existing infrastructure.

Information Security Concepts, Frameworks, and Standards

In order to successfully sit for the CRISC exam, you should be familiar with some basic information security concepts. You can't be expected to know how to manage risk in a security environment if you don't understand the basics of information security in the first place. Now, we're going to assume you have some level of experience already as an information security professional, since risk management is a significant portion of (and a logical career progression from) the information security profession. You may also have had some level of experience in specific risk management processes at some point during your career. As such, we're not going to go into great detail on the basic information security concepts in the upcoming sections; this will just serve as a quick refresher to remind you of certain security concepts. We'll also review a few key control frameworks in detail, including the NIST Risk Management Framework (RMF) and COBIT 2019, and how these frameworks are used in managing risk. Additionally, you'll find that this chapter covers more material than you might find on the exam; this is for two important reasons. First, it's important that you understand foundational and conceptual knowledge about controls and some of the relevant control frameworks you will find on both the exam and in the real world as a risk and control assessor. Second, this book is intended to be not only a study guide for the exam but also a comprehensive reference you will use even after you have passed the CRISC exam.

You may learn traditional information security doctrine, as well as fundamental information security knowledge, from various training courses and on-the-job experience over the years. One such doctrine teaches that there are three fundamental information security goals. These goals are what we're striving for as risk and information security professionals; they are *confidentiality*, *integrity*, and *availability*. You'll sometimes see these three terms strung together as an acronym, such as the *CIA triad* or, occasionally, the *AIC triad*, depending on the different information security literature you read. In any event, these three goals are what we want to achieve for all our information systems and data. They are also characteristics we want to ensure all our systems, processes, procedures, methods, and technologies display.

Popular security theory sets forth these three overarching security goals but also provides for auxiliary elements that support these goals in various ways. These are concepts that, both individually and combined, help us as security professionals to ensure we maintain data confidentiality, integrity, and availability, as well as protect our systems from unauthorized use or misuse. We'll discuss all these different security elements and other concepts, as well as how they support three primary goals of information security, in the next few sections.

Confidentiality, Integrity, and Availability

Confidentiality is the goal of keeping information systems and data from being accessed by people who do not have the authorization, need-to-know, or security clearance to access that information. In other words, confidentiality means that only authorized individuals and entities should be able to access information and systems. Confidentiality can be achieved through a number of security protection mechanisms, such as rights, privileges, permissions, encryption, authentication, and other access controls. If confidentiality of data or information systems is breached, we get the opposite of confidentiality, which is unauthorized disclosure. Unauthorized disclosure is a risk to data and information systems, and one we as security professionals struggle very hard to protect against.

Integrity is the characteristic of data that describes the state in which a system or its data has not been subject to unauthorized modification or alteration. Data integrity means that data is left in the same state as it was when it was stored or transmitted. Therefore, when it is accessed again or received, it should be identical to the data that was originally stored or transmitted. Integrity is achieved in several ways, by using checksums, message digests, and other verification methods. Data alteration is the opposite of integrity, particularly when the modification has not been authorized by the data owner. Data modification or alteration can happen accidentally, such as when it is inadvertently changed due to human error or faulty transmission media. It can also happen intentionally (which is usually malicious in nature when this modification is unauthorized) by direct interaction with data during storage or transmission (during an attack, for example). This risk to data affects whether the data can be trusted as authentic or true, whether it can be read as intended, or whether it is corrupt.

Availability is the property of systems and data to be accessible to authorized users at any time or under any circumstances. Even if data is kept confidential, and its integrity is kept intact, it still does us no good if we can't access it when we need it to perform critical business functions. Availability ensures we have this data (and the information systems that process it) at our fingertips. Just as confidentiality and integrity have their opposites, *data destruction* and *denial of service* are the opposite of availability. These risks to our information systems could prevent authorized consumers of that data or users of that information system from performing their jobs, thus severely impacting our business operations.

 EXAM TIP   You will need to understand the definitions of the goals of information security—confidentiality, integrity, and availability—very well for the exam. Almost everything in information risk management supports those three goals, either directly or indirectly.

Access Control

As an information security professional, you probably already know that a *security control* is a security measure or protection applied to data, systems, people, facilities, and other resources to guard them from adverse events. Security controls can be broken down and categorized in several ways. *Access controls* directly support the confidentiality and integrity goals of security, and indirectly support the goal of availability. Access control essentially means that we will proactively ensure that only authorized personnel are able to access data or the information systems that process that data. Access controls ensure that only authorized personnel can read, write to, modify, add to, or delete data. They also ensure that only the same authorized personnel can access the different information systems and equipment used to store, process, transmit, and receive sensitive data.

There are several different types of access controls, including identification, authentication, and authorization methods, encryption, object permissions, and more. Remember that access controls can be administrative, technical, or physical in nature. Administrative controls are those implemented as policies, procedures, rules and regulations, and other types of directives or governance. For example, personnel policies are usually administrative access controls. Technical controls are those we most often associate with security professionals, such as firewalls, proxy servers, VPN concentrators, encryption techniques, file and folder permissions, and so on. Physical controls are those used to protect people, equipment, and facilities. Examples of physical controls include fences, closed-circuit television cameras, guards, locked doors, gates, and restricted areas.

In addition to classifying controls in terms of administrative, technical, and physical, we can also classify access controls in terms of their functions. These functions include preventative controls, detective controls, corrective or remedial controls, deterrent controls, and compensating controls. All the different controls can be classified as one or more of these different types of functions, depending on the context and the circumstances in which they are being used. Controls were described in more detail in Chapter 3.

Data Sensitivity and Classification

Asset is a general, all-encompassing term that could include anything of value to an organization. The term *asset* can be applied to data, systems, capabilities, people, equipment, facilities, processes, proprietary methods, and so on; it is anything the organization values and desires to protect. Organizations normally determine how important their assets are to them and how much protection should be afforded to those assets. For example, intellectual property is an extremely valuable asset to the organization and is normally well-protected. This is really the basic fundamental concept of risk management: how much security or protection a particular system or piece of data requires, based on how likely it is that something bad will happen to it, balanced with what the organization can really afford to spend on the protection for that asset. In order to make reasonable decisions on how much security an asset needs, the organization has to decide how much the asset is worth to it. We'll discuss worth in terms of dollars a bit later in the chapter, but for now let's look at it from a perspective of asset sensitivity. In terms of sensitivity, you'll usually see the term *data sensitivity* in particular, but we could also broadly apply sensitivity to any asset in an organization.

Data (or other asset) sensitivity refers to how much protection the organization feels a particular system or piece of data requires, based on its value to the organization and the impact if it were lost, stolen, or destroyed. For example, information published on the organization's public website or in the company newsletter is public knowledge and is usually easily retrievable if, for some reason, the hard disk containing that data fails or is erased. Since the data is public, we may not consider that data to be very sensitive in nature and therefore require less protection for it than other types of data. On the other hand, customer order data is extremely important to the organization, simply because its business operations depend on that data in order to function and turn a profit, so it makes reasonable sense that the organization would spend a little bit more time, money, and effort in protecting that particular data. Therefore, its sensitivity, or *classification level,* would be considered somewhat higher than public data. Generally, the higher the sensitivity of the data, the more protection it is given.

In basic security classes, you typically learn about the different classifications of data found in both commercial organizations and government ones. In commercial organizations, typical data sensitivity labels include Private, Company Sensitive, Proprietary, and so on. In the U.S. government, data sensitivity levels include Confidential, Secret, and Top Secret, and are classified based on the level of damage to the security of the United States that could be incurred if data at these various classification levels was disclosed or lost. Remember that data sensitivity is driven by the value of the data to the organization, the impact if it is lost, stolen, or destroyed, and balanced by the commitment of resources the organization is willing to provide to protect that data. Data sensitivity and classification policies specify the different formal levels of sensitivity in the organization and what those levels require in terms of protection.

Identification and Authentication

Identification and authentication are often misunderstood terms. They are related, to be sure, but they are not the same thing and really shouldn't be used interchangeably by a knowledgeable security professional. *Identification* refers to the act of an individual or entity presenting valid credentials to a security system in order to assert that they are a specific entity. When you enter a username and password into a system, for example, or insert a debit card into an automated teller machine and enter a personal identification number (PIN), you are identifying yourself. *Authentication*, on the other hand, is the second part of that process, where your identity is verified with a centralized database containing your authentication credentials. If the credentials you have presented match those in the authentication database, you are authenticated and allowed access to the network or resource. If they do not match, you are not authenticated and are denied access to the resource.

There are several different methods of identification and authentication, including single factor (such as username and password, for example) and multifactor, which consists of two or more of the following: something you *know* (knowledge factor), something you *have* (possession factor), or something you *are* (biometric or inherence factor). Authentication also uses a wide variety of methods and technologies, such as Kerberos and 802.1X.

Authorization

Authentication to a resource doesn't automatically guarantee you have full, unrestricted access to a resource. Once you are authenticated, the system or resource defines what actions you are authorized to take on a resource as well as how you are allowed to interact with that resource. *Authorization* is what happens once you've successfully identified yourself and have been authenticated to the network. Authorization dictates what you can or can't do on the network, in a system, or with a resource. This is usually where permissions, rights, and privileges come in. In keeping with the concept of *least privilege*, users should only be authorized to perform the minimum actions they need in order to fulfill their position's responsibilities. Authorization has a few different components. First, there is *need-to-know*. This means that there must be a valid reason or need for an individual to access a resource, and to what degree. Second, an individual may have to be trusted, or *cleared*, to access a resource. This may be accomplished through a security clearance process or non-disclosure agreement, for example.

EXAM TIP   Understand the differences between identification, authentication, and authorization. Remember that identification is simply presenting credentials, whereas authentication is verifying them. Authorization dictates what actions an individual can take on a system once authentication has occurred.

Accountability

Accountability means that a person is going to be held responsible for their actions on a system or with regard to their interaction with data. Accountability is essentially the traceability of a particular action to a particular user. Users must be held responsible for their actions, and there are different ways to do this, but it is usually ensured through *auditing*. First, there must be a unique identifier that is tied only to a particular user. This way, the identity of the user who performs an action or accesses a resource can be positively established. Second, auditing must be properly configured and implemented on the system or resource. What we are auditing is a user's actions on a system or interactions with a resource. For example, if a user named Sam deletes a file on a network share, we want to be able to positively identify which user performed that action, as well as the circumstances surrounding the action (such as the time, date, from which workstation, and so on). This can only be accomplished if we have auditing configured correctly and take the time to review the audit logs to establish accountability.

NOTE   Although related, accountability is not the same thing as auditing. Accountability uses auditing as just one method to ensure that the actions of users can be traced to them and that they are held responsible for those actions. Other methods, such as non-repudiation, are used as well.

Non-Repudiation

Non-repudiation is closely related to accountability. Non-repudiation ensures that the user cannot deny that they took an action, simply because the system is set up such that no one else could have performed the action. The classic example of non-repudiation is given as the proper use of public key cryptography. If a user sends an e-mail that is digitally signed using their private key, they cannot later deny that they sent the e-mail since only they are supposed to have access to the private key. In this case, the user can be held accountable for sending the e-mail, and non-repudiation is ensured.

Note that there is no hard and fast rule about mapping security elements and access controls to security goals; all of these elements and controls can support any one or even more than one goal at a time. For example, encryption, a technical access control, can support both confidentiality and integrity at the same time.

NOTE Although other texts may describe the supporting elements of the security goals differently, the basic ones we've described here are very common and directly support the three goals of confidentiality, integrity, and availability.

Frameworks, Standards, and Practices

Managing risk is not an ad-hoc process. It can be a complex effort and involves establishing a formal program with responsible people leading it. It requires developing procedures and processes that are defined, repeatable, and defendable. Fortunately, you don't have to reinvent the wheel; most of this work has already been done for you in the form of established frameworks, methods, standards, and practices. One of the first things you'll want to do when establishing a risk program is to understand what type of framework, processes, standards, and practices you will use since there is a variety to choose from. You must try to use the one that fits your organization the best, and you can't do that unless you have at least a basic understanding of the more defined, standardized ones used in the industry. Let's take a moment and discuss the difference between frameworks, standards, and practices.

Frameworks

A *framework* is a generally overarching methodology for a set of activities or processes. It may not get into the detailed processes and procedures; instead, it provides for a 500-foot view of the general direction and steps used to build a more detailed program or process. A framework is used as an overall architecture for a greater effort. A framework has characteristics that include defined steps and repeatability, and it can be tailored based on the organization's needs. In terms of a risk management framework, you may have a set of general steps defining how to approach risk management, which include listing the processes and activities necessary to build such a program or effort. You would then break down these larger steps into specific supporting procedures for this effort based on the needs of your organization and using standards (described next). Frameworks are typically selected and adopted at the strategic level of corporate management and governance.

Standards

A *standard* is a mandatory set of procedures or processes used by the organization and usually fits into an overall framework. Standards often define more detailed processes or activities used to perform a specific set of tasks. Standards are used for compliance reasons and made mandatory by an organization or its governance. The National Institute for Standards and Technology (NIST) standards are mandatory for use by the United States federal government, for instance, but are published as an option for private organizations and industries to adopt if they so choose. If an organization adopts the NIST standards for risk management, for example, the organization may make them mandatory for use by its personnel. Then all processes and activities for a given effort within the organization would have to use and meet those standards. Some standards define the level of depth or implementation of a security control or measure. The Federal Information Processing Standards (FIPS) for cryptography and encryption are an example of this; they set forth the different levels of encryption strength for various cryptography applications that may be required in certain circumstances. So, if you create security policies and procedures for implementing cryptography within the organization, the FIPS standard could tell you to what level those policies and procedures must be implemented.

Practices

A *practice* is a normalized process that has been tried and proven as generally accepted within a larger community. Practices could also be developed by a standards organization or a recognized authority regarding a particular subject or particular process. Professional industry organizations or vendors often develop practices documents. You might also see "best practices" promulgated by various industries or organizations, for example. Practices are not usually mandatory but could be made mandatory by the corporate management or other governance if they were so inclined.

The next few sections give more detailed examples of some of the formal frameworks and standards you should be familiar with for the exam and in real life as a risk management professional. We recommend you pay particular attention to the ones developed and published by ISACA; these will likely be present in some form on the exam. Of course, in this book, we're only going to give you a brief overview of each, and you should take the time to review the actual standards and frameworks in depth before you sit for the exam.

NIST Risk Management Framework

The NIST Risk Management Framework (RMF) is a seven-step methodology that provides for risk management all the way through the information systems life cycle. The steps for the RMF are briefly described in the following sections.

Step 1: Prepare

The first step, Prepare, has the purpose of carrying out essential activities to help prepare all levels of the organization to manage its security and privacy risks using the RMF. It involves identifying key risk management roles, establishing the organizational risk management strategy, determining the organization's risk tolerance, assessing the organization's risk assessment, developing the organizational strategy for continuous monitoring, and identifying the implemented common controls.

Step 2: Categorize

Step 2, Categorize, involves inventorying the types of information on target systems and assigning categorization levels to that information based on the level of impact if the security goals of confidentiality, integrity, and availability were affected or compromised for the information on the system. This step uses subjective values of high, medium, and low to assign values to each of the three goals for a particular type of information.

Types of information processed on the system could include business-sensitive, financial, protected health information, and so on. FIPS 199, "Standards for Security Categorization of Federal Information and Information Systems," as well as NIST Special Publication 800-60, "Guide for Mapping Types of Information and Information Systems to Security Categories," provide detailed guidance on categorizing information systems.

Step 3: Select

Based on these individual values, as well as an aggregate of them, the applicable security controls you would assign to this information system would be accomplished in Step 3, Select. This step provides baselines of security controls based on the high, medium, and low values assigned during step 2. If the aggregate value of information or system has been rated as *high*, for example, the high baseline of security controls is employed for that system. Once a security control baseline has been established, the organization has the latitude and flexibility to add or subtract security controls from the baseline as it sees fit based on different factors, including the applicability of some controls, the environment the system operates within, and so on. The selected controls can be found in the supporting NIST Special Publication 800-53, revision 5, "Security and Privacy Controls for Information Systems and Organizations," which contains a catalog of all the NIST controls.

Step 4: Implement

In Step 4 of the RMF, Implement, the selected controls are applied to the information systems and data is processed on those systems. This is a large process that can cover a good deal of the life cycle of the system in question, and it may take significant time and resources. In this step, the organization is essentially securing the information system against any validated threats and protecting identified vulnerabilities.

Step 5: Assess

Step 5, Assess, is where a lot of security professionals who manage certification and accreditation activities or perform risk assessments come into the picture. During this step, the controls the organization selects for the information system are formally assessed, verifying that they were implemented correctly and validating whether they perform as they were designed. They are assessed based on their effectiveness in protecting against the threats they were implemented to protect against. During this step, the system is assessed in its current state, with all existing controls and mitigations in place. Based on the assessment findings, there may be recommendations for further controls and mitigations, as well as alterations to the existing security posture for the system. In this step, the level of risk to the system and its data is normally analyzed and determined.

Step 6: Authorize

Step 6, Authorize, involves the decision from the entity in charge to authorize a system to be implemented and put into operation. This decision is based on various factors, including the level of risk assessed during step 5, the risk appetite the organization has settled on, and the tolerance for risk the organization is willing to accept. The decision to authorize a system for use may also come with caveats, including conditional authorization based on the continued mitigation and reduction of risk by the system or data owner. This authorization is a formal authority for the system to operate, made by someone with the legal authority to make that decision. It is typically in writing and only valid for a specified period, after which the system must be reassessed for risk and control compliance.

Step 7: Monitor

Continuous monitoring of security controls defines step 7 in the RMF; just because an authorization decision is rendered doesn't mean the system will now be operated forever without continually monitoring its security posture for new or changed risks. Existing controls should be monitored for continued compliance and effectiveness against identified threats. New risks will be occasionally discovered for the system as new threats and vulnerabilities are identified, and the system will have to be reauthorized after a certain period. Note that the RMF is a cyclical process; all these steps will be accomplished again for each system at various times over its life cycle.

ISO 27001/27002/27701/31000

Whereas the NIST RMF is very much an American framework, the International Organization for Standardization (ISO) frameworks are used globally. The ISO family is largely focused on keeping information assets secure, ensuring privacy, and managing risk across the following major documents:

- **ISO/IEC 27000:2018** Provides the overview of information security management systems (ISMS).
- **ISO/IEC 27001:2013** Specifies the requirements for establishing, implementing, maintaining, and continually improving an ISMS within the context of the organization. It also includes requirements for the assessment and treatment of information security risks tailored to the needs of the organization.
- **ISO/IEC 27002:2022** Gives guidelines for organizational information security standards and information security management practices, including the selection, implementation, and management of controls, taking into consideration the organization's information security risk environment(s).
- **ISO/IEC 27701:2019** Specifies requirements and provides guidance for establishing, implementing, maintaining, and continually improving a privacy information management system (PIMS).
- **ISO 31000:2018** Provides guidelines on managing risk faced by organizations.

COBIT 2019 (ISACA)

COBIT (formerly an acronym for Control Objectives for Information and Related Technologies) is a framework developed by ISACA and facilitates the governance of enterprise information and technology. This framework has been around for several years and through several iterations. It also provides for integration of other popular frameworks and standards, including The Open Group Architecture Framework (TOGAF), the Project Management Body of Knowledge (PMBOK), the Information Technology

Infrastructure Library (ITIL), PRojects IN Controlled Environments 2 (PRINCE2), the Committee of Sponsoring Organizations of the Treadway Commission (COSO), and the many International Organization for Standardization (ISO) standards. This interoperability enables new users of COBIT to leverage any of these other standards they have already been using in their adoption of COBIT.

COBIT consists of two layers in its model, governance and management, which further break down into a total of 40 separate objectives. Table 4-3 quickly summarizes these layers and their respective objectives.

Governance: Evaluate, Direct, and Monitor (EDM)				
EDM01: Ensured Governance Framework Setting and Maintenance	EDM02: Ensured Benefits Delivery	EDM03: Ensure Ensured Risk Optimization	EDM04: Ensured Resource Optimization	EDM05: Ensured Stakeholder Engagement
Management: Align, Plan, and Organize (APO)				
APO01: Managed I.T. Management Framework	APO02: Managed Strategy	APO03: Managed Enterprise Architecture	APO04: Managed Information	APO05: Managed Portfolio
APO06: Managed Budget and Costs	APO07: Managed Human Resources	APO08: Managed Relationships	APO09: Managed Service Agreements	APO10: Managed Vendors
APO11: Managed Quality	APO12: Managed Risk	APO13: Managed Security	APO14: Managed Data	
Management: Build, Acquire, and Implement (BAI)				
BAI01: Managed Programs	BAI02: Managed Requirements Definition	BAI03: Managed Solutions Identification and Build	BAI04: Managed Availability and Capacity	BAI05: Managed Organizational Change
BAI06: Managed IT Changes	BAI07: Managed IT Change Acceptance and Transitioning	BAI08: Managed Knowledge	BAI09: Managed Assets	BAI10: Managed Configuration
BAI11: Managed Projects				
Management: Deliver, Service, and Support (DSS)				
DSS01: Managed Operations	DSS02: Managed Service Requests and Incidents	DSS03: Managed Problems	DSS04: Managed Continuity	DSS05: Managed Security Services
DSS06: Managed Business Process Controls				
Management: Monitor, Evaluate, and Assess (MEA)				
MEA01: Managed Performance and Conformance Monitoring	MEA02: Managed System of Internal Control	MEA03: Managed Compliance with External Requirements	MEA04: Managed Assurance	

Table 4-3 COBIT 2019 Governance and Management Objectives

Note that while COBIT covers a variety of business and IT processes and areas, those specific to risk management happen at both layers—governance and management—and are tightly integrated with other processes. COBIT, in this regard, is not a risk management framework per se, as is the NIST RMF, but offers more of a broader view of management and governance across all major areas of a business. The next topic we cover, ISACA's Risk IT Framework, supports COBIT and provides a more granular view of risk management practices and activities.

 NOTE Understand that while COBIT is important to the overall risk discussion, it is not a risk framework itself. It does, however, support management and governance of IT as well as other critical business areas. It also leads to a more detailed discussion on the ISACA Risk IT Framework, which does deal with IT risk.

The Risk IT Framework (ISACA)

The Risk IT Framework is a more concise, risk-related set of processes than that offered by the related framework COBIT 2019. While COBIT covers the "big picture" of governance and management processes that support risk management programs in the organization, the Risk IT Framework gets more into the key processes of risk management, such as risk governance, evaluation, and response. The Risk IT Framework is also a mere summary of ISACA's *The Risk IT Practitioner Guide*, available to ISACA members, which is an even more in-depth treatment of the processes and activities encountered during risk management.

The Risk IT Framework comes from traditional risk management principles of various enterprise risk management (ERM) standards and describes activities and processes thought of as best practices in the industry. It provides a starting place for the establishment of these processes—sort of a map to navigate from a nonexistent or immature risk management program to a formalized, defined set of processes. The Risk IT Framework focuses more on the business risks of using IT in the organization's structure and how risk is involved with the gap often found between IT implementation and business goals. Table 4-4 lists the different domains of the Risk IT Framework model, with each of their three major processes.

Keep in mind we've only covered a few of the risk-related frameworks and standards available in the industry. Also, be aware that we've only scratched the surface of these bodies of knowledge here in this chapter; a full discussion of each one of them is quite beyond the scope of this book. You should obtain and review these publications in depth

Risk Governance (RG)	RG1: Establish and maintain a common risk view	RG2: Integrate with ERM	RG3: Make risk-aware business decisions
Risk Evaluation (RE)	RE1: Collect data	RE2: Analyze risk	RE3: Maintain risk profile
Risk Response (RR)	RR1: Articulate risk	RR2: Manage risk	RR3: React to events

Table 4-4 Domains and Processes of ISACA's Risk IT Framework

before you sit for the exam. There are also many other available frameworks and standards developed and promulgated by other professional organizations, government entities, industries, vendors, and so on. You should be familiar with as many of these as is relevant to your work since they help you turn risk management from "magic" into an art and science for your organization. The frameworks and standards we have described earlier are the ones most relevant to your studies for the CRISC exam.

 EXAM TIP While you may not be expected to know the intricate details of each framework described here, it will be helpful to know at least the basic characteristics and descriptions of each. You may be asked to identify a particular characteristic of a framework on the exam.

Security and Risk Awareness Training Programs

Both security awareness and risk awareness training programs are critical controls to reduce risk within an organization. They can cover a whole range of topics, including phishing, data handling, data sensitivity, compliance requirements, wireless challenges, how data is lost, how to submit incidents, and so on. Both help to improve the risk posture of organizations at an individual level by increasing general employee awareness of threats and required practices as well as leader awareness of organizational risks. Not having any training is an indication, from a risk perspective, that people may not know how to handle different types of risks or even how to recognize risks.

Awareness programs are a very necessary part of risk management. They can't be viewed as simply just another two-hour training session to check a box for management or compliance. Awareness is essential because it helps form and maintain the organization's risk culture. It also educates personnel at all levels of the organization, including employees and other workers, managers, and senior leadership, on the organization's risk strategy, its appetite and tolerance levels for risk, its risk management plan, and other relevant topics necessary to manage risk in the organization. Beyond the education on organizational governance and risk management processes, awareness training can give all members of the organization the knowledge they need to better identify, assess and evaluate, and respond to risk. Awareness training may be required for compliance with governance in some cases, but even if it's not, it should be considered critical to the overall risk management strategy in the organization and given due consideration in the organizational priority list. The next two sections discuss the different tools and techniques used in awareness training and how to develop an awareness program within an organization.

Awareness Tools and Techniques

Like most training, awareness training should meet several criteria. First, it should be geared toward specific groups of audiences. This might include basic training that everyone receives, more advanced training for managers or senior leaders, and in-depth training for personnel with assigned risk management responsibilities, such as risk owners, risk analysts, and so on. Second, training shouldn't be a one-time event. Periodic, recurring training is a good idea simply because it can be used to reinforce and refresh stale knowledge and bring workers up to date on the latest tools, techniques, and risk considerations. Finally, awareness training should be well organized and conducted by knowledgeable instructors, both from inside and outside the organization. Internal trainers can give the benefit of the organization's specific views on risk culture, appetite, and tolerance, while external trainers bring the benefit of objective knowledge and risk management methods from the industry.

The subject of the training depends on the audience, of course. The basics may include familiarization training with rules and regulations regarding risk within the organization as well as the basic steps of risk management. Basic concepts and definitions may also be provided in familiarization training. Specific training on risk management techniques and tools may be reserved for those workers who have direct risk management responsibilities. There also may need to be training for senior leadership on how to develop risk management strategies and plans for the organization.

An organization can deliver awareness training in several different ways, and using various combinations of training types can help to deliver an effective training program. Classroom training is, of course, one standard method. Other methods might include individual-based training that comes from reading, computer-based training, and so on. Workers might also be required to read a risk management handbook that defines the different rules and regulations covering risk within the organization. Specialized training on risk management might have to be provided by an external training provider for those individuals with defined risk management responsibilities.

Developing Organizational Security and Risk Awareness Programs

Establishing the security and risk awareness programs in an organization can be a challenge. One way organizations fail is to simply direct someone to develop a training program, when the organization has not even established its risk management strategy or plans. Developing the organization's approach for risk is an essential first step before implementing awareness training. The organization must develop, formally if possible, its stance on risk appetite and tolerance as well as its risk management strategy. It should decide what risk management methodologies it will use as well as what standards and frameworks. Only then can a training program be developed based on a good, solid risk management framework within the organization.

Establishing the awareness training programs also requires buy-in from management at all levels. The program should be adequately funded, and allowances should be made for workers to be able to take part in the training. Management should be committed to awareness training as part of its overall risk management strategy. Sufficiently trained and experienced instructors or a training program manager should be selected to develop and maintain the program. Finally, the training program should articulate not only the risk culture of the organization but also the different risk management needs the organization has. These might include specific risk factors, threats, vulnerabilities, and so on, considered when the training is developed. Workers that participate in awareness training should be able to easily put into practice the concepts, tools, and techniques they learn.

Additionally, the training program should be periodically evaluated for effectiveness, as well as updated with current risks, governance, tools, and techniques.

Beyond initial or recurring awareness training, ongoing communication within the organization is a must for effectively managing both security and risk awareness. Workers in general, but also specifically those with key risk management duties, should be given information on an ongoing basis regarding organizational risks and how to manage and deal with them. Obviously, some information would be restricted from the general organizational population, but specific instances of threats and vulnerabilities, risk factors, and so on should be provided to risk managers in key areas so they can keep updated on the most current risk posture for the organization.

 EXAM TIP While training programs are sometimes the first things that are cut from the budget or the last things to be developed in a program, don't underestimate the importance of awareness training within the overall risk management strategy. Training not only can make the risk management process within the organization more effective, it can also actually help to reduce or mitigate risk because it educates people about the subject, and this alone may minimize risk.

Data Privacy and Data Protection Principles

Throughout this chapter, we have discussed the core concepts of information security that any program should be striving for. This section outlines key data privacy and data protection principles and associated policies and procedures that organizations should consider when aiming to reduce risk.

Security Policies

Security policies and procedures are official organization communications created to support those critical principles of data privacy and data protection. These policies and procedures define how the workers must interact with the organization's computer systems to perform their job functions, how to protect the computer systems and their data, and how to service the organization's clients and constituents properly. Essentially, these policies define how an organization will implement the principles that must be upheld.

Access Control

The following access control principles and policies help provide a consistent organizational structure and procedures to prevent internal fraud and corruption in your organization:

- **Least privilege** The *least privilege* principle grants users only the access rights they need to perform their job functions. This requires giving users the least amount of access possible to prevent them from abusing more powerful access rights.

- **Separation of duties** The *separation of duties* principle ensures that one single individual isn't tasked with high-security and high-risk responsibilities. Certain critical responsibilities are separated between several users to prevent corruption.

- **Job rotation**   *Job rotation* provides improved security because no worker retains the same amount of access control for a position indefinitely. This prevents internal corruption by workers who might otherwise take advantage of their long-term position and security access.

- **Mandatory vacation**   A *mandatory vacation* policy requires employees to use their vacation days at specific times of the year or to use all their vacation days allotted for a single year. This policy helps detect security issues with employees, such as fraud or other internal hacking activities, because the anomalies might surface while the user is away. Increasingly, organizations are implementing a policy requiring mandatory administrative leave for situations in which an employee is under any sort of investigation, systems related or otherwise.

Physical Access Security

As part of its overall access control, your organization must have strong physical access controls and an associated policy, and it must ensure that all workers are educated on the policy's use.

Depending on the security level of the organization, physical security may include guarded or unguarded entrances. Even on guarded premises, the use of security access cards ensures that only identified, authenticated, and authorized persons can enter a facility. Each security access card is coded with the authorization level of the user, who will be able to access only areas of the facility required by their job function. For example, only network and systems administrators would be able to access a server and network communications room with their access card.

Workers must be trained to always close automatically locking doors behind them and not allow unidentified people to follow them through (known as *tailgating*). Most security access cards include a photograph of the cardholder to further identify users in the event they are challenged for their identity. Workers must be encouraged to report suspicious individuals within the premises who are unfamiliar and do not have proper identification.

A published organizational security policy that addresses physical access allows your workers to have proper knowledge of security procedures and to be equally active in the responsibility for physical security.

Network Security

Several policies provide standard guidelines for implementing network security principles within an organization and encompass areas such as the use of the Internet and internal network, data privacy, security incident response, human resources (HR) issues, and document security. These policies are often enforced by technical controls such as data loss prevention (DLP) tools that monitor for breaches of policy and issue a report when a breach occurs. Other tools may alert an administrator to machines joining the network that don't meet security requirements (having out-of-date antivirus signatures, for example) or report to an administrator when an unauthorized machine has been added to the network or an inappropriate website has been visited.

Acceptable Use

An *acceptable use policy (AUP)* is a policy consisting of a set of established guidelines for the appropriate use of computer networks within an organization. The AUP is a written agreement, read and signed by workers, that outlines the organization's terms, conditions, and rules for Internet and internal network use and data protection.

An AUP helps educate workers about the kinds of tools they will use on the network and what they can expect from those tools. The policy also helps to define boundaries of behavior and, more critically, specifies the consequences of violating those boundaries. The AUP also lays out the actions that management and the system administrators may take to maintain and monitor the network for unacceptable use, and it includes the general worst-case consequences or responses to specific policy violations.

Developing an AUP for your organization's computer network is extremely important for both organizational security and limiting legal liability in the event of a security issue. An AUP should cover the following issues:

- **Legality**   The organization's legal department needs to approve the policy before it's distributed for signing. The policy will be used as a legal document to ensure that the organization isn't legally liable for any type of Internet-related incident and any other transgressions, such as cracking, vandalism, and sabotage.

- **Uniqueness to your environment**   The policy should be written to cover the organization's specific network and the data it contains. Each organization has different security concerns—for example, a medical facility needs to protect data that differs significantly from that of a product sales organization.

- **Completeness**   Beyond rules of behavior, the AUP should also include a statement concerning the organization's position on personal Internet use on company time.

- **Adaptability**   Because the Internet is constantly evolving, the AUP will need to be updated as new issues arise. You can't anticipate every situation, so the AUP should address the possibility of something happening that isn't outlined.

- **Protection for employees**   If your employees follow the rules of the AUP, their exposure to questionable materials should be minimized. In addition, the AUP can protect them from dangerous Internet behavior, such as giving out their names and e-mail addresses to crackers using social engineering techniques.

The focus of an acceptable use policy should be on the responsible use of computer networks and the protection of sensitive information. Such networks include the Internet—for example, web, e-mail (both personal and business), social media, and instant messaging access—and the organization's intranet. An AUP should, at a minimum, contain the following components:

- A description of the strategies and goals to be supported by Internet access in the organization

- A statement explaining the availability of computer networks to workers

- A statement explaining the responsibilities of workers when they use the Internet

- A code of conduct governing behavior on the Internet

- A description of the consequences of violating the policy
- A description of what constitutes acceptable and unacceptable use of the Internet
- A description of the rights of individuals using the networks in the organization, such as user privacy
- A description of the expectations for the access and use of information
- Proper use of social media
- A disclaimer absolving the organization from responsibility under specific circumstances
- A form for workers to sign indicating their agreement to abide by the AUP

Note that many organizations' websites contain an acceptable use policy or terms of use statement that protects them from any liability from users of the site.

Social Media

Websites such as Facebook, Twitter, and Instagram are more popular than ever, and workers often use these sites, sometimes during the workday, to keep up with friends, family, and activities. While keeping your workers' morale high is a plus, it's important to limit social media usage at work, as it can be a hit to overall productivity. Perhaps even more importantly, workers who are posting negative comments about your organization, or even posting potentially private intellectual property, can be a competitor's dream. For example, consider a disgruntled employee who begins tweeting about your organization's secret spaghetti sauce recipe, which is then copied by a competitor. Not good!

However, some pleasant scenarios for an organization can be directly attributed to workers' social media usage. That's why it's important to determine what level of social media use your organization is comfortable with while workers are on the clock. Many organizations have a policy that social media use during work is only allowed on breaks and lunch hours and that workers may not discuss or disclose any information regarding their workplace or intellectual property.

Personal E-Mail

As with social media, many workers have personal e-mail accounts they may want to keep an eye on throughout the day; this lets them know that bills are being paid, packages have been delivered, and so on. Maybe they even use e-mail to keep up with friends. Although this can be positive for workers' morale, it is important that an organization understands how personal e-mail is being used throughout the workday. An important consideration is a potential threat associated with sophisticated adversaries in cyberspace who know a great deal about the organization's workers and may use their personal e-mail account for spearfishing and other nefarious activities. If malware is introduced through this personal e-mail usage during the workday, it then becomes your problem—assuming they're using one of the organization's systems to read their personal e-mail. That malware could potentially leak trade or other secrets about your organization. Again, as with social media, it is important for an organization to dictate the terms of how personal e-mail will be used throughout the workday and whether personal e-mail is allowed to be used on the organization's more sensitive systems. For example, it is generally considered bad practice to allow personal e-mail to be used on production computers, where malware could have a catastrophic effect if introduced into the environment.

Due Care, Due Diligence, and Due Process

Due care, due diligence, and *due process* are terms that apply to the implementation and enforcement of organization-wide security policies. An organization practices *due care* by taking responsibility for all activities that take place in corporate facilities. An organization practices *due diligence* by implementing and maintaining these security procedures consistently to protect the organization's facilities, assets, and workers. Although many organizations outline plans for security policies and standards, they often never officially implement them or don't properly share the information with workers. Without direction from management in the form of training, guidelines, and manuals, and without workers input and feedback, security policies will not be successful.

By practicing due care, the organization shows it has taken the necessary steps to protect itself and its workers. By practicing due diligence, the organization ensures that these security policies are properly maintained, communicated, and implemented. If the organization doesn't follow proper due care and due diligence initiatives, it might be considered legally negligent if organization security and customer data are compromised.

Due process guarantees that in the event of a security issue by a worker, the worker receives an impartial and fair inquiry into the incident to ensure the worker's employment rights are not being violated. If during an investigation or inquiry, the worker's rights are violated, the organization may face legal ramifications via lawsuits or governmental employment tribunals.

Privacy

Privacy policies are agreements that protect individually identifiable information. An organization engaged in online activities or e-commerce has a responsibility to adopt and implement a policy to protect the privacy of personally identifiable information (PII). Increasingly, regulations such as the European Union's General Data Protection Regulation (GDPR), the California Consumer Privacy Act (CCPA), and the U.S. Health Insurance Portability and Accountability Act (HIPAA) require a privacy policy that is acknowledged before use. Organizations should also take steps to ensure online privacy when interacting with other organizations, such as business partners. Privacy obligations also extend to an organization's use of the PII of its workers.

The following recommendations pertain to implementing privacy policies:

- An organization's privacy policy must be easy to find, read, and understand, and it must be available prior to or at the time the PII is collected or requested.

- The policy needs to state clearly what information is being collected; the purpose for which that information is being collected; possible third-party distribution of that information; the choices available to an individual regarding the collection, use, and distribution of the collected information; a statement of the organization's commitment to data security; and what steps the organization takes to ensure data quality and access.

- The policy should disclose the consequences, if any, of a person's refusal to provide information or the refusal to permit its processing.

- The policy should include a clear statement of what accountability mechanism the organization uses, such as procedures for dealing with privacy breaches, including how to contact the organization and register complaints.

- Individuals must be given the opportunity to exercise choice regarding how PII collected from them online can be used when such use is unrelated to the purpose for which the information was collected. At a minimum, individuals should be given the opportunity to opt out of such use.

- When an individual's information collected online is to be shared with a third party, especially when such distribution is unrelated to the purpose for which the information was initially collected, the individual should be given the opportunity to opt out.

- Organizations creating, maintaining, using, or disseminating PII should take appropriate measures to ensure its reliability and should take reasonable precautions to protect the information from loss, misuse, or alteration.

Each organization must evaluate its use of the Internet and its internal systems to determine the type of privacy policy it needs in order to protect all involved parties. The privacy policy will protect the organization from legal issues, raising employees, customers, and constituents' comfort levels regarding the protection of their information. A privacy policy should include the following elements:

- **Information collection**   Collect, use, and exchange only data pertinent to the exact purpose, in an open and ethical manner. The information collected for one purpose shouldn't be used for another. Notify persons of information you have about them, its proposed use and handling, as well as the enforcement policies.

- **Direct marketing**   The organization can use only non-PII for marketing purposes and must certify that the persons' personal information won't be resold to third-party organizations.

- **Information accuracy**   Ensure the data is accurate, timely, and complete and has been collected in a legal and fair manner. Allow people the right to access, verify, and change their information in a timely, straightforward manner. Inform people of the data sources and allow them the option of removing their names from the marketing lists.

- **Information security**   Apply security measures to safeguard the data on databases. Establish worker training programs and policies on the proper handling of PII. Limit the access to a need-to-know basis on personal information and divide the information so that no one worker or unit has the whole picture. Follow all government regulations concerning data handling and privacy.

EXAM TIP   Privacy policies must be easy to find, and they must provide information on how to opt out of any use of personally identifiable information.

Human Resources

An organization's HR department is an important link regarding the organization and worker security. The HR department is responsible for hiring employees, tracking contractors, consultants, and other temporary workers, ensuring workers conform to company codes and policies during their term of work, and maintaining organization security in case of a worker termination. The following sections outline the responsibility of human resources during the three phases of the employment cycle: hiring, maintenance, and termination.

Hiring

When hiring employees for a position within the organization, the HR department is responsible for the initial employee screening. This usually takes place during the first interview: an HR representative meets with the potential employee to discuss the organization and to get a first impression, gauging whether this person would fit into the organization's environment. This interview generally is personality based and nontechnical. Further interviews are usually more oriented toward the applicant's skill set and are conducted by the department advertising the position. Both types of interviews are important because the applicant could possess excellent technical skills for the position, but their personality and communications skills might not be conducive to integration with the work environment.

During the interview process, HR also conducts *background checks* of the applicant and examines and verifies their educational and employment history. Reference checks are also performed, where HR can obtain information on the applicant from a third party to help confirm facts about the person's past. HR will also verify professional licenses and certifications. Depending on the type of organization, such as the government or the military, the applicant might have to go through security clearance checks or even a credit check, medical examination, and drug testing.

To protect the confidentiality of organization information, the applicant is usually required to sign a *non-disclosure agreement (NDA)*, which legally prevents the applicant from disclosing sensitive organization data to other organizations, even after termination of employment. These agreements are particularly important with high-turnover positions, such as contract or temporary employment.

When an employee is hired, the organization also inherits that person's personality quirks or traits. A solid hiring process can prevent future problems with new employees.

Tracking Temps, Contractors, and Consultants

Many organizations have more than just employees in their workforce. Most will have a few contractors, consultants, and temps—and some will have a lot! In organizations where these "non-employee" workers have managed identities to regulate their access to computers and workspaces, it's necessary for organizations to carefully track them with the same precision as regular employees.

Who better to do this than HR? For legal reasons, many organizations' HR departments are reluctant to also track the non-employee workforce, but information security requirements demand centralized, competent tracking just the same.

Today's human resource information systems (HRISs) have the ability to segregate employees from other types of workers. This helps HR departments manage employees and non-employee workers separately, as often they must.

Codes of Conduct and Ethics

The HR department is also responsible for outlining an organization's policy regarding codes of conduct and ethics, which are general lists of what the organization expects from its workers in terms of everyday conduct—dealing with fellow workers, managers, and subordinates, including people from outside the organization such as customers and clients.

These codes of conduct could include restrictions and policies concerning drug and alcohol use, theft and vandalism, sexual harassment, and violence in the workplace. If a worker violates any of these policies, they could be disciplined, suspended, or even terminated, depending on the severity of the infraction.

Termination

The dismissal of workers can be a stressful and chaotic time, especially because terminations can happen quickly and without notice. A worker can be terminated for a variety of reasons, such as performance issues, personal and attitude problems, or legal issues such as sabotage, espionage, or theft. Alternatively, the worker could be leaving to work for another organization. The HR department needs to have a specific set of procedures ready to follow in case a worker resigns or is terminated. Without a step-by-step method of termination, some procedures might be ignored or overlooked during the process and thus compromise the organization's security.

A termination policy should exist for each type of situation where a worker is leaving the organization. For example, you might follow slightly different procedures for terminating a worker who's leaving to take a job in an unrelated industry than a worker who's going to work for a direct competitor. In the latter case, the worker might be considered a security risk if they remain on the premises for their two-week notice period, where they could transmit organization secrets to the competition.

Similarly, terminating a contractor or consultant will involve different policies and procedures since their employment relationship is with another organization. Finally, organizations with one or more labor unions must navigate those waters according to collective bargaining agreements and rules.

A termination policy should include the following procedures for the immediate termination of a worker:

- **Securing work area** When the termination time has been set, the worker in question should be escorted from their workstation area to the HR department. This prevents them from using their computer or other organization resource once notice of termination is given. Their computer should be turned off and disconnected from the network. When the worker returns to their desk to collect personal items, someone should be with them to ensure that they do not take private organization information. Finally, the worker should be escorted out of the building.

- **Return of identification**   As part of the termination procedure, the worker's identification should be returned. This includes identity badges, pass cards, keys for doors, and any other security device used for access to organization facilities. This prevents the person from accessing the building after being escorted from the premises.

- **Return of equipment**   All organization-owned equipment must be returned immediately, such as desktops, laptops, cell phones, tablets, organizers, or any other type of electronic equipment that could contain confidential information.

- **Suspension of accounts**   An important part of the termination procedure is the notification to the network administrators of the situation. They should be notified shortly before the termination takes place to give them time to disable any network accounts and phone access for that worker. The network password of the account should be changed, and any other network access the worker might have, such as remote access, should be disabled. The worker's file server data and e-mail should be preserved and archived to protect any work or communications the organization might need for operational or legal reasons.

 EXAM TIP   All user access, including physical and network access controls, needs to be disabled for a worker once they have been terminated. This prevents the worker from accessing the facility or network.

Chapter Review

The enterprise architecture within an organization affects the risk of the business in several different ways. Aspects of enterprise architecture risk include interoperability, supportability, security, maintenance, and how the different pieces and parts of the infrastructure fit into the systems development life cycle.

Key areas in IT operations management include server and infrastructure management, end-user support, help desk, and problem escalation management, and, of course, cybersecurity.

Organizations use project, program, and portfolio management to oversee and sustain both short- and long-term aspects of systems and processes.

At the core of a project are three primary drivers. These are *scope* (amount or range of work), *schedule* (when work is to be done and its completion date), and *cost* (including all the resources expended toward the completion of the project).

Business continuity is concerned with the careful planning and deployment of resources involved in keeping the mission of the business going (that is, keeping the business functioning regardless of negative events). *Disaster recovery* is primarily concerned with the quick reaction involved with preserving lives, equipment, and data immediately following a serious negative event.

Resilience refers to the ability of the business to survive negative events and continue with its mission and function.

Data lifecycle management is a lifecycle process concerned with the creation, protection, use, retention, and disposal of business information.

The *systems development life cycle*, or SDLC, is essentially the entire life of a system or product, from concept to development, from implementation to disposal. Security should be a part of every step in the SDLC, thus ensuring security by design.

New or emerging technologies can present risks to organizations simply because there are several different important considerations when integrating the latest technologies into an existing environment.

Access controls ensure that only authorized personnel can read, write to, modify, add to, or delete data. They also ensure that only the same authorized personnel can access the different information systems and equipment used to store, process, transmit, and receive sensitive data.

The three goals of security, known as the CIA triad, are confidentiality, integrity, and availability. Supporting these three goals are other elements of security, such as access control, data sensitivity and classification, identification, authentication, authorization, accountability, and, finally, non-repudiation.

Standards, frameworks, and practices relevant to risk management include NIST RMF, COBIT 2019, and the various ISO standards.

Data classification policy defines data sensitivity levels, as well as handling and disposal procedures to ensure adequate protection of sensitive information.

Industry frameworks, standards, and practices can be adopted when building an information security program, as opposed to building these elements from scratch.

The NIST Risk Management Framework (RMF) is a seven-step methodology that provides for risk management all the way through the information systems life cycle.

COBIT is a management framework developed by ISACA and facilitates the governance of enterprise information and technology. COBIT consists of two layers, governance and management, which further break down into a total of 40 separate objectives.

The Risk IT Framework comes from traditional risk management principles of various enterprise risk management (ERM) standards and describes activities and processes thought of as best practices.

Information security awareness training ensures an organization's workforce is aware of policy, behavior expectations, and safe computer and Internet usage.

Security policies and procedures are official organization communications that are created to support those critical principles of data privacy and data protection.

Effective physical access controls ensure that only authorized personnel are permitted to access work centers, processing centers, and other work areas. This contributes to an environment with better information security as well as workplace safety.

An organization practices *due care* by taking responsibility for all activities that take place in corporate facilities.

An organization practices *due diligence* by implementing and maintaining these security procedures consistently to protect the organization's facilities, assets, and workers.

Due process guarantees that in the event of a security issue by a worker, the worker receives an impartial and fair inquiry into the incident to ensure the worker's employment rights are not being violated.

Each organization must evaluate its use of the Internet and its internal systems to determine the type of privacy policy it needs in order to protect all involved parties.

An organization's HR department is an important link regarding organization and worker security. The HR department is responsible for hiring employees, tracking contractors, consultants, and other temporary workers, ensuring workers conform to company codes and policies during their term of work, and maintaining organization security in case of worker termination.

Quick Review

- Two common enterprise architecture frameworks are The Open Group Architecture Framework (TOGAF) and the Zachman framework.

- Business continuity and disaster recovery are primarily concerned with the goal of business resilience.

- Two of the key processes involved in business continuity planning are conducting a *business impact assessment (BIA)* and determining a recovery strategy.

- Two key areas of concern in business continuity are the *recovery point objective (RPO)* and the *recovery time objective (RTO)*.

- *Resilience* is the ability of an organization to resist the effects of negative events and its ability to bounce back after one of these events.

- *Data classification* refers to policies that define the proper use, handling, and protection of data at various sensitivity levels.

- The term *systems development life cycle* represents an evolution of the original term *software development life cycle*, reflecting an earlier age when most organizations wrote their own custom business applications.

- Some of the risks associated with emerging technology involve staff unfamiliarity, resulting in improper implementation or use.

- *Access controls* directly support the confidentiality and integrity goals of security and indirectly support the goal of availability.

- *Identification* refers to the act of an individual or entity presenting valid credentials to a system. *Authentication* involves the verification of one's identity with a centralized database. *Authorization* refers to the access rights or privileges assigned to a user account. *Non-repudiation* is a record-keeping property of a system whereby a user will not be able to deny having performed some action.

- A *framework* is a generally overarching methodology for a set of activities or processes.

- A *standard* is a mandatory set of procedures or processes used by the organization and usually fits into an overall framework.

- A *practice* is a normalized process that has been tried and proven as generally accepted within a larger community.

- Periodic security awareness training can be used to reinforce and refresh stale knowledge and bring workers up to date on the latest tools, techniques, and risk considerations.

- The *least privilege* principle grants users only the access rights they need to perform their job functions.

- *Separation of duties* ensures that one single individual isn't tasked with high-security and high-risk responsibilities.

- *Job rotation* provides improved security because no worker retains the same amount of access control for a position indefinitely.

- *Mandatory vacations* enable security and audit staff to examine absent workers' procedures and records to identify signs of misbehavior or fraud.

- An *acceptable use policy (AUP)* is a policy consisting of a set of established guidelines for the appropriate use of computer networks within an organization.

- Social media policy governs acceptable use regarding the sharing of organization information and representation of the organization.

- The use of personal e-mail is a potential distraction as well as a risk for information leakage and the introduction of malware into an environment.

- *Privacy policies* are agreements that protect individually identifiable information.

- Human resources should track not only employees but temporary workers, contractors, and consultants to ensure the integrity of access controls.

Questions

1. You are managing a project that involves the installation of a new set of systems for the accounting division of your organization. You have just been told that there have been budget cuts and the project will not be able to purchase additional equipment needed for the installation. You now have to find other areas to cut in order to fund the extra equipment. Which element of project management is most affected by this threat?

   A. Schedule

   B. Scope

   C. Cost

   D. Quality

2. As a risk practitioner in a larger organization, you have been asked to review the company's SDLC model for potential risk areas. The model includes the Requirements, Design, Development, Implementation, and Disposal phases. Software and systems are moved from the development environment immediately into the production environment and implemented. Which SDLC phase would you recommend that the business add to reduce risk of integration or functionality issues as the system is implemented?

   A. Initiation

   B. Test

   C. Sustainment

   D. Maintenance

3. Lack of a well-written work breakdown structure document can contribute to a vulnerability that affects which aspect of project management?

   A. Cost

   B. Schedule

   C. Scope

   D. Quality

4. Which of the following is the major risk factor associated with integrating new or emerging technologies into an existing IT infrastructure?

   A. Security mechanisms

   B. Data format

   C. Vendor supportability

   D. Interoperability

5. Which of the following is a short-term process primarily concerned with protecting personnel, facilities, and equipment immediately following a disaster or major incident?

   A. Disaster recovery

   B. Business continuity

   C. Business impact analysis

   D. Recovery point objective

6. Which of the following would be a vulnerability that stems from the business not identifying its critical assets and processes during the continuity management process?

   A. Failure to adequately consider system requirements during the SDLC

   B. Failure to perform a business impact analysis

   C. Failure to consider interoperability with integrating new technologies

   D. Failure to maintain redundant systems or data backups

7. Your business just went through a major storm, which has flooded your data center. Members of your recovery team are attempting to salvage equipment as well as locate critical data backups. No one seems to know exactly what they're supposed to do, and they don't have the right equipment available to them. Additionally, there is no coordinated effort within the team to perform specific tasks. Which of the following vulnerabilities most likely led up to this scenario?

   A. Failure to back up sensitive data

   B. Failure to acquire an alternate processing site

   C. Lack of a business impact analysis

   D. Failure to test the disaster recovery plan

8. After a few incidents where customer data was transmitted to a third party, your organization is required to create and adhere to a policy that describes the distribution, protection, and confidentiality of customer data. Which of the following policies do you create?

    A. Privacy

    B. Due care

    C. Acceptable use

    D. Service level agreement

9. You need to create an overall policy for your organization that describes how your users can properly make use of company communications services, such as web browsing, e-mail, and File Transfer Protocol (FTP) services. Which of the following policies do you implement?

    A. Acceptable use policy

    B. Due care

    C. Privacy policy

    D. Service level agreement

10. Which of the following security goals is concerned with ensuring that data has not been modified or altered during transmission?

    A. Confidentiality

    B. Availability

    C. Integrity

    D. Non-repudiation

11. Which of the following is most concerned with ensuring that users cannot deny that they took an action?

    A. Accountability

    B. Non-repudiation

    C. Auditing

    D. Authorization

12. Which of the following describes a set of mandatory procedures or processes used by an organization?

    A. Standard

    B. Framework

    C. Practice

    D. Policy

13. Which of the following frameworks might be used in business governance and IT enterprise management?

    A. NIST RMF

    B. COBIT 2019

    C. The Risk IT Framework

    D. ISO 27001

14. You are implementing an organization-wide risk management strategy, and you are using the NIST Risk Management Framework (RMF). You have just completed step 1 of the RMF, "Categorize information systems." Which of the following steps should you complete next in the RMF sequence?

    A. Authorize system.

    B. Assess security controls.

    C. Continuous monitoring.

    D. Select security controls.

15. Which of the following statements most accurately reflects the effect of information technology (IT) on risk to the business enterprise? (Choose two.)

    A. Information technology is a serious risk to the mission of the organization.

    B. Information technology is used to protect the organization's information.

    C. Information technology is used to eliminate risk to the mission of the organization.

    D. Information technology is used to generate the organization's information.

Answers

1. **C.** Cost is the element of project management that is most affected by the threat of not enough funding.

2. **B.** A test phase introduced into this model would reduce risk by ensuring that a system or software application meets performance and functionality standards before it is introduced into the production environment, potentially eliminating costly issues before they occur.

3. **C.** Lack of a well-written work breakdown structure document can contribute to a vulnerability that affects a project's scope.

4. **D.** Interoperability is the major risk factor associated with integrating new or emerging technologies into an existing IT infrastructure. It covers a wide range of factors, which typically include backward compatibility, data format, security mechanisms, and other aspects of system integration.

5. **A.** Disaster recovery is a short-term process primarily concerned with protecting personnel, facilities, and equipment immediately following a disaster or major incident.

6. B. Failure to perform a business impact analysis could cause a vulnerability in that the organization would not be able to adequately identify its critical business processes and assets.

7. D. Failure to test the disaster recovery plan on a periodic basis—as well as make sure people are trained and have the right equipment—can result in poor or ineffective recovery efforts.

8. A. A privacy policy concerns the protection and distribution of private customer data. Any company, especially one engaged in online activities or e-commerce, has a responsibility to adopt and implement a policy for protecting the privacy of individually identifiable information.

9. A. An acceptable use policy establishes rules for the appropriate use of computer networks within your organization. The policy describes the terms, conditions, and rules of using the Internet and its various services within the company's networks.

10. C. Integrity is concerned with ensuring that data has not been modified or altered during transmission or storage.

11. B. Non-repudiation is concerned with ensuring that users cannot deny that they took a particular action.

12. A. A standard is a set of mandatory procedures or processes used by an organization.

13. B. COBIT is used in business governance and IT enterprise management.

14. D. Step 2 of the RMF is "Select security controls" and is accomplished after information systems have been categorized.

15. B, D. Information technology is used to generate the business's information as well as protect it.

Implementing and Managing a Risk Management Program

This appendix takes a more pragmatic view of building and managing a risk management program. Rather than the somewhat academic view in the CRISC job practice, we draw directly from our experience building several risk management programs in our careers.

We have built or improved numerous risk management processes and programs between the three of us. The process and technique are not overly complicated. The most challenging part of building a risk management process is figuring out how to engage with executives in the organization—so that they understand what the process is all about and participate meaningfully. After all, it's their business, and we just want to make sure they make informed decisions related to various types of risks.

Today's Risk Landscape

It's a crazy world for an IT or cyber risk leader. While we find the profession both challenging and rewarding, increasing pressures on all sides are making the job more difficult (see Figure A-1). Some of the factors at play include the following:

- **Innovation and chutzpah of cybercrime**   Cybercriminal organizations are thriving. Ransomware, extortion, social engineering, and DDoS are highly successful, drawing even more into this dark industry. Intruders develop new attack methods in shorter periods of time, indicating the presence of increases in research and development.

- **Upward pressure on regulations**   The success of cybercriminals is putting pressure on governments to pass laws requiring organizations (and governments) to do more to protect sensitive information. Industry sector regulations like GLBA and HIPAA, along with emerging privacy regulations like GDPR and CCPA, are building layers of regulation on already strained businesses.

Figure A-1
Pressure comes
from all sides on
security and risk
programs today.

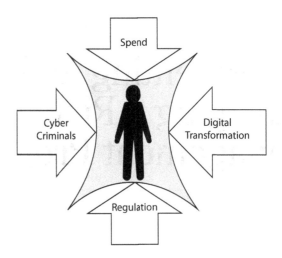

- **Downward pressure on spend**   Despite the two factors mentioned, management is trying to keep a lid on rising costs and hold the line on spending increases while expecting security organizations to better defend them from attack. A related problem is the limited talent pool of qualified security and risk professionals to guide organizations out of the mess they're in.

- **Increasing complexity of digital transformation**   Organizations' IT environments have never been more complex. Despite pressure to standardize on tools and technologies, the move to cloud services and cloud infrastructure means IT organizations have more kinds of technologies, more types of services, and more kinds of operations to manage.

- **Introduction of IoT devices**   Increasingly, IT departments have to deal with more than just servers, desktops, laptops, printers, and mobile devices on their networks. Many other devices are plugged into internal networks, including "smart" devices, appliances, and voice-activated assistants. The so-called "attack surface" expands faster than a security team can ever hope to monitor and protect it.

- **BYOD**   Increasingly, organizations' workers use personally owned devices, mainly smartphones, to access and manage business information and systems. Such organizations have effectively ceded control of their information and information systems if these devices are not actively managed.

- **Telework**   The COVID-19 pandemic thrust new working conditions on virtually every enterprise in the world, many of which were unprepared to deal with this and related changes. Organizations that were already stretched and accepting too much risk had still more risk to take on.

- **Cloud-based services**   Cloud-based services decrease the effort and friction of acquiring new information systems. Sometimes, however, this goes too far, resulting in individuals and workgroups that unilaterally decide to employ cloud-based services, escaping the scrutiny of legal and cybersecurity professionals. Corporate information has escaped the control of IT and risk owners in many cases.

- **Increasing variety of security tooling**   Many thousands of security software companies compete in the marketplace with their tools. Security leaders are increasingly distracted by these vendors and their promises of stopping whatever the latest attack techniques happen to be at the moment.

- **Difficulty in finding qualified security professionals**   Most organizations struggle to find enough qualified security professionals to fill their teams. Organizations take months, half a year, or more to find new hires. We won't argue or debate the finer points on this matter, except to say that companies have a hard time finding the people they want to hire on their security teams.

These factors weigh heavily on security organizations, resulting in sub-par security architecture, planning, monitoring, and response, with too few personnel working on important issues.

Allegory of the Battlefield
Consider the following photograph that shows Major General Alexander M. Weyand poring over a battlefield map in Korea:

(Image courtesy U.S. National Archive)

Imagine, if you will, that General Weyand is taking in information from scouts on the enemy's position and discussing where and when to deploy troops to counter the enemy's moves and even gain territory. This is all about the allocation of scarce resources to provide the maximum margin of victory.

(continued)

> The soldiers on the front line depend on this strategizing—their very lives depend on it. Political leaders depend on this strategizing as well so that their armies will meet their objectives of countering the enemy's objectives.
>
> Imagine, for a moment, that an army lacked this planning and decision-making function. Without it, lower-level officers would be commanding their regiments to go this way and that, based on what they could see within their limited purview. Lacking big-picture information and purpose, they may succeed or fail, but they won't be operating with a clear, central purpose.
>
> Risk management is the modern equivalent of those field commanders. In risk management, security specialists are examining threat intel, considering available internal capabilities, and making decisions on which of many issues are the most important to discuss and take action on. Formal risk management is the modern equivalent of field commanders studying the enemy's plans, available resources, and most effectively applying their resources to meet their objectives.
>
> Most organizations do not do this, at least not in any repeatable way. Instead, when decisions are made, they usually lack any analysis or triage to determine the best way forward on any given issue. The result: high-risk matters get little attention, while other issues get more than their fair share. Scarce resources are applied to the wrong issues, while the highest risk issues go poorly resolved or entirely unaddressed.

What Is a Risk Management Program?

To fully describe a risk management program, first we'll step back and describe what a *program* is. In business today, a program is a set of defined roles and responsibilities as well as processes or procedures that are carried out indefinitely.

A risk management program is simply a process or set of processes through which

- Risks are discovered.
- Risks are cataloged.
- Risks are analyzed.
- Business decisions about what to do about risks are made.

Also, follow-up is performed to ensure these business decisions are carried out on time and as agreed upon.

The primary artifacts found in a typical risk management program include the following:

- **Program charter** This document defines the purpose and scope of the risk management program, roles and responsibilities, and describes its processes and records.

- **Process or procedures**   This document describes the steps in various risk management processes and procedures, who carries them out, and what records are maintained.

- **Risk register**   This is the central repository of risks that have been identified. The risk register is one of the historical records of a risk management program.

- **Risk analyses**   Individual risks are often studied in greater detail, with additional risk analysis to help decision-makers decide what to do about these risks.

- **Minutes**   This is a business record of decisions and other actions taken.

So far, this may sound formal. Risk management should be consistent and methodical so that its proceedings are managed and recorded.

The Purpose of a Risk Management Program

Many kinds of threats and risks demand the attention of cybersecurity leaders. Even the best-equipped organizations have insufficient resources to deal effectively with every identified risk. A risk management program facilitates informed decision-making that helps to prioritize resources to deal with identified risks.

When properly designed and implemented, a risk management program serves as a *triage* apparatus to help identify and distinguish more significant risks from lesser risks. Instead of going into the detail of determining the actual probability and financial impact of threats, risk management's triage sorts out risks to help management understand which risks are more critical to deal with sooner and which can be dealt with later.

A common mistake made in risk management programs is the time spent in detailed analysis to determine accurate probabilities of threat events and actual costs of threat events. While, at times, it may be helpful to determine estimates of probability and impact, this is not the sole purpose of risk management. Instead, the triage function of risk management identifies those risks needing prompt attention versus those whose attention can wait.

In this respect, a qualitative analysis method can be far more useful than a quantitative one. If risks are considered still "very high," it really doesn't matter if it's 85.2 percent versus 95.7 percent; it's still coming, and it's still bad.

When properly designed and implemented, risk management identifies the most critical risks and facilitates business-level decision-making by business leaders to deal with those risks.

Not Only IT Risk Management

Many in the business think of risk management as consisting primarily of cyber risk and increasingly of privacy risk. The scope of risk in the CRISC certification consists of all IT risk, which goes beyond cyber to include various aspects of operational risk, such as the capacity and availability of IT systems to continue running properly.

(continued)

> The methodology of risk management, however, transcends IT altogether. Other risk domains include workforce risk, economic risk, market/competitive risk, currency exchange risk, geopolitical risk, natural hazards risk, fraud risk, and more. The techniques used in risk management are agnostic to the context of risk.
>
> Risk management is risk management, regardless of the focus or the context. It's only necessary for a risk management program to have someone skilled in the techniques of risk management and someone skilled in the subject matter of the risk management program. The program can succeed, whether both of these are a single person or two people.

The Risk Management Life Cycle

Like many business activities, risk management is a life-cycle process. Risks are identified in many ways, and specific activities are performed for each of those risks. The entire life cycle is described in detail in this section.

Risk Discovery

In Chapter 2, we made a list of the ways in which new IT risks can be discovered, with complete explanations for each. We'll provide just the summary here:

- Audits
- Penetration tests
- Security advisories
- Whistleblowers
- Threat modeling
- Risk assessments
- Security and privacy incidents
- Operational incidents
- News and social media articles
- Professional networking
- Passive observation
- Risk-aware culture

This list should not be construed as complete. Instead, it should help you understand that there are many ways in which a risk manager will discover new risks. Put another way, it would be dangerous to limit the identification of new risks to a fixed set of inputs, as this could artificially eliminate a source that is critical for some. Risk discovery is sometimes methodical and sometimes spontaneous. The spontaneity of risk discovery compels us to advise you to consider all possible likely and unlikely sources of risk. We can no more tell you the types of risk sources to include than we can tell you which of those sources will be related to your next risk event.

The Risk Register

The *risk register* (sometimes known as a *risk ledger*) is the centerpiece of business records in a risk management program. Each entry in the risk register represents a different IT risk that has been identified at some point in time, as recently as earlier today or as distant as a year or two in the past.

Since this appendix focuses on establishing a risk management program, we recommend implementing an initial risk register using a spreadsheet program such as Microsoft Excel or Google Sheets. It's our style to build a program or a process using largely manual procedures and then introduce automation later.

A risk register starts quite simply, with columns like these:

- Risk name
- Risk description in terms of the risk context
- Threat description
- Vulnerability description

As you accumulate records in the risk register, you'll find it helpful to add more columns. These columns indicate when the entry was recorded, its context, and a business-centric explanation:

- Entry date
- Entered by
- Risk description in business terms
- Risk context

While the description of risk in business terms appears to be just another bullet item, it is perhaps the most important field in the risk register. Without it, risk managers will have a more difficult time describing the risk in business terms to executives who may be asked to decide on the disposition of the risk. Including this column in the risk register compels the risk manager to begin thinking about the risk in business terms early, giving them time to ponder and develop the risk story.

Rating risks for severity is a topic all its own, discussed in more detail in the following subsections.

You will need to add more columns as you move through the life cycle and make risk treatment decisions. These columns describe basic risk treatment parameters:

- Risk status
- Risk treatment selection
- Risk treatment description
- Risk treatment owner
- Risk treatment commit date

As risk treatment activities reach their conclusions, you'll need additional columns:

- Risk treatment completion date
- Risk closure date

Over time, you'll be spending considerable time in the risk register. You'll want to view risks in various contexts and categories at times. Some columns that help classify risks include the following:

- Location.

- Business unit.

- Technology type. This may consist of one or more columns that enable you to view risks in discrete categories. For instance, you may wish to view all risks related to mobile devices, endpoints, specific types of servers, database management systems, network devices, or other components.

Rating Risks—Qualitative

Not all risks are created equal. Some may be nearly trivial, while others represent an existential threat to the organization. A risk register must contain some columns used to describe the level of risk for each entry.

The two basic qualitative measures of risk are probability and impact, as detailed next:

- **Probability**   This specifies the likelihood of an actual occurrence of the risk. In qualitative terms, probability is typically expressed as High, Medium, or Low or in basic numeric terms such as 1 (Low) to 3 (High), 1 to 5, or 1 to 10.

- **Impact**   This specifies the impact on the organization due to an actual occurrence of the risk. Like probability, impact in qualitative risk ratings is expressed as High, Medium, or Low or on a numeric scale such as 1–3, 1–5, or 1–10.

Note that, in qualitative risk rating, no attempt at an actual probability or impact is being made. Instead, the purpose of qualitative risk ratings is one of *triage*—these ratings help the risk manager distinguish entries with higher risks from entries with lower risks.

Qualitative Terms Help with Ratings

Rating the probability and impact of risks on numeric scales of 1–3 or 1–5 can, at times, be too abstract. For this reason, we recommend a list of terms be associated with these levels for both probability and impact. Using these terms as a guide can help the risk manager perform more consistent risk ratings for risk register entries.

For event probability on a scale of 1–5, these terms can be used:

- 5 = Certain
- 4 = Likely
- 3 = Possible
- 2 = Unlikely
- 1 = Rare

Similarly, these terms can be used for impact:

- 5 = Global
- 4 = Country
- 3 = Department
- 2 = Team
- 1 = Individual

These impact terms describe the scope of impact for a risk event. The highest-rated events would affect the entire organization, while the lowest-rated events would affect only a single worker.

Two additional qualitative measures can be introduced that help the risk manager better understand the overall risk for each entry:

- **Asset value**   This qualitative term expresses the value of the asset(s) involved in a specific risk. Like other qualitative terms, asset value is expressed as High, Medium, or Low or on a numeric scale. Generally, this represents an asset that would have to be recovered or replaced should a relevant threat occur.

- **Operational criticality**   This term expresses the operational importance of an asset or function. An asset that the organization depends on for high-value operations (even if the value of the asset itself is low) would be assigned a higher value.

While these two measures are not seen as often in qualitative risk analysis, they help distinguish risks in that all-important triage used to identify the most critical risks.

Calculating Overall Risk   The four qualitative risks explained here can help the risk manager sort out various risks in the risk register. One final column can help tie them all together that would simply be called "Risk." This column can easily be calculated by multiplying the ratings of the four risk columns together. For example, a risk item in the risk register is rated as follows:

- Probability = 4
- Impact = 2
- Asset value = 2
- Operational criticality = 1

The risk value in this example is $4 \times 2 \times 2 \times 1 = 16$.

Using Qualitative Risk Ratings   In qualitative risk analysis, the individual risk columns, as well as the column representing overall risk, exist to help the risk manager better understand how various risks compare to one another. No attempt is made to calculate the actual probability of occurrence or the costs incurred if a risk event occurs. Instead, qualitative risk ratings help the risk manager understand which risks warrant more focus and attention.

Other columns in the risk register provide opportunities for focus, including those columns specifying the type of asset or system, the business unit, the geographic location, and more. The ability to focus on a portion of the risk register associated with a specific part of the organization, a particular location, or other distinguishing characterization helps the risk manager focus on the risks that matter more versus the ones that matter less.

In a sample risk management scenario, a risk manager is preparing to have a conversation with the part of IT that manages end-user endpoints—primarily laptop and desktop computers—in a particular region of the world. To prepare, the risk manager can filter the risk register to view just the risks associated with end-user endpoints as well as risks in particular global regions. The resulting risk will contain just those items, which the risk manager can then examine more deeply to distinguish the items of greater concern from those of lesser concern. Now, the risk manager can have a more meaningful conversation with the IT leaders about risks directly associated with their work.

NOTE   The purpose of qualitative risk analysis is *triage*—to distinguish risks from one another and to more easily identify larger risks.

Rating Risks—Quantitative

Sometimes, a risk manager is asked to go beyond qualitative risk rating and provide actual probabilities and financial impacts of risks. "How much will it cost us if customer data is stolen?" is a reasonable question that an executive may pose to a risk manager. Arguably, the risk manager should attempt to arrive at an estimate to help the executive better understand the consequences of a security breach.

In our practice, we do not attempt to uplift every item in the risk register from qualitative to quantitative terms. Doing so would take a considerable amount of time and not result in much additional insight. Instead, we embark on quantitative risk analysis when examining individual risks. We discuss this further in the section "Performing Deeper Analysis."

The Risk Register Is a Living Document

The risk register is a living document, and even when risks are reduced, this is recorded and reflected in the document; they are not simply deleted. This provides a history of risk management within the organization. The contents of the risk register should be managed accordingly.

Types of Risk Registers

Many kinds of risks are present everywhere in an organization, and it makes little sense to put them all together in one risk register. Imagine if there was a risk entry associated with currency exchange risk, and adjacent to it is another entry that expresses the misconfiguration of a server. Both are useful, even valuable, but they are vastly different in their context and importance. Further, particularly in larger organizations, other individuals will manage these risks and discuss them with different executives.

Layers of Risk Registers

Different levels of risk are typically maintained in separate risk registers. Most often, these basic three risk registers will exist:

- **Entity-level risk**   These are the overall "big picture" risks that affect an entire organization. The types of subject matter in an entity-level risk register generally include the following:
  - Workforce-related risks
  - Currency exchange risks in organizations operating in multiple countries, or with suppliers in other countries
  - Economic risks having to do with macroeconomic business cycles
  - Risks that exist as an aspect of organizational culture
- **Program-level risk**   These are risks most often associated with business processes throughout the organization. Examples of the types of risks found at this level include the following:
  - **Effectiveness of vulnerability management**   If, for instance, the IT department is lackadaisical in its security patching, an entry may be created in the risk register that describes this systemic problem.
  - **Identity management**   An organization may have little discipline in its access request, fulfillment, and termination procedures.
  - **BYOD**   An organization may not have controls to prevent employees' use of personally owned devices for managing critical data, leading to a significant data leakage risk.
- **Asset-level risk**   These risks are associated with individual assets and groups of assets. Often, these risks are identified with scanning tools and other tooling. Examples of risks at this level include the following:
  - Misconfiguration of critical devices
  - Missing critical patches
  - Newly discovered unmanaged devices

Communicating Between the Layers

A single risk manager may be involved in two or all three of these risk registers in smaller organizations. More often, however, different persons manage each risk register separately. One might think that these risk registers would be isolated from each other. While this may be true, organizations are wise to be cognizant of opportunities for communication between those who manage various risk registers.

Classic examples of the crossover between risk registers include the following:

- Chronic occurrence of an IT department exceeding patching SLAs may compel a risk manager to create a program-level risk item describing a risk with the operational process of patching.
- Chronic occurrence of a product engineering group avoiding engagement with security and privacy teams may compel a risk manager to create an entity-level risk describing a culture that lacks the essential cultural ingredient of "security and privacy by design."

The most frequent communication between risk register layers is a chronic or repeated failure of processes at lower layers that suggests a systemic problem at a higher layer.

NOTE Our frequent use of the term *risk manager* signifies a *role* rather than a job title. The job title of risk manager is generally seen only in larger organizations, whereas those with other job titles fulfill the role.

Reviewing the Risk Register

Risk managers should have intimate familiarity with the contents of their risk register(s). This requires a risk manager to frequently examine the contents of the risk register, using various filtering ("slicing and dicing") techniques to view subsets of the entire risk register. This attention could approach what we would call "preening," where a risk manager examines and periodically adjusts contents in the risk register.

Most often, a risk manager will occasionally adjust an aspect of risk rating of a risk register item. As the risk manager becomes intimately familiar with the risk register, sometimes the risk manager will realize that a particular risk entry's risk rating should be adjusted a bit up or down, making risk ratings more credible and reasonable.

NOTE A risk program aspiring to higher maturity should require recording rating changes and other changes to the risk register, or perhaps use a change control process requiring two or more persons to understand and agree to changes to the risk register.

In an example described earlier in this appendix, a risk manager is preparing for a conversation with a particular leader in an organization by examining risk register items relevant to that leader's mission. This is a helpful example, but a risk manager should not wait for a conversation to focus on those relevant risks. Instead, the risk manager should routinely examine smaller sets of risks in logical groupings such as location, type of asset, and business unit to become even more familiar with the risk landscape in different parts of the organization.

Formal Risk Register Reviews

While the risk manager may be spending quality time alone with the risk register, formal reviews with one or more additional people are warranted. These reviews can help improve the quality of the risk register through consensus. Reviews strengthen the integrity of the risk register, as they will represent the opinion of a group rather than a single individual.

Few other persons may have skills or experience in risk management in smaller organizations. Risk register reviews with others are still valuable: as the risk manager describes risks to others, opportunities for improvements can still be identified.

Better organizations will document risk register reviews and record any changes to risk register entries.

Reviewing Risks with Staff   It is often appropriate for the risk leader to review the contents of the risk register with other security, privacy, and risk staff members. Generally, these discussions will consist of a closer look at the details in the risk register, including a look at ratings, and any completed work on risk analysis that includes potential risk treatment options.

Staff members can be a good source of new material for the risk register. Reviews may, at times, remind staff members of other matters that may be good candidates for the risk register. Frontline personnel are often aware of good and poor practices in technology operations and business processes; earning their trust and using them for intel on new risks can be a valuable pursuit.

When possible, staff reviews should not be limited to personnel in cybersecurity but could include staff from IT and other departments.

 NOTE   Risk-averse organizations may consider employing reminders of confidentiality before reviewing risk register contents with staff.

Reviewing Risks with Business Leaders   At times, it is appropriate for the risk leader to review the contents of the risk register with business leaders. This discussion can take many forms, including the following:

- A detailed review of all relevant risks
- A high-level review of the "Top N" risks
- A high-level review of the nature of top risks

These reviews may be considered formal or informal, depending on many factors, including the maturity of the risk program and governance in the organization.

These reviews are not a part of risk treatment but instead are an assessment of the universe of relevant risks. These reviews help business leaders be better informed of the risks that have been identified, and possibly would include discussion on what risks may be the subject of focus in the near term.

Identifying Candidates for Deeper Analysis

The purpose of risk register reviews is about reaching an agreement on each risk's ratings and other data as well as overall risk reduction in the organization. Risk reduction is accomplished by selecting risks that are considered suitable candidates for next steps: deeper analysis and, eventually, risk treatment.

The purpose of deeper analysis is to help the risk manager decide if a specific risk is ready for risk treatment—the decision made by business leaders on the final disposition of the risk. Before that decision can be made, the risk manager must first analyze the risk in more detail.

In the risk management program, the risk manager may establish formal criteria or rely more on gut instinct for selecting risks to study in more detail. A blended approach will likely be used in this selection, where risks meet criteria and are more "visible" than others. This visibility may be related to applicable regulation, internal politics, market reputation, service profitability, or other factors.

A risk manager may select less politically charged risks in a new risk management program. Business leaders may then be more comfortable making risk treatment decisions due to the absence of emotional or political factors. When business leaders are more familiar with the risk treatment process, risks with greater visibility (whatever that may mean) can be selected and treated.

Performing Deeper Analysis

When a risk has been selected for deeper analysis, it's time for the risk manager to begin working on it. The purpose of this deeper analysis is to determine one or more viable risk treatment options that, hopefully, business owners will agree with and ratify.

Individual risks are generally not simple: discerning risk treatment options may require much thought and discussion. We prefer the ideal small group discussion, where the risk manager and one or two subject matter experts brainstorm to identify feasible risk treatment options.

There is no ideal number of options to analyze, although, pragmatically, we prefer three to five options to be considered. If more than five options are selected, risk analysis will take additional time; with fewer than three, management may feel that too few options were considered.

NOTE In our continuing discussion of risk management, risk analysis, and risk treatment, we use terms that imply a simple spreadsheet program for recording risks and performing risk analysis. The use of a spreadsheet may be practical for an emerging risk management program.

The Analysis Worksheet

The worksheet used for additional analysis compares the untreated risk score with the risk score for each of several possible risk treatment options. We like to use a simple model, as described here:

Untreated risk:

- The same columns from the risk register, including likelihood, impact, criticality, asset value, and risk score.

Treated risk:

- An additional set of risk score columns, including likelihood, impact, criticality, asset value, and risk score.
- Additional columns that express the time, effort, and cost required to perform the risk treatment.
- Columns that express the reduction in risk and residual risk.

Risk treatment:

- One or more columns that would specify who or what department or team would perform the risk treatment.

Each risk treatment option occupies a new row in the worksheet. Each option is scored, with the scores representing the levels of likelihood, impact, criticality, and asset value, as well as the new calculated risk score, as though the risk treatment was in place.

Once each risk treatment option is scored, the risk reduction and residual risk are shown. The risk reduction and residual risk, together with other columns showing hard costs and impact on the workforce, can help the risk manager better understand the feasibility of each risk treatment option.

Depending on the complexity of the risk, a detailed analysis may require many hours of research and study. The amount of time available for this work will depend on the risk manager's availability compared with other tasks. In some cases, detailed risk analysis may be considered a luxury.

Figure A-2 depicts a simple risk analysis worksheet that includes the initial risk rating, plus a description of various risk treatment options with their ratings.

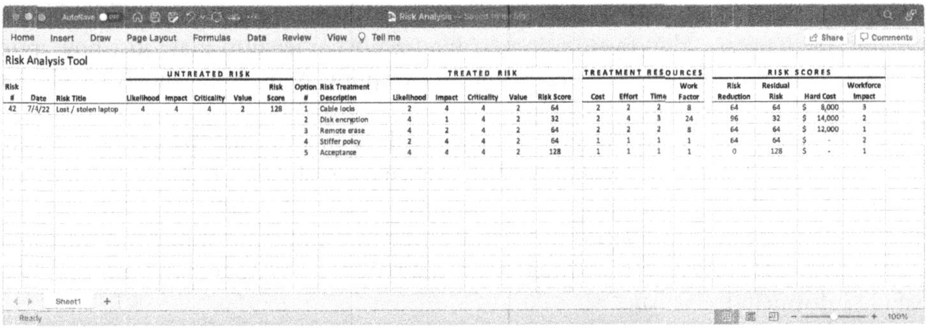

			UNTREATED RISK							TREATED RISK					TREATMENT RESOURCES				RISK SCORES			
Risk #	Date	Risk Title	Likelihood	Impact	Criticality	Value	Risk Score	Option #	Risk Treatment Description	Likelihood	Impact	Criticality	Value	Risk Score	Cost	Effort	Time	Work Factor	Risk Reduction	Residual Risk	Hard Cost	Workforce Impact
42	7/4/22	Lost / stolen laptop	4	4	4	2	128	1	Cable locks	2	4	4	2	64	2	2	2	8	64	64	$ 8,000	3
								2	Disk encryption	4	1	4	2	32	2	4	3	24	96	32	$ 14,000	2
								3	Remote erase	4	2	4	2	64	2	2	2	8	64	64	$ 12,000	1
								4	Stiffer policy	2	4	4	2	64	1	1	1	1	64	64	$ -	2
								5	Acceptance	4	4	4	2	128	1	1	1	1	0	128	$ -	1

Figure A-2 A simple risk analysis worksheet showing risk treatment options

NOTE We prefer to use a separate workbook for performing detailed risk analysis; otherwise, the central risk register workbook will soon be overcrowded with numerous risk analysis tabs.

Qualitative and Quantitative Risk

For risks that involve relatively low costs, it may be sufficient for the risk manager to rely only on qualitative risk analysis techniques to portray which treatment options are more effective than others at reducing risk. However, when the costs of the risk and risk treatment are significant, the risk manager may need to perform a quantitative risk analysis to determine estimates of actual risk treatment costs. Quantitative risk analysis is instrumental when the risk treatment option includes significant hard and/or soft costs.

Selecting Treatment Options

For the risk analysis to contribute to successful risk treatment, the risk manager needs to understand how the business leaders in their organization think about risk. The risk manager should select one or more risk treatment options that business leaders can understand. Business leaders need to feel that their decision is not forced or coerced, and that the options represent a range of reasonable options.

As the risk manager ponders risk treatment options, they need to remember the goal is to bring the elements together to tell a story.

Considering Risk Appetite and Risk Tolerance

Organizations are all over the place regarding risk appetite and risk tolerance. It is our experience (through many years of consulting) that most organizations have no formal statement or practice of risk appetite. In other words, management has not drawn a line in the sand stating that risks above a certain magnitude will not be routinely accepted.

Organizations lacking a formal risk appetite policy or statement must rely instead on gut feel for determining whether to accept any particular risk. While not ideal, as long as the risk manager properly facilitates the risk treatment conversation, business leaders can still make an informed risk decision, even without formal risk guardrails.

A better situation is when the organization has formally defined risk appetite, which states the highest risks that the organization is permitted to accept. We advise another caution here: risk managers should resist the call to reclassify specific risks to a lower level, just to facilitate acceptance. Suppose a particular risk exceeds the allowable risk appetite. In that case, the organization's *risk tolerance* comes into play: just how much more risk will the organization accept on an exception basis, and who is required to approve such an exception?

Understand that we're still in the risk analysis phase but are anticipating possible outcomes for risk treatment discussions and an eventual decision. Risk managers should be prepared with talking points to argue for and against each risk treatment option as well as the array of risk mitigation options. Remember that it is not the risk manager's responsibility to make risk decisions but rather to facilitate discussions leading to business leaders making informed decisions.

Developing a Risk Treatment Recommendation

We like to think about the risk analysis of a risk register item as the development of an entire package of information to be presented to senior management. The package will typically consist of the following:

- A brief description of the risk
- The context of the risk
- Typical risk scenarios, with their probability and impact, if and when realized
- Risk treatment options
- The recommended risk treatment option
- Backup information should management wish to explore the matter further

When taking risk treatment options to senior management, we have reduced this to a single presentation slide and speak to the matter in business terms. Typically, there will be some discussion and a few questions. Depending on the formality of the organization, there may be a formal vote or verbal support for or against a decision.

It's vital to develop talking points, anticipate questions, and rehearse the briefing with a trusted peer. You generally have one opportunity to tell the story of the risk, its potential impact on the organization, and what you propose be done about it.

NOTE   It's always better to be prepared with more information than is used in a risk treatment proceeding.

Risk Treatment Overruled

As a risk manager in a public company, I (Peter) brought to senior leadership in one of our risk management reviews a matter of workplace security and safety: a particular business office had no access control that segregated work areas from the reception area. Visitors during business hours could simply walk through the door and into the entire office suite where about 100 employees worked. My recommendation was to accept this risk.

The company president stood up and said, "No, I will not accept this risk. We should have a wall and door constructed to keep visitors out of the work area unless they are permitted to enter."

While this may at first appear to have been a correction or a reprimand, I took it as an engaged senior executive taking a different point of view and making an informed risk decision. At this point, I knew that senior leaders were engaged and not merely rubber-stamping my recommendations.

The Risk Treatment Decision

Up to this point, the risk manager has been analyzing one or more risks, developing viable risk treatment and risk mitigation options, and preparing a package to present to senior management. During the meeting in which the risk manager has presented the story of the risk and the recommended course of action (or inaction, in the case of risk acceptance), senior leaders should be allowed to ask questions about the matter before being asked to ratify the recommendation (or decide otherwise). Note the questions, who asked them, and how they were answered—this will help in future proceedings.

The call for the actual decision may range from formal to informal. An accurate accounting of the decision is critical, as it should be a part of officially published meeting minutes used to document the decision. Note those present and (optionally) who agreed and who disagreed.

NOTE In some cases, it may be wise to discuss the risk treatment matter with senior executives in one-on-one discussions, where they may be more apt to ask questions to understand the situation better. These discussions will also help the risk manager better prepare for the risk treatment discussion, and in some cases, it may even sway the risk manager to pursue a different remedy.

Risk Mitigation   When the risk treatment decision is *mitigation,* the decision should also include the naming of the person responsible for performing the risk treatment and executives' desire for the timing of risk treatment. This is particularly important if the risk treatment owner is not present in the discussion.

Any discussion about risk treatment options should be captured so that the risk treatment owner will have additional background and insight into why the particular risk treatment option was selected. This may help the risk treatment owner proceed more quickly with planning and execution without circling back to decision-makers to better understand the rationale behind the decision.

All of the basic facts about risk mitigation (who made the decision, when the decision was made, who the risk treatment owner is, when the risk treatment should be completed, and so on) should be entered into the risk register. Then, the risk manager can conduct effective follow-up over the coming weeks, months, and quarters and report on the progress to the decision-makers.

Risk Acceptance   If the risk treatment decision is *acceptance,* we recommend that this decision not be perpetual but instead have an expiration date. After that expiration date, the risk will be reopened and a new risk treatment decision made. The reason for expiring risk acceptance is this: conditions related to the risk may change in a year, so much so that a different decision may be needed in the future. Many things can change in a year:

- How the organization uses information systems
- The organization's reliance on critical business processes on information systems
- Changes in underlying information technology

- Changes in threats
- Changes in tools that help mitigate threats
- Changes in business priorities

One year may seem like a short period, but a lot can happen in a year. Make sure executives are on board with this concept.

Organizations with formal risk management programs sometimes utilize a *risk acceptance letter*—a signed memo in which a business unit leader or department head chooses to accept a specific, identified risk versus another risk treatment option such as mitigate, transfer, or avoid. In the risk acceptance letter, the signatory accepts the potential consequences if an event related to the risk occurs in the future.

CISOs Are Not Risk Owners

Many organizations have implicitly adopted the mistaken notion that the chief information security officer (CISO) is the de facto risk owner for all identified risk matters.

In a properly run risk management program, risk owners are business unit leaders and department heads who own the business activity where a risk has been identified. For instance, if a risk is identified regarding the long-term storage of full credit card numbers in an e-commerce environment, the risk owner would be the executive who runs the e-commerce function. That executive would decide to mitigate, avoid, transfer, or accept that risk.

The role of the CISO is to operate the risk management program and facilitate discussions and risk treatment decisions, not to make those risk treatment decisions. A CISO can be considered a risk *facilitator* but not a risk owner.

Even when embraced and practiced, this concept does not always stop an organization from sacking the CISO should a breach occur. A dismissal might even be appropriate, for example, if the risk management program that the CISO operated was not performing as expected.

Risk Transfer   One of the four basic risk treatment options, *risk transfer* means that some outside organization is willing to take on the risk. Often, this comes in the form of cyber insurance, but it could just as easily be a business process outsourcing (BPO) arrangement in which a service provider is willing to accept certain risks.

We provide a note of caution here. While an organization can outsource risk, no organization can outsource accountability. Here is an example: a successful service business specializing in water damage mitigation outsources its entire IT and IT security functions to a large service provider, including information systems where customers register and request one-time or recurring services. The IT service provider suffers a breach, resulting in the exposure of its customers' personal information and numerous identity theft and fraud cases. The service business attempts to explain that the external service provider is the party responsible for the breach. However, the customers are unhappy, blame the service business, and threaten to organize a class-action lawsuit for the damages.

In this example, the service business cannot absolve itself because the IT outsourcer's lapse resulted in the breach. The service business decided to use this particular IT outsourcer and cannot absolve itself of responsibility because of an unfavorable outcome.

Cyber insurance is similar to this example. An organization with cyber insurance may suffer a breach, and the cyber insurance company may compensate the organization for particular losses. However, the organization will have lost some goodwill and may have a long-lasting tarnished reputation that can take years to undo.

It is imperative that senior executives fully grasp the complete picture of risk transfer.

Risk Avoidance   *Risk avoidance* is often the least understood risk treatment option. With risk avoidance, the activity that causes the risk is itself discontinued.

Here is an example: a risk assessment reveals the use of an unsanctioned cloud service provider to process sensitive information. End users decided to employ a free online service to perform language translation and use it for translating sensitive documents, including contracts. In its end-user licensing agreement (EULA), the service provider claims ownership over any content that it translates. When this matter was brought to light in a risk treatment discussion, business executives directed the organization to immediately discontinue use of the service provider, thus avoiding the risk.

The Fifth Option in Risk Treatment

For decades, risk management frameworks have cited the same four risk treatment options: accept, mitigate, transfer, and avoid. There is, however, a fifth option that some organizations select: *ignore the risk*.

Ignoring a risk situation is a choice, although it is not considered a wise choice. Ignoring a risk means doing nothing about it, not even making a decision about it. It amounts to little more than pretending the risk does not exist. It's off the books. It is not even added to a risk register for consideration, but it represents a risk situation nonetheless.

In some cases, such as for minimal risk items, this may be perfectly acceptable. A theft of a paperclip may simply be too small for consideration for a risk register. It would probably be wise to leave this off of a risk register unless there is a specific reason to add it. In some cases, listing minimal risk is very critical because compliance requirements dictate that specific risks be considered in risk evaluations. Developing the right level of detail for a risk register requires experience, listening to an organization's culture, and striking the right balance.

Organizations without risk management programs may implicitly ignore all risks, or many of them at least. Organizations might also be practicing informal and maybe even reckless risk management—risk management by gut feel. Without a systematic framework for identifying risks, many are likely to go undiscovered. This practice could also be considered as ignoring risks through the implicit refusal to identify them and treat them properly.

Note that ignoring risk, particularly when governance requires that you manage it, is usually a violation of the principles of due diligence and due care. Many organizations can be legally charged with "willful negligence" if they have a duty to manage risk, and they simply don't.

Other Risk Response Options   Other common risk response options include contingency, enhance, and exploit.

Contingency is all about creating contingency plans in case a risk materializes. For instance, an organization might develop a playbook within its security incident response or business continuity planning process to respond to a specific type of event.

Enhance may be a response to a positive risk such as a project coming in under budget. If a few dollars spent earlier in the project will save some money long term, it may make sense to enhance the risk. In another example, a security engineering team determines that a new detective control helps to reduce other risks not considered initially.

Exploit can be very much related to the same situation. If a project finishes early, the resources may be reassigned to another project. Note that this use of the term *exploit* is different from that of malware or an attacker exploiting a vulnerability in an information system, business process, or worker.

Publishing and Reporting

Like any formal business program, risk leaders publish periodic reports and metrics from the risk management program. The risk program needs to inform business executives on the state of risk in the organization and proceedings in the program. Several aspects of risk reporting are discussed here.

Risk Register

The risk register itself is considered a detailed, operational business record. Reporting about the risk register generally consists of high-level depictions of risk instead of reporting the detail. Challenges in reporting risk include the following:

- **Trends**   Changes in the size of the risk register, or the aggregate or average risk levels, may be misleading, particularly in newer risk programs that still identify risk.

- **Completeness**   A risk register should not be considered a complete record of risk, as there may be numerous undiscovered and unidentified risks.

New Risks

Risk leaders may opt to disclose the number of, or even some details about, new risks identified in the reporting cycle. This reporting is a good indication that the risk program continues to keep its risk radar operating and open to risk discovery.

Risk Review

Reporting and metrics on risk reviews are an indication of engagement and involvement. Executives should expect risk leaders to periodically engage business leaders and department heads throughout the organization and may want to know how often (and with whom) this occurs.

Risk Treatment

The rate at which risk treatment decisions are made, and trends in risk treatment options, shows that the risk leader continues to work through the risk register.

Risk Mitigation Follow-Up

When mitigation is the chosen risk treatment for a given risk, the risk leader needs to track that risk mitigation and report on whether mitigation is performed on schedule. Mitigation activities that are behind schedule can be highlighted so that executives can understand where their directives are falling short and which are being completed on time.

Risk Renewals

As discussed earlier in this appendix, risk acceptance should not be perpetual but should expire. Risk leaders may want to publish, as a leading indicator, the number of risks nearing renewal. Those risks will be redeliberated and new decisions made, whether to continue to accept the risks for another year or take a different approach.

Risk Prioritization

In risk reporting, leaders often care only about the top-priority risk, such as a top 5, 10, or 20 risks. These may not be precisely the top risks, according to the risk manager. However, these priorities represent an articulation of risk appetite and risk tolerance, as well as leadership's culture and focus on risk. All too often, risk prioritization with managers boils down to nothing more than cost, unfortunately.

The Sensitivity of Risk Reporting Information

In most organizations, detailed information about risk, particularly vulnerabilities and safeguards, is treated as highly confidential. If it became public, that information might allow the organization to be attacked. Further, this information would reveal clues about the organization's risk culture. This is especially true in government and healthcare, in our experience.

About the Online Content

This book comes complete with TotalTester Online customizable practice exam software with 300 practice exam questions.

System Requirements

The current and previous major versions of the following desktop browsers are recommended and supported: Chrome, Microsoft Edge, Firefox, and Safari. These browsers update frequently, and sometimes an update may cause compatibility issues with the TotalTester Online or other content hosted on the Training Hub. If you run into a problem using one of these browsers, please try using another until the problem is resolved.

Your Total Seminars Training Hub Account

To get access to the online content you will need to create an account on the Total Seminars Training Hub. Registration is free, and you will be able to track all your online content using your account. You may also opt in if you wish to receive marketing information from McGraw Hill or Total Seminars, but this is not required for you to gain access to the online content.

Privacy Notice

McGraw Hill values your privacy. Please be sure to read the Privacy Notice available during registration to see how the information you have provided will be used. You may view our Corporate Customer Privacy Policy by visiting the McGraw Hill Privacy Center. Visit the **mheducation.com** site and click **Privacy** at the bottom of the page.

Single User License Terms and Conditions

Online access to the digital content included with this book is governed by the McGraw Hill License Agreement outlined next. By using this digital content you agree to the terms of that license.

Access   To register and activate your Total Seminars Training Hub account, simply follow these easy steps.

1. Go to this URL: **hub.totalsem.com/mheclaim**
2. To register and create a new Training Hub account, enter your e-mail address, name, and password on the **Register** tab. No further personal information (such as credit card number) is required to create an account.

   If you already have a Total Seminars Training Hub account, enter your e-mail address and password on the **Log in** tab.
3. Enter your Product Key: `cqpq-9s9f-3fbz`
4. Click to accept the user license terms.
5. For new users, click the **Register and Claim** button to create your account. For existing users, click the **Log in and Claim** button.

   You will be taken to the Training Hub and have access to the content for this book.

Duration of License   Access to your online content through the Total Seminars Training Hub will expire one year from the date the publisher declares the book out of print.

Your purchase of this McGraw Hill product, including its access code, through a retail store is subject to the refund policy of that store.

The Content is a copyrighted work of McGraw Hill, and McGraw Hill reserves all rights in and to the Content. The Work is © 2022 by McGraw Hill.

Restrictions on Transfer   The user is receiving only a limited right to use the Content for the user's own internal and personal use, dependent on purchase and continued ownership of this book. The user may not reproduce, forward, modify, create derivative works based upon, transmit, distribute, disseminate, sell, publish, or sublicense the Content or in any way commingle the Content with other third-party content without McGraw Hill's consent.

Limited Warranty   The McGraw Hill Content is provided on an "as is" basis. Neither McGraw Hill nor its licensors make any guarantees or warranties of any kind, either express or implied, including, but not limited to, implied warranties of merchantability or fitness for a particular purpose or use as to any McGraw Hill Content or the information therein or any warranties as to the accuracy, completeness, correctness, or results to be obtained from, accessing or using the McGraw Hill Content, or any material referenced in such Content or any information entered into licensee's product by users or other persons and/or any material available on or that can be accessed through the licensee's product (including via any hyperlink or otherwise) or as to non-infringement of third-party rights. Any warranties of any kind, whether express or implied, are disclaimed. Any material or data obtained through use of the McGraw Hill Content is at your own discretion and risk and user understands that it will be solely responsible for any resulting damage to its computer system or loss of data.

Neither McGraw Hill nor its licensors shall be liable to any subscriber or to any user or anyone else for any inaccuracy, delay, interruption in service, error or omission, regardless of cause, or for any damage resulting therefrom.

In no event will McGraw Hill or its licensors be liable for any indirect, special or consequential damages, including but not limited to, lost time, lost money, lost profits or good will, whether in contract, tort, strict liability or otherwise, and whether or not such damages are foreseen or unforeseen with respect to any use of the McGraw Hill Content.

TotalTester Online

TotalTester Online provides you with a simulation of the CRISC exam. Exams can be taken in Practice Mode or Exam Mode. Practice Mode provides an assistance window with hints, explanations of the correct and incorrect answers, and the option to check your answer as you take the test. Exam Mode provides a simulation of the actual exam. The number of questions, the types of questions, and the time allowed are intended to be an accurate representation of the exam environment. The option to customize your quiz allows you to create custom exams from selected domains or chapters, and you can further customize the number of questions and time allowed.

To take a test, follow the instructions provided in the previous section to register and activate your Total Seminars Training Hub account. When you register, you will be taken to the Total Seminars Training Hub. From the Training Hub Home page, select your certification from the Study drop-down menu at the top of the page to drill down to the TotalTester for your book. You can also scroll to it from the list of Your Topics on the Home page, and then click the TotalTester link to launch the TotalTester. Once you've launched your TotalTester, you can select the option to customize your quiz and begin testing yourself in Practice Mode or Exam Mode. All exams provide an overall grade and a grade broken down by domain.

Technical Support

For questions regarding the TotalTester or operation of the Training Hub, visit **www.totalsem.com** or e-mail **support@totalsem.com**.

For questions regarding book content, visit **www.mheducation.com/customerservice**.

acceptable use policy (AUP)   Organizational policy that describes both acceptable and unacceptable actions when using organizational computing resources, as well as the consequences of violating the policy.

access control   The processes and technologies involved in protecting information, systems, and data against unauthorized disclosure, modification, or loss through the control of access to those resources physically and/or logically.

accountability   The ability to trace an action or event to a specific subject and to hold that subject responsible for their actions.

AIC triad   *See* CIA triad.

assessment   The process of determining whether a program, project, or control is meeting specified objectives as well as determining whether the controls selected to protect the system are performing their desired function to the level required.

asset   Anything of value to an organization; assets can include tangible items such as information, data, equipment, supplies, facilities, and systems as well as intangible items such as customer loyalty and reputation.

asset valuation   The practice of assigning a monetary value to an asset.

attack   An offensive action that results in potential harm to an asset.

attack surface   The set of components that could be the target of attack by an adversary.

audit   A formal inspection of a control, process, or system to determine whether it is being followed, operates effectively, and meets its objectives.

authentication   The process of validating credentials a user has supplied to verify that they are the actual authorized user and that the credentials belong to that user.

authorization   The process of giving authenticated users the proper accesses to systems, data, and facilities.

availability   The goal of having information and systems available to authorized users whenever and however they need them.

bow-tie analysis   A risk analysis technique used to depict the relationships between various elements of risk.

brainstorming   A problem-solving technique in which participants spontaneously generate potential ideas for discussion and analysis.

business case   In the context of risk management, a written or oral presentation that explains the reasoning for the expense and effort associated with risk response.

business continuity   The process, generally detailed in a supporting plan, that keeps the company operating and functioning in the event of a power outage, IT malfunction, or major disaster.

business impact assessment (BIA)   The process of analyzing critical business processes, as well as the assets used to support them, and determining the impact to them when a loss of or disruption in access to those assets occurs.

business process outsourcing (BPO)   The process of outsourcing one or more business processes to a service provider.

business triage   A decision-making system used to prioritize resources to maximize outcomes.

capability   The ability for the organization to implement a risk response.

capability maturity model integration (CMMI)   A business process maturity model developed by Carnegie Mellon University and now owned by ISACA.

change management   The overall process used to manage the request, review, approval, and execution of changes to IT systems or business processes.

CIA triad   The three security principles of confidentiality, integrity, and availability.

COBIT   A management and governance framework developed and used extensively by ISACA in its various risk management and business process frameworks.

code review   A manual examination of software source code to identify defects, including those that may be exploited by an attacker. *See also* code scan.

code scan   An automated examination of software source code to identify defects. *See also* code review.

common control   A control spanning the entire organization that protects multiple assets rather than only a specific asset. A physical control is a good example of a common control, and the responsible entity for that control would be the common controls provider.

confidentiality   The goal of protecting systems and information from unauthorized disclosure.

configuration management   The use of recordkeeping to record changes made to configuration settings in an information system.

control   A measure put in place to increase protection for an asset, to make up for a lack of protection for an asset, or to strengthen a weakness for an asset. Controls can be administrative, technical, or physical and operational. They can also be further divided by functionality (deterrent, preventative, detective, and so on).

control baseline   The initial set of controls selected, based on the security categorization to be applied to systems and data and maintained throughout their life cycle.

control deficiency analysis   The process of determining the difference between the existing state of a control's effectiveness and its desired state.

control gap   A situation where controls do not exist or are insufficiently designed to meet a control objective.

control objective   An overarching statement describing the intent of a group of controls.

control ownership   The person or entity responsible for the proper implementation and maintenance of security controls within the organization.

cost   The financial impacts of any decision as well as the less-easily quantified aspects such as loss of goodwill, loss of brand status, and other hard-to-define attributes. Cost also includes the maintenance of the responsive mitigation over its required life span.

criticality analysis   A study of each system and process, a consideration of the impact on the organization if it is incapacitated, the likelihood of incapacitation, and the estimated cost of mitigating the risk or impact of incapacitation

culture   The values and norms in an organization that define how people treat each other and work together to achieve organization objectives.

data classification   Policies that define sensitivity levels and handling procedures, and controls used to protect information at various levels.

data destruction   The willful or malicious destruction of data that renders it unavailable for intended uses.

data discovery   A manual or automated technique in which a target system is examined to determine the presence of specific types of data; additionally, this may include an examination of access rights to particular sets of data.

data sensitivity   The level of protection required for information or data based on its impact to the organization if it were disclosed to unauthorized people, subject to unauthorized modification, or otherwise lost.

Deming cycle   A generic business life cycle model consisting of Plan, Do, Check, and Act.

denial of service (DoS)   An attack on a system that renders it unavailable for legitimate uses.

design review   The examination of the design of a system or process to determine whether it is sound and meets stated objectives.

disaster recovery (DR)   The process of reacting to an incident or disaster and recovering an organization, its personnel, and systems to a functioning state.

due care   The process of taking the necessary responsibility and steps to protect an organization and its workers.

due diligence   The reasonable amount of investigation taken prior to entering into a legal agreement.

due process   An impartial and fair inquiry of violations of organization policy.

economy of use   The design principle that states that you should attempt to design and implement controls that can be applied to more than one system or set of data or that provide more than one function in effectively mitigating risk. The goal is to minimize single-use controls (controls that apply only to a specific system or set of data) because they can be more expensive and specialized to implement.

effectiveness   The extent to which the response reduces the likelihood or the impact of the risk event to the organization; also, the degree and depth to which a control fulfills its security requirements.

efficiency   The interaction of a control with its environment, affecting factors such as cost, reliability, supportability, and interoperability.

enterprise risk management (ERM)   The practice of identifying and managing strategic risk in an organization.

event   An instance of threat realization.

event-tree analysis   A bottom-up risk analysis technique that focuses on all possible risk impacts and looks for all possible risk events.

exception management   The process of accepting, documenting, and tracking exceptions to security policies and risk mitigation strategies.

exploit   1) A specific tool or method that can be used to carry out a threat. 2) The act of attacking an asset, made possible by the presence of a vulnerability.

Factor Analysis of Information Risk (FAIR)   A risk analysis methodology used to analyze the factors that contribute to individual risks.

false negative   A situation where a vulnerability isn't detected but does actually exist.

false positive   A situation where a vulnerability is reported that isn't actually legitimate.

fault-tree analysis   A top-down risk analysis technique that focuses on risk events and looks for all possible causes of the event.

Federal Information Processing Standards (FIPS)   Public standards published by the National Institute of Standards and Technology (NIST) for use in U.S. government systems.

Federal Information Security Management Act (FISMA)   A U.S. federal law requiring federal agencies to develop information security programs and capabilities aligned to NIST Special Publication 800-53.

framework   An overall methodology prescribing higher-level processes or controls.

fuzzing   A technique used to generate various forms of input to a system to identify potential vulnerabilities that could allow an attacker to compromise the system.

gap assessment   An examination of a system or process to determine whether it complies with established requirements or standards.

governance   The legal or corporate standards that prescribe how an organization will conduct itself with regard to its behavior in handling information and data.

governance, risk, and compliance (GRC) system   *See* integrated risk management (IRM) system.

Gramm-Leach-Bliley Act (GLBA)   U.S. law that requires financial institutions (including banks, loan companies, insurance, and investment companies) to protect sensitive financial data and make their information-sharing practices known to their customers. Of particular interest to security professionals is the Safeguards Rule incorporated into GLBA, which requires institutions under the jurisdiction of the Federal Trade Commission to have specific measures in place to protect customer information.

Health Insurance Portability and Accountability Act (HIPAA)   Law passed in 1996 requiring the U.S. government's Health and Human Services Department to establish requirements for protecting the privacy and security of personal health information (PHI). The two important elements of HIPAA of interest to security professionals are the HIPAA Privacy Rule and the HIPAA Security Rule, which set forth specific standards to protect electronic PHI.

identification   The process of initially presenting credentials to a system to identify an authorized user.

impact   The level of potential harm or damage to an asset or the organization if a given threat were to exploit a given vulnerability.

inherent risk   The level of risk associated with a specific activity or function, prior to applying any protective controls or safeguards.

integrated risk management (IRM) system   An information system used to track and manage various governance, risk, and compliance activities, including risk management.

integrity   The goal of preventing unauthorized modification to a system or data.

ISO/IEC   The International Organization for Standardization (ISO) and the International Electrotechnical Commission (IEC), which together are responsible for a majority of the information technology standards used worldwide, including several that apply to information security and risk management.

IT general control (ITGC)   A control that is applied across all information systems and supporting processes in an organization.

job rotation   A practice where an organization occasionally moves personnel from one job to another to help prevent practices contrary to policy.

key control indicator (KCI)   A specific indicator that shows the relative effectiveness of a control.

key performance indicator (KPI)   An indicator that is used to understand and enable the measurement of a control's performance.

key risk indicator (KRI)   A highly probable indicator designed to accurately predict an important level of risk based on a defined threshold.

least privilege   A security principle that dictates that subjects should be given only the minimum level of rights, permissions, and privileges necessary to perform their designated functions or jobs, and no more than that.

life cycle   A characteristic of a business process where a sequence of activities is repeated.

likelihood   The certainty that an incident will occur; often expressed statistically as a probability of occurrence.

mandatory vacation   A practice where an organization requires that each employee use a minimum amount of vacation each year to provide the opportunity for audit, security, and privacy specialists to examine the employee's practices or records during their absence.

materiality   A quantitative or qualitative expression of significance.

maturity   The degree of formality and optimization of a business process or capability.

maturity assessment   An assessment of processes or capabilities to determine their maturity. *See also* maturity.

maximum tolerable downtime (MTD)   A theoretical period, measured from the onset of a disaster, after which the organization's ongoing viability would be at risk.

multifactor authentication   Any means used to authenticate a user that is stronger than just the use of a user ID and password. Examples of multifactor authentication include digital certificates, tokens, smart cards, and biometrics.

need-to-know   A security concept that requires a subject have an actual requirement to access systems or data, based on their job requirements.

NIST   The U.S. Department of Commerce's National Institute of Standards and Technology, a standards development organization.

NIST Risk Management Framework (RMF)   The overall risk management methodology published and promulgated by the National Institute of Standards and Technology (NIST) in Special Publication 800-37.

non-repudiation   The security concept that requires a subject to be accountable for their actions, such that they cannot deny that they took an action.

OCTAVE   The Operationally Critical Threat, Asset, and Vulnerability Evaluation (OCTAVE) methodology developed by Carnegie Mellon University and the U.S. government to assist organizations in identifying and assessing information security risk.

Payment Card Industry Data Security Standard (PCI DSS)   A set of security requirements levied on merchants that process credit card transactions by the major payment card industry providers, including Discover, Visa, MasterCard, and American Express. PCI DSS was developed to impose security requirements and controls on retailers (merchants and service providers) to reduce credit card fraud and identity theft.

penetration test   An authorized assessment that actively identifies and exploits vulnerabilities or weaknesses in a system or process.

personally identifiable information (PII)   Data elements that uniquely identify a natural person.

platform   A hardware, software, or cloud infrastructure upon which to base computing operating systems, applications, and networks. It may involve different operating systems, network protocols, or particular types of hardware.

port scanner   A software program that determines which ports on a target system are listening for incoming requests. *See also* vulnerability scanner.

portfolio   A grouping of programs managed as a whole. Portfolio management involves the oversight of several different programs by a senior person in the organization.

practice   A proven, standardized methodology or way of performing particular tasks or processes.

privacy   The principles and practices of ensuring the protection and proper use of the personally identifiable information (PII) of customers, constituents, and workers.

probability   The chance that an event will occur.

program   1) A grouping of similar projects; programs are usually ongoing and longer term in nature and may also encompass several individual projects. 2) Activities specific to processes that may have an indefinite duration.

project   A limited-duration set of activities geared toward a particular goal; projects have definitive start and stop dates, resource allocations, scopes, schedules, and costs.

project management   A set of processes covering a defined project from start to finish, generally looking to cut costs such as time, scope, and overall project cost.

protocol analyzer   A hardware or software tool that collects network traffic for the purpose of examination, either for determining network issues or for capturing plaintext usernames, passwords, or other sensitive information being sent in the clear.

qualitative assessment   An assessment technique that uses subjective values, such as low, moderate, and high, to describe various components of risk, such as likelihood and impact. Qualitative techniques rely on data that is often not easily described in numerical terms.

quantitative assessment   An assessment technique that uses nonsubjective values, such as numerical or other measurable data, to describe various components of risk, such as likelihood and impact. Quantitative techniques rely on data that is numerically derived and not easily subject to individual opinion.

quick win   A high-reward, low-cost risk response that is both effective and efficient.

recovery point objective (RPO)   The maximum tolerable period in which data can be lost by the organization because of an incident or disaster.

recovery time objective (RTO)   The maximum amount of time allowed to pass between an incident and recovering a business process to an operational state.

residual risk   The risk that remains after the application of risk treatment, acceptance, or transfer.

resilience   The ability of the business to survive negative events and continue with its mission and function.

return on investment (ROI)   The ratio between investment and value received.

risk   The possibility of harm that can come to an asset or an organization.

risk acceptance   An active decision made to assume risk (either inherent or residual) and take no further action to reduce it.

risk acceptance letter   A formal memo in which a business leader agrees to accept an identified risk.

risk analysis   The detailed examination of an individual risk identified in a risk assessment.

risk appetite   The organization's overall acceptable level of risk for a given business venture.

risk assessment   The process of identifying and assessing various factors, including threats, threat actors, vulnerabilities, assets, and likelihood to determine their impact on the organization.

risk avoidance   A risk treatment option taken when the level of risk is still not acceptable after controls have been considered, resulting in an activity being canceled or not being started.

risk capacity   The amount of loss that an organization can incur without seriously affecting its ability to continue as an organization.

risk culture   The overall attitude toward risk, promulgated and supported by the organization's leadership.

risk factor   Any factor that may contribute to an increase or decrease in risk; risk factors could be external or internal, and they could affect either likelihood or impact should a risk event actually occur.

risk identification   The realization of a new risk to an organization, its systems, or its processes.

Risk IT Framework   ISACA's own risk management methodology; it is strongly tied to and integrated with COBIT. The Risk IT Framework merges traditional IT models with a more risk-focused mindset.

risk ledger   *See* risk register.

risk management   The life cycle process of managing risk within an organization at all levels, according to the organization's risk appetite, tolerance, and strategy.

risk mitigation   Involves the application of controls that lower the overall level of risk through the reduction of the vulnerability, the likelihood of the threat exploit, or the reduction of the impact to the asset, if the risk were to be realized.

risk monitoring   Ongoing risk assessment activities in which risks are periodically reviewed to determine whether the nature of threats, threat actors, vulnerabilities, impact, or probabilities of occurrence have changed.

risk owner   The person ultimately responsible and accountable for a risk.

risk ownership   The state of being responsible and accountable for a risk.

risk profile   A collection of detailed data on identified IT risks, typically applied to a specific system or groups of systems.

risk ranking   The process of placing risks into a sequence, usually with the greatest risks appearing first.

risk realization   The awareness that a potential risk scenario has become actualized.

risk register   The master product or document that reflects the different risk scenarios and factors for the organization; it could be broken down by asset or system and reflects the different risk factors, including threats, vulnerabilities, assets, likelihood, and impact to assets.

risk response action plan   A list of the risk responses that have been chosen, and the charts of their progress and associated timeline, with an appropriate action owner or owners.

risk scenario   An identified risk event possibility, which consists of a threat actor, threat, vulnerability, and asset.

risk sharing   Often referred to as *risk transference,* risk sharing entails the use of a third party to offset part of the risk. It can involve the outsourcing of some activities to a third party to reduce the financial impacts of a risk event.

risk tolerance   The organization's level of acceptable variation from the risk appetite.

risk transference   *See* risk sharing.

root-cause analysis (RCA)   A method of problem-solving that seeks to identify the root cause of an event or problem.

Sarbanes-Oxley Act of 2002 (SOX)   U.S. law passed in 2002 establishing requirements for public companies in the United States, as well as auditors and accounting firms, to improve the accuracy and reliability of corporate disclosures concerning securities laws. The law is enforced by the U.S. Securities and Exchange Commission (SEC) and provides governance for the integrity and accuracy of data produced by an organization. For security professionals, this has the effect of imposing specific integrity and protection controls on information systems and processes.

scope   The set of systems, processes, personnel, data, or work centers to be included in an assessment.

security categorization   The process of determining the impact to the organization regarding the confidentiality, integrity, and availability of information and systems. The security categorization uses qualitative benchmarks of low, moderate, and high. FIPS 199 and NIST Special Publication 800-60 offer a defined process for the security categorization of information.

security control   A security measure or protection applied to data, systems, people, facilities, or other resources to protect them from adverse events. *See also* control.

segregation of duties   *See* separation of duties.

separation of duties   The process design and access control concept that enforces the rule that no single individual can carry out certain high-value or high-risk tasks.

service level agreement (SLA)   A contractual agreement, signed by an organization and a third-party provider, that details the level of security, data availability, and other protections afforded the organization's data held by the third party.

sniffer   *See* protocol analyzer.

Software as a Service (SaaS)   A third-party cloud-based service that offers outsourced use of software; this allows an organization to use licensed software at a lower cost than buying, installing, and maintaining hardware and software.

stakeholder Any business-related individual, department, or entity directly affected by risk to the organization.

standard A prescribed set of detailed processes, which may include specific levels of performance or function, used to complete and measure a given task or function.

statement of impact A qualitative or quantitative description of the impact on an organization if a process or system is incapacitated for a time.

systems development life cycle (SDLC) A framework describing the entire useful life of a system or software, which usually includes phases relating to requirements definition, design, development, acquisition, implementation, operations, and disposal.

tailgating A practice of unauthorized persons following authorized persons through a security door or entrance.

The Open Group Architecture Framework (TOGAF) A life-cycle enterprise architecture framework used for the designing, planning, implementation, and governance of an enterprise architecture.

third-party risk management (TPRM) The set of activities used to identify and manage risks associated with the use of external suppliers and service providers.

threat An event or occurrence that has the potential to cause harm or damage to people, places, or things or to adversely affect operations.

threat actor A threat agent that is one or more people. *See also* threat agent.

threat agent An entity that has the intent to initiate a threat event. This doesn't have to be a person; it could also be nature, in the case of a natural disaster.

threat assessment An assessment that attempts to determine all potential threat actors and threats that may affect a given asset or its vulnerabilities.

threat landscape The set of threats that have been identified that are associated with a business activity or business asset.

threat modeling A threat assessment that attempts to determine all possible vectors of attack and includes risk factors that may affect the ability of a threat actor to initiate or complete a threat event.

threat realization A threat that is carried out that causes harm or damage to people, places, or things.

three lines of defense The concept of defense within a risk management framework that consists of operational management, risk and compliance management, and audit and accountability.

triage *See* business triage.

vulnerability A weakness in a system, asset, or process, such as a flaw in software code; it can also be considered a lack of protection for an asset, such as an unlocked server room door.

vulnerability analysis   Examination of a vulnerability in a system, asset, or process.

vulnerability assessment   An assessment that attempts to discover potential weaknesses for an asset. This involves identifying the assets that will be covered within the scope of the assessment, conducting scans and other tests against those assets, and providing a report of the vulnerabilities that have been found.

vulnerability scanner   A software program designed to scan a system to determine what services the system is running and whether any unnecessary open ports, operating systems and applications, or back doors can be exploited because of a lack of patching or other flaws. *See also* port scanner.

walkthrough   An interview with a control, process, or system owner as a part of an assessment.

work breakdown structure (WBS)   A detailed decomposition of the work to be performed during the project, including specific step-by-step tasks, as well as required resources.

workers   An inclusive term that means employees (full-time and part-time), temporary workers, contractors, consultants, and others who are a part of an organization's workforce.

Zachman framework   An enterprise architecture framework used to describe an IT architecture in increasing levels of detail.

INDEX

I